D0939053

THE MEMOIRS OF JAMES II
1652–1660

THE DUKE OF YORK AS A SOLDIER

The Memoirs of
JAMES II

His Campaigns as Duke of York
1652–1660

Translated by
A. LYTTON SELLS
from the Bouillon Manuscript
Edited and collated with the Clarke edition

With an Introduction by
Sir Arthur Bryant

GREENWOOD PRESS, PUBLISHERS
WESTPORT, CONNECTICUT

The Library of Congress has catalogued this publication as follows:

Library of Congress Cataloging in Publication Data

James II, King of Great Britain, 1633-1701.
    The memoirs of James II.

    Includes bibliographical references.
    1. Europe--History--1648-1715--Sources. I. Sells,
Arthur Lytton, 1895-   ed.
DA450.A3 1972   940.2'52   71-163544
ISBN 0-8371-6209-2

*Campagnes Tirées mot pour mot des memoires de
Jacques Stuart Pour Lors Duc d'Yorck, et depuis Roy
d'Angleterre Jacques Second: depuis 1652 inclusivement, iusquen 1660*

Originally published in 1962
by Indiana University Press, Bloomington

Reprinted with the permission
of Indiana University Press

First Greenwood Reprinting 1972

Library of Congress Catalogue Card Number 71-163544

ISBN 0-8371-6209-2

Printed in the United States of America

CONTENTS

ILLUSTRATIONS

PLATES

ACKNOWLEDGEMENTS

The frontispiece is taken from a portrait by an unknown artist of James II when Duke of York which was almost certainly painted in Flanders in the late 1650s. It is in the royal collection and is reproduced by gracious permission of Her Majesty the Queen. Plates 1, 2 and 3 are from the Bouillon Manuscript of the Memoirs in the Lilly Library, Indiana University. Plates 4 and 5 are from A. M. Ramsay's *Histoire du Vicomte de Turenne* (Paris, 1735). Plate 6 is from an engraving in the British Museum and is reproduced by permission of the Trustees. Plate 7 is from a painting by Wissing and is reproduced by kind permission of Earl Spencer. Plate 8 is from a painting by Lely in the royal collection and is reproduced by gracious permission of Her Majesty the Queen.

Figures 1, 2, 3 and 4 are from Ramsay's *Histoire du Vicomte de Turenne* (Paris, 1735).

INTRODUCTION

By

SIR ARTHUR BRYANT

JAMES the Second of England and the Seventh of Scotland was neither a great man nor a great king. But he was a prince of firm integrity, strong religious faith, a loyal master and friend—perhaps, in the light of his own interests, too loyal a friend—and, within the limits imposed by his royal birth and calling, a fine administrator, especially in naval and military matters in which from his earliest years he had had much experience. With the help of his lieutenant, Samuel Pepys, he did more personally for the Royal Navy than any other English Sovereign, past or future. And that was no small service to his country, even if it was his only one. With his ancestor, Edward III, he shared, too, the unique privilege for a King of England of commanding her Fleet in action. He not only took part, like King George VI and the Duke of Edinburgh, in one of the major battles of British sea history, but he directed it victoriously as Commander-in-Chief. Not only did he command Britain's Fleet in action and preside over her Admiralty for many years. At one time, as a very young man, he temporarily commanded the French army in the field while acting as deputy for the great Turenne. Later, though also for a very brief period and as a deputy, he commanded the Spanish army in the Netherlands. Many years afterwards, when King of England, he commanded the English Army in the abortive and, for him, disastrous campaign of 1688. He also commanded the Irish Army before the battle of the Boyne. This must surely be a record of command, however checkered, for any Sovereign. James, too, was the last Roman Catholic to reign in England. And he has yet another claim to fame: that the greatest city of the modern world, New York, was re-christened after him and bears his name.

James was born on October 14th, 1633, six months after the Fleet Street tailor's son, Samuel Pepys, who was one day to help him establish England's Navy on a new model. Unlike his elder brother, Charles, who was dark and took after his Medici maternal forbears, James was fairish with a long lantern jaw and a rather stolid, phlegmatic temperament, inherited possibly from his father's mother, who was a Danish princess. The second son of Charles I by his French Queen, Henrietta Maria, his birth was proclaimed by the heralds with the usual pomp appertaining to a 17th century Prince of the Blood:

> Almighty God of his infinite grace and goodness preserve and blesse with long life in health, honor and all happiness the most high, mighty and excellent Prince James Duke of York, second sonne to the most high, most mighty and most excellent Prince Charles, by the grace of God King of England, Scotland, France and Ireland, Defender of the Faith.

He was christened by Archbishop Laud—the arch-champion of the Anglican Church of which his father was Head—and his godparents were two of the leading figures of contemporary European Protestantism: his aunt, the exiled Queen of Bohemia—the one-time 'Queen of Hearts', in honour of whose wedding festivities Shakespeare's *Tempest* had been played seventeen years before—and the Prince of Orange, grandson of the man who had defied the might of Spain and the Counter-Reformation during the reign of Elizabeth and whose grandson, half a century later, was to invade James's kingdom and assume his vacant throne as the saviour of English Protestantism.

James's earliest years were spent in the atmosphere of a brilliant royal Court, mainly at the palaces of Hampton Court, Richmond and Greenwich. At the age of five, according to the customary protocol of his age, he was appointed Lord-Admiral of England. Three years later, while he was still only a child, the stately and ceremonious world in which his earliest impressions were formed crumbled around him, as the pent-up anger of his father's Puritan and libertarian subjects boiled over against the authoritarianism of his Government and Laud's high-handed episcopal church discipline. The boy heard the London mob howling for Strafford's blood, listened with horror to the reports that daily reached Whitehall of the doings of 'the mighty terrible Parliament' that was seeking to wrest power from the Crown and substitute the rule of contumacious lords, country squires and lawyers, and learnt with tears of his father's surrender and betrayal of his faithful servant—an act which he ever afterwards regarded as a fatal parental weakness. Soon afterwards, in the depth of winter, he was forced to fly from London with his parents to Hampton Court. A few months later, after various vicissitudes, he joined his father at York where he was, rather forlornly, invested with the Garter. He was an eyewitness that summer of the defiance of the Governor of Hull to the royal summons —another consequence, he always afterwards believed, of a lack of resolution in the monarchical councils—and was present when the Royal Standard was raised at Nottingham against the Parliamentary leaders who, with the support of the Puritan faction in the country, were now openly defying the Crown.

A week after his ninth birthday, James experienced his first battle. Together with his elder brother Charles, throughout a long October day, he watched his father fighting for his throne against Lord Essex's army in the Warwickshire meadows below Edgehill. According to Aubrey, whose evidence is uncorroborated, the two princes were in the charge of one of the royal physicians, the famous William Harvey—discoverer of the circulation of the blood—who, also according to Aubrey, spent most of the day under a hedge reading a book and oblivious of his charges. For the next three years James lived in an armed city—the Oxford of Prince Rupert and the Cavaliers, given over, in G. M. Trevelyan's words, 'to the use of a Court whose days of royalty were numbered, its walks and quadrangles filled, as the end came near, with men and women learning to accept sorrow as their lot through life, the ambitious abandoning hope of power, the wealthy hardening themselves to embrace poverty, those who loved England preparing to sail for foreign shores and lovers to be parted for ever'. It was James's fate, as a boy, to endure that agony to the end, for he remained at Oxford until its hopeless surrender and long after his mother, his father and his elder brother had all left the doomed city.

After the King's defeat at Naseby and the fall of Oxford the young Duke's lot was a very sad one. For the next two years he was a prisoner, with his younger brother, Henry, and his little sister, Elizabeth, in the old palace of St. James's. Here he waited

3

while his captors, the Puritan army of Fairfax and Cromwell and the Presbyterian Parliament at Westminster, quarrelled with one another for the control of the kingdom they had wrested from his father. His mother was in exile in France, the King a prisoner, first at Hampton Court and later at Carisbrooke in the Isle of Wight. But in the spring of 1648, on the eve of the second Civil War, James, in obedience to a secret message from his father, succeeded in escaping to Holland. With the help of a Royalist colonel, his sister's maid, and a barber, the fourteen-year-old lad slipped out of the palace through a garden door into St. James's Park, disguised himself in cloak and perriwig and took a coach to one of the lanes leading to the river where a waiting wherry bore him to a secret rendezvous near London Bridge. Here he changed into girl's clothes and took passage on a barge to Gravesend where a ship was about to sail for Holland. But going down the Thames the master of the barge, who knew nothing of his passenger's identity, surprised him tying up his garter 'in so unwomanish a manner' that his suspicions were aroused. James was only able to continue his journey by instantaneously making a clean breast of the matter. Fortunately the barge-owner was loyalist enough to be prepared to risk his neck for the young prince, and James reached Gravesend in safety. Hence he sailed at daybreak for Holland and, after escaping shipwreck on the Middleburgh sandbanks and capture by a Parliamentary frigate, landed on the continent. He was to remain on it, an exile, for the next twelve years.

After nine months at the Hague at the Court of his eldest sister, Mary, who was married to Prince William of Orange, the young Duke joined his mother at Paris where she was living in straitened circumstances in the Louvre. Her sister-in-law, the French Queen Regent, and her nephew, the boy king, Louis XIV, has just been driven from the capital by rebellious nobles and the Paris mob, and it looked at that moment as though the French Crown was going to go the way of the English. A few days after James's arrival at the Louvre, the dreadful news arrived of King Charles's death on the scaffold at Whitehall. To the young prince and his family and to the English and Scottish exiles who surrounded them it seemed as if the very foundations of the earth had been shaken. 'This sad and execrable murder of our blessed master', wrote one of them, 'hath so disordered me that I shall hardly ever recover true quiet of mind. My soul abhors the thought of it of which no age ever heard the like. Yet, through all distractions, I must force myself to action when it may conduce to avenge the blood of that royal and glorious martyr upon those base inhuman murderers.'

Such was the school of adversity, exile and longing for revenge in which James grew to manhood. It was to prove, for the next decade, a school also of chronic poverty. 'Nothing,' the young Duke wrote on the first page of these memoirs, 'was so rare as money.' The leading figure among the exiles who formed the shadow court of Charles II in Paris, Edward Hyde, his Chancellor, confessed that his young master owed for all he had eaten for months:

I am not acquainted with one servant of his who hath a pistole in his pocket. Five or six of us eat together one meal a day for a pistole a week but all of us owe for God knows how many weeks to the poor woman that feeds us ... I do not now know that any man is yet dead for want of bread, which really I wonder at.

For James there was only one resort: to earn his living by his sword. After a short interlude in Jersey, the last dominion to remain loyal to the fallen Crown of England, and a further visit to Holland to see his widowed sister's new-born child—the infant William of Orange who one day was to supplant him on the Throne—the Duke at the age of eighteen took service in the French royal army. For the next four years he kept himself as a soldier of fortune. They were the most formative years of his life and, in some ways, the happiest.

This was the period covered by the main and most detailed part of the memoirs printed in this volume. James had the good fortune to be apprenticed to one of the great captains of all time, and one of the noblest of men, the great Henri, Vicomte de Turenne, Marshal of France, who commanded the royal armies in the Civil Wars of the Fronde against the brilliant rebel soldier, the Prince of Condé, and the Spanish invaders of his divided country. The two men—the forty-one year old Marshal and the young volunteer whose father had perished on the scaffold—became firm friends, and to his dying day, as the Cardinal de Bouillon's preface to the manuscript shows, James held the memory of Turenne in affectionate honour.

It was a regard and affection which Turenne fully reciprocated. For James proved an excellent lieutenant – brave, enduring, eager to learn and amenable to discipline. Phlegmatic, except when his deepest emotions were aroused, with a passion for order and routine, yet bold and, within his unimaginative limits, resourceful, James had many of the basic qualities of the good soldier. With all his faults, the code of honour he learnt in the profession of arms was to give dignity to his character and invest with a touch of nobility the many humiliations and vicissitudes of his checkered life.

James's experiences during the wars of the Fronde and the campaigns in northern France against the invading Spanish armies were not dissimilar to those of thousands of young Englishmen who fought over the same ground in the First World War of the twentieth century. The names encountered in the record of his marches, sieges and battles are those with which men of my own generation became familiar in the years 1914–1918.

There was on the right a brook which comes from Roiset and falls into the Somme a little above Péronne. There was in front a little valley and on the side of the brook a water course which the cavalry could not pass without great difficulty; the nearest village was called Tincour or Buires.

The young Duke was a modest and straightforward recorder of the campaigns in which he served; his journal is 'crew cut' and almost entirely free of emotion. Yet, between the lines, a soldier can recognise the authenticity of his experience. Witness his account of the march across the Champagne plain in the December of 1652.

The troops had to be quartered in the villages as the rigours of winter made it impossible to camp. The day they came to Sommyeur the frost was so very sharp that all the horsemen were forced to march on foot to keep warm; thirty or forty soldiers perished the same day through the extremity of cold; for, so soon as any of them who were not warmly clothed sat down for ease, the frost pierced them and they were never able to raise (*sic*) again. The Duke of York saw several frozen to death and a much greater number would have perished but for the care taken by the officers to put on horseback those whom they saw ready to succumb and carried them to the first villages where they saved several of them by giving them brandy and other kinds of liquor. What made this frost keener and more penetrating was that they were then marching over the vast plains of Champagne, where there was no shelter against the piercing north-east wind which was blowing directly in their faces.

Or of a struggle with mud, which will bring back many memories to veterans of both the first and second German Wars.

Never did soldiers or even officers march on an enterprise with more repugnance and murmuring. After enduring all the rigours of the frost, it was only with great impatience that they could endure the fatigue caused by the thaw in a hilly country where the clay made the roads impracticable, particularly between Pont-à-Vere and Laon, where the baggage nearly remained in the mud.

As befits a soldier James says little in his Memoirs of his personal part in these transactions. But the trust reposed in him by Turenne and his speedy promotion, as well as the testimony of those who served with him, shows how well he acquitted himself. Writing of his conduct in action against the Dutch fleet fourteen years later, his secretary, Sir William Coventry, described him as being 'more himself and more of judgment . . . in the middle of a desperate service, that at other times . . . and though he is a man naturally martial to the hottest degree, yet a man that never in his life talks one word of himself or service of his own, but only that he saw such or such a thing'. Had he fallen in action at the Battle of Lowestoft or in these early campaigns in Champagne and Picardy he might have gone down to history as one of the noblest and bravest of British princes.

In 1656, to his intense chagrin, the Duke was forced to resign his commission in the French Army. A treaty negotiated between Commonwealth England and France made it a condition of peace between the two countries that he should do so. His brother, the King, after a brief sojourn in Germany, found a refuge in the Spanish Netherlands, and James, recalled to his side, served for a time with the Spanish armies against his old comrade in arms, Turenne. While so engaged he was present at the Battle of the Dunes and left us a laconic, but moving, account of the dogged courage of Cromwell's Ironsides serving, 'at push of pike', with the French. 'Not so much as one single man of them ask'd quarter, or threw down his armes, but every one defended himself to the last; so that we ran as great danger by the butt end of their muskets as by the volley which they had given us.' More than thirty years later, watching the English seamen he had once commanded destroying his last hopes of recovering his kingdom as they boarded the French warships off La Hogue, the exiled James paid a similar tribute to the martial qualities of his countrymen: 'None but my brave English could do so brave an action.'

The rest of James's story is familiar enough. In May 1660 he returned with his brother to England as Heir Presumptive to the Throne – a position he was to hold until his accession a quarter of a century later. Yet even amid the rejoicings of the Restoration, with the nation beside itself at the sudden recovery of its ancient Crown, Parliament and Laws, the Duke found himself in trouble. For the daughter of the Lord Chancellor, to whom in exile he had given a secret promise of marriage, proved in child by him, and he was faced by the dilemma of either disgracing the family of his brother's chief Minister or of contracting a match which was bound, by the standards of the age, to outrage the country. In the upshot, with the King's support but to the fury of his mother and sister, James married Anne Hyde and publicly acknowledged her as his wife. The *mésalliance*, as it seemed at the time – the start of which is referred to in these memoirs – gave England two future Sovereigns, Mary II and Anne.

During the next decade – the only prolonged period in James's life when he was free from major trouble – the young Duke, as Lord High Admiral, directed the country's naval affairs and commanded her fleet in two great naval engagements against the Dutch. Pepys, who as an official of the Navy Board was undergoing a similar sea-change, describes in his diary James's transformation from a rather idle young prince, spoilt by an oversudden accession of good fortune – 'applying himself but little to the affairs of the country and attending to nothing but his pleasures' – into a painstaking administrator, 'concerned to mend things in the Navy himself and not leave it to other people' and who 'do follow and understand business very well and is mightily improved thereby'. For a short period at the beginning of the first Dutch war James was, indeed, the hero of the nation. And his vigour and presence of mind during the Fire of London enhanced the reputation he had won in battle.

Yet within a dozen years of the Restoration James had made himself the most distrusted man in the country. By publicly embracing the Roman Catholic faith he committed what seemed the greatest of all political blunders in an age when to the ordinary Englishman Catholicism, or Popery as it was called, was as hated and feared as Fascism today. The King—who himself had Catholic leanings but was too wise to admit them—did his best to persuade James to keep his religious convictions to himself but, partly out of honesty and partly out of affection for his wife, who had been received into the Catholic Church before her death in 1671, James insisted on blazoning the matter out. As a result he was forced to resign the Admiralty after an alarmed Parliament had brought in a Test Act requiring attendance at Anglican Communion as a pre-requisite to the holding of every high office in the State. What was worse, his open change of religion made the nation suspect, not without truth, that there was a secret design on the part of the King and Court to restore England to the Catholic fold. During the years following his enforced retirement, James was faced by a growing national movement—fostered and led by the great Protestant or 'Whig' Parliamentarian, Lord Shaftesbury—to exclude him from the succession to the Throne and legitimise the King's bastard, the young Duke of Monmouth, in his place. For a time he was forced, at his brother's command, to leave the country and live in exile, first in Brussels, and then, as Viceroy and High Commissioner, in Scotland. During this period, while the false accusations of Titus Oates agitated and terrorised the country, even the life of the Catholic Heir Presumptive would have been in danger had he remained in London. Saved by his brother's consummate political skill—an adroitness that James despised, never understood and regarded as weakness —he was recalled in 1682 on the rising crest of an astonishing loyal reaction against the excesses of the Whig extremists. Following an escape from drowning by shipwreck off the Yorkshire coast, the Duke was hailed on his return by the London mob—who earlier had been ready to hound him to death—with the refrain,

9

INTRODUCTION

The glory of the British line,
Old Jimmy's come again!

Two years later, in February 1685, Charles died and James succeeded to the Throne. In little more than three years, by his tactlessness, his inability to compromise or judge of human motive and character, and by the rigidity with which he upheld and sought to extend the rights of his unpopular co-religionists, James II threw away all the advantages won by his brother's political strategy. Acclaimed by the ruling Anglican High Tory Party as the uncompromising son of the martyred King who had died for the Church of England and as the champion of monarchical legitimism and Divine Right, he persisted in outraging their strongest beliefs and prejudices by suspending the laws in order to grant office to Roman Catholics and Dissenters, by governing without a Parliament—since no Parliament would endorse his policy—and by maintaining a standing army, partly recruited from Irish Papists and destined, it was believed (though probably unjustly) to enslave the nation. When in the summer of 1688 a son was unexpectedly born to his Catholic Queen, Mary of Modena—whom he had married fifteen years before—abandoning the hope that their dilemma was only temporary and putting their religion before their loyalty, his disillusioned Tory supporters joined with their Whig opponents in secretly inviting the King's Protestant son-in-law, William of Orange, to invade England with a Dutch fleet and army to save the religion and laws of the country. This, with the support of the majority of the English people, William did, landing at Torbay as 'Liberator' in November 1688.

Betrayed by those whom he most trusted, including his daughters, Mary of Orange and Anne, and the leading officers of his Army, James lost his head and, for once, his courage, and, after five weeks of uncertainty, retreat and confusion, attempted to fly the country. He thereby gave those who wished, not merely to restrain, but to dethrone him, the chance to declare the throne vacant. A second attempt to escape—encouraged by William—proved successful, and at three o'clock on the morning of Christmas Day 1688 the hapless King landed in France, once more a fugitive, never to return to England.

Henceforward until his death James was the pensioner of his

cousin, Louis XIV, in whose armies he had fought forty years before and who had now become Britain's declared enemy and, with his vast armed hosts and dreams of 'universal monarchy', a threat to the liberties of all Europe. With Louis's help James landed in Ireland in the spring of 1689 in an attempt to recover his throne which, in his absence, had been conferred by Parliament jointly on William and Mary. Hailed by the Catholic Irish as a saviour, he remained there till July of the following year when his Franco-Irish army was routed by William at the Battle of the Boyne.

For the remainder of his life James lived in retirement at St. Germain, increasingly given over to religious devotion and meditation. He died on September 17th, 1701, a few months before the Protestant nephew and son-in-law who had supplanted him on the throne. To Catholics, as well as to a little group of loyal English Tories who refused to acknowledge his successor, he seemed a martyr who had given up everything for his faith and the principles of monarchical right which he had so stubbornly refused to compromise.

PREFACE

THE announcement in 1951 that Charles Scribner's Sons, of
New York, with whom I was associated for many years as
Rare Book expert, had acquired the most 'legendary' Shuckburg
copy of the Gutenberg Bible from a member of the British Royal
Family aroused interest in other than bibliographical circles.
Press associations carried the story, articles were written, interviews given, and offers of 'family treasures' swelled to full flood
from all continents. As a result of this publicity, a young French
girl in New York telephoned to inquire about the value of some
first editions of Robert Browning, Lord Tennyson, and Walter
Savage Landor.

The first book examined, the Browning, was inscribed by the
author to Walter Savage Landor, as was the Tennyson volume.
The books by Landor were his own copies, annotated throughout
in his waspish style and of considerable bibliographical interest.
They were purchased upon mutually satisfactory terms and
promptly found suitable homes.

One's first reaction to material of this kind is naturally: 'Where
did it come from?' and 'Is there any more of it to be had?' The
answers were that they came from the family library in France,
which was a large one, and that other similar material *might* be
there, that these particular books had been brought to America as
they seemed the most likely to be saleable here, and that Mademoiselle was descended from Walter Savage Landor, which satis-
factorily explained their provenance. This was exciting, of course,
but it developed that the library was in a somewhat inaccessible
spot, the castle was closed, and there was no one locally capable of
making even the briefest kind of inventory.

In 1954 I made arrangements to go to England and the continent on a rare-book hunting expedition, and my companion on the
trip to France was to be Percy Muir, of the firm of Elkin Mathews,
a long-time friend whose knowledge of French booksellers, French
books, and, in short, France is encyclopedic. The forthcoming
trip recalled the memory of the Landor library and, after some in-

vestigation, I found that the daughter was now living in Paris. Arrangements were made at last to visit the castle in the Midi, where Mademoiselle's mother was now in residence.

The castle is very old and had somehow—probably from its isolated position far off the traditional invasion routes—escaped the desolation of the wars that had devastated other parts of France in past ages and in our own day. Among its proud traditions, and they are many, is the fact that Richard Lion-Heart had visited it. The library and many other rooms contained—on the walls, in closets and cupboards—important and interesting documents associated with the castle's long history, but most were connected with the family's history and were understandably not to be parted with under any circumstances.

Only one book of real value, the rare first edition of Henry D. Thoreau's first book *A Week on the Concord and Merrimac Rivers* (Cambridge, Massachusetts, 1849), in fine condition and inscribed by Thoreau to Landor, turned up and it was discovered by Muir. This book the Countess parted with reluctantly, obviously disappointed that nothing of importance (aside from the French works with which she would not part) had come to light.

Two evenings before our departure I went prying around some of the old closets, partly to see if something had not been overlooked and partly to prove to Muir that I was as good a needle-in-a-haystack hunter as he. On top of a large pile of seventeenth- and eighteenth-century books and documents, I chanced to pick up the manuscript of the present volume. Had it been at the bottom, I would never have reached for it. Opening the manuscript in the middle, I was certain that, being in French, it was another document with which the family would not part; but something made me glance at the title page. This, I thought, requires consideration, and retiring to my rooms I meditated on it, skimming through it with my faulty French.

The book, 145 folio pages, written on both sides, was bound in eighteenth-century blind-tooled calf without lettering. The title page read in part: 'Campagnes Tirées mot pour mot des memoirs de Jacques Stuart Pour lors Duc d'Yorck, et depuis Roy d'Angleterre Jacques Second. . . .' Bound in were four folio leaves, written on both sides, headed 'Preface du Cardinal de Bouillon', and an attestation with seal, dated 1734, and signed by five members of

the Scots College of the University of Paris. There was a book-
plate of Turenne Aynac and the name 'M[arqu]is de Turenne
d'Aynac' written on the flyleaf.

It was obvious what it was, but I was hazy as to its true importance. Though not particularly well-informed about this period, I
was familiar with Winston Churchill's *Marlborough*. I recalled
his vivid chapter on James II's memoirs, the romantic tale of
the attempt to smuggle them from France to England during
the French Revolution, their destruction at St. Omer, and
the subsequent controversies over the authenticity of various
texts.

The next morning, with Muir translating, we discovered that
the preface was written by Emmanuel-Théodose de la Tour
d'Auvergne, Cardinal de Bouillon, nephew of Henri de la Tour
d'Auvergne, Vicomte de Turenne, the famous French Marshal. In
1695, when the Cardinal had met King James II, then in exile at
St. Germain-en-Laye, the King had told the nephew of his experiences as a young man serving in the French Army under Marshal
Turenne. Since most of this information was unknown to the
Cardinal, he requested the King to set down a record. The King
replied that he had already written memoirs of his early years,
that he would extract from these all references to the Marshal
together with his experiences in the Low Countries down to the
Peace of the Pyrenees and the Restoration of his brother Charles
II to the throne of England, and that he would have them translated into French for presentation to the Cardinal.

On January 27, 1696, James sent for the Cardinal and presented him with this manuscript, with the injunction that it was to
be shown to no one during the King's lifetime. This injunction
was faithfully observed by the Cardinal, not only during the life of
the King, but during his own lifetime also. Not until 1715, the
year of his death, did he write the preface, giving its history and
adding his intention to bequeath it to the next in seniority in the
family of Turenne, with the hope that it would remain in the
possession of the senior member of his family from generation to
generation in perpetuity.

His heir was his nephew, Henri-Oswald de la Tour d'Auvergne,
Comte de Turenne, who inherited from the Cardinal not only this
manuscript but the whole of his very considerable library. The

library was eventually dispersed, but the manuscript remained with the family. Although King James had promised the Cardinal a translation of only those parts of the memoirs that would be of interest to him, it became apparent from the certificate of authentication that the manuscript is a remarkably faithful version of the English original. This certificate of authentication, bound between the Cardinal's preface and the body of the manuscript, was prepared for and given to the Cardinal's nephew. It is signed by five officials of the Scots College of the University of Paris, where the papers of James II had been deposited by his order. The most important of the signers is Louis Inesse, who used the French form of his name, originally Lewis Innes. He had succeeded Robert Barclay as principal of the Scots College in 1682 and devoted himself to the preservation and arrangement of the records in the college library. He was one of the five men who acted as James II's Cabinet at St. Germain after the King's return from Ireland in 1690.

The certificate reads:

These Memoirs of the late King James II of Great Britain conform to the original English Memoirs written in H.M.'s own hand which, in accordance with a Minute signed by his hand, are preserved in our said college. And we, the aforesaid, certify further that the present Manuscript, revised and corrected by the said King James, translated by his order, given by his hand to the late Cardinal de Bouillon on January 27, 1696, and written in the hand of Dempster, one of the Secretaries of his said Majesty, conforms in fact, circumstances, reflections, and generally in every way (the turn of style and method of relation excepted) to a second translation of the same English Memoirs, made by order of the late Queen of Great Britain, signed in her hand, sealed with her Seal bearing her arms, countersigned by my Lord Caryl Secretaire d'Etat on November 14, 1704, and given on January 15, 1705, by the said Louis Inesse to S.A.R. the Cardinal de Bouillon, to be used in the Histoire du Vicomte de Turenne. . . .*

This was a discovery indeed, but what could be done with it? I thought from the first that the family could be persuaded to part with the manuscript if I advanced the theory that it had very little

---

* See the Bibliographical Note, pp. 19, 20, 22 below, for a discussion of this second manuscript.

French interest, since it was merely the translated memoirs of an Englishman who later became King. But we were leaving the next morning and how to persuade the owners and arrange the innumerable details (assuming they were willing to part with the manuscript) was a puzzle. The problem was solved in the simplest manner. I returned to London and left Percy Muir to attend to the details. His account follows.

Randall's discovery of the James II manuscript, coming after our experience in purchasing the Thoreau book, was not discussed at once with the Countess. I was convinced that it would be wise to await a psychological moment at which to broach the subject.

The moment arose soon after a late supper on our last evening at the chateau, when the Countess announced that we must inspect the countryside by moonlight from the battlements. We climbed a spiral staircase in one of the towers, and as we emerged into a kind of loft under the roof we found the floor covered with an amazing variety of receptacles. There were buckets, baths, chamberpots—even a bedpan or two. Our hostess explained that this was a precaution against a repetition of the experience during the previous year's rainy season, when water had streamed through the roof and brought down ceilings. She reminded us of the water-stained walls in the rooms below, which were indicative of the intensity of the flood.

As we emerged onto the roof, the Countess pointed out that all the lead was porous and needed replacing. She had had an estimate for renewing it, but it was a sum entirely beyond her means to provide.

'And you had hoped, perhaps,' I suggested, 'that Landor's books might provide for the possibility.'

'Yes!' she said. 'But you have removed that foolish idea from my head. I am sure your valuation is an honest and accurate one. But the money would go nowhere. Perhaps you will still find something, somewhere in the house, that will keep a roof over my head.'

'We have,' I said. And at three o'clock in the morning, on that moonlit roof, I told her what we had found. I was not surprised to learn that she had no idea of the existence of the document; and its nature had to be described to her in detail. She wanted to see it at once and we went down to examine it. She was quite indefatigable and would have sat up the rest of the night poring over it and discussing it. I finally succeeded in persuading her to retire to her bedroom with the manuscript, and we were able to sleep for a few hours.

The next morning Randall announced that his schedule required that he return to London immediately, so that, while I was able to stay, he was forced to leave with the great purchase still uncompleted. The Countess was torn between reluctance to part with a family document and anxiety about the roof. She had decided that her daughter must be consulted about the manuscript. It was a part of her inheritance and she must make the decision.

'But without a proper roof,' I said, 'neither this manuscript nor anything else in the chateau may be worth inheriting.'

'Of course, you are right,' she answered. 'You will see her in Paris on your return there. She is a very sensible girl. She will see the point. But if she says I am not to sell I shall be glad.'

I had to leave without a decision and without the manuscript, although we did agree to abide by the daughter's future decision. A further condition was made. If we did buy the manuscript, a complete facsimile in a copy of its original eighteenth-century binding was to be made and given to the Countess at our expense.

Since the daughter did approve the purchase, there was a second journey to the chateau, when I did acquire the manuscript. For the conclusion of the story, we must return to Randall's part of this preface:

The delivery of the manuscript to America occurred just prior to my leaving Scribner's to become Librarian of the remarkable collection of rare books and manuscripts which Mr. J. K. Lilly, Jr., of Indianapolis, had given to Indiana University. It became my first major addition to that collection.

The best and most exhaustive account of King James's Memoirs is in Winston Churchill's *Marlborough*.* In it he published for the first time a letter from Thomas Inesse, brother of Louis Inesse,

* George G. Harrap, London, and Charles Scribner's Sons, New York.

and his successor as Principal of the Scots College, to James Edgar, secretary to the Old Pretender, dated Paris, October 17, 1740.

There were, it appears, four manuscripts of the Memoirs, two in English and two in French, which may be described as follows: (1) The original English manuscript written in the hand of King James himself and (2) an English transcription thereof. These are referred to by Thomas Inesse in this way:

Now the Orig. Memoires having been at first all written upon paper of different Seizes such as his late Maty had about him or at hand during his Campagnes or in the different parts he happened to be; were in no kind of order till by his late Maties directions, my Brother arranged them and caused bind them up in three vols with references to mark the suitte [sequence]. Besides this, they are in some places by length of time and bad ink become almost illegible so that M. Carte sometimes not a little puzzled to make them out: To remedy this I thought properr to communicate to him a fair copy we have of these Memoires ending, as the Orgls do, at the Restoration in 3 vols in 4°, upon the first Volume of which is the following notte in my Brothers hand ... [transcribed in 3 volumes in 4° from the King's Original Memoires by M. Dryden the famous Poet,[1] in the year 1686, and afterwards revised by his Majesty, and in Severall places corrected in his own hand].

There are besides some other Markes upon this copy of Mr. Dryden by which it would appear that A.D. 1686 when it was making ready for the Press and probably it had been published, if the unhappy Revolution had not soon after fallen out.

'... The chief differences between this Copy and the Original consist in this that whereas in the Origl Memoires H.M. speaks always of himself in the third person [2] ... in this copy of M. Dryden he is made always to speak in the first person. ...'

(3) The present French version and (4), as detailed in the Certificate of Attestation, a second French translation made after the King's death for his widow, Mary of Modena.

Churchill's account disposes of many previously accepted inaccuracies, for example, the highly misleading account in the

---

[1] Assumed to be Charles Dryden, the poet's son.
[2] A study of the copy of James II's Memoirs published by J. S. Clarke in 1816 leads one to doubt this statement (Editor).

bibliographical notes to A. W. Ward's article in the *Dictionary of National Biography*. This article sets down and summarizes as fact many views or statements which are challenged by Churchill. It is suggested, for example, that James II either wrote or supervised the preparation of the Memoirs down to the year 1678. Churchill argues that the only Memoirs written by the King were those contained in the present manuscript which ends with the Restoration of Charles II.[3]

Churchill discusses the fate of the original English Memoirs.

'There is no doubt about the existence of the Memoirs nor where they lay during the whole of the eighteenth century. On the outbreak of the French Revolution the Scots College tried by various channels to send these historical treasures to England for safety. In 1793 it is believed that a Monsieur Charpentier finally undertook the task. He was arrested at Saint-Omer, and his wife, fearing lest the Royal Arms of hostile England on the bindings might be compromising, first buried the volumes in the garden of her house, and later dug them up and burned them. Thus ended the travels of the Memoirs, the only original memoirs " writ in the King's own hand ".'

It is not clear from Churchill's account whether the second English transcription (2, above) and the last French translation (4, above) were also destroyed in like manner. It seems most likely that they were. In any event they have never been recovered and were not at the Scots College in Paris when Charles James Fox visited there in 1802.

Now arises the question of the printing of the various manuscripts. During the eighteenth century some access was had to James's Memoirs and other papers deposited in the Scots College and several works, a 'Life', etc., were written from them. First, the English. Ward, in *D.N.B.*, states categorically: 'Of the materials used by the compilers [of the *Life of James II*] genuine remains exist in the extracts made from the Memoirs by Carte—as well as in those by Macpherson....'

These references are to three different sources:

---

[3] Evidence has now come to light to suggest that James continued to write memoirs, though not perhaps continuously, after 1660 and even into the 1680's (Editor).

(1) *The Life of James II collected out of Memoirs writ in his own hand.* By James Clarke. 1816.

(2) *The Life of the Duke of Ormonde.* By Thomas Carte. 1736.

(3) *Original Papers containing the secret history of Great Britain from the Restoration to the accession of the House of Hanover.* By James Macpherson. 1775.

James Macpherson is best known for his equivocal fostering of the poems of 'Ossian', an association which is hardly a recommendation in an historian. Churchill disposes of his claim to authority summarily and effectively. His labours are 'irrelevant and redundant' and may be allowed 'to pass without further comment from the account'.

Churchill also clears up the confusion about the Memoirs and a 'Life'. About 1707 James II's son, the Old Pretender, caused a detailed biography of his father to be compiled by a Jacobite gentleman named Dicconson, which was deposited at the Scots College for many years. A copy of his manuscript was acquired by an English Benedictine community in Italy. It was purchased during the Napoleonic Wars by the Prince of Wales, afterwards George IV, who had it edited by the Rev. James Clarke, his historiographer, and printed in 1816. This is source-reference (1) above.

Carte's claim to have quoted or copied any considerable portion of the original Memoirs is disposed of by the letter from Thomas Inesse, quoted above. Inesse had made available to Carte the rewritten version made by Dryden in 1686, and it was from this version that Carte's extracts were made.

From this bibliographical material, several interesting points emerge. First, it is clear that at no time has the original English manuscript been printed, only the passages quoted or condensed by Dicconson have survived. Secondly, at no time when printing of the Memoirs was feasible were they in a fit state to be printed, because of their haphazard compilation and their illegibility. Finally, and most important of all for our present purpose, the only redaction of the Memoirs, made under the King's personal supervision, known to have survived in any form is the present manuscript.

Admittedly the King supervised the Dryden version; but Inesse expressly mentions 'the differences in it from the Original' and specifies for example, that Dryden's version was written in the first person throughout,[4] whereas the original was in the third person, thereby disposing of any possible notion that this might be a translation of Dryden's version, rather than the original.

The reference to a second French translation in the certificate from the Scots College which accompanies the present manuscript is confusing. Two dates are mentioned in connection with it, 1704, when it was sealed by 'My Lord Caryl', Secretary of State, and 1705, when it was said to have been given by Louis Inesse to the Cardinal de Bouillon to be used in the *Histoire du Vicomte Turenne*.

These dates are not without interest and significance. In 1701, after the death of James II, John Caryll was appointed as one of the Old Pretender's Secretaries of State and created Baron. And that same year he wrote to James II's widow, Mary of Modena, that he was engaged with the King's Memoirs. There can be little doubt that this refers to the commissioning of the second French translation, and the affixing of his seal to it in 1704 probably signifies its completion.

There remains the mystery of why it should have been entrusted to the Cardinal in 1705, when he had been given his own manuscript of the Memoirs nine years before. The probable explanation is that the second manuscript was lent to him for purposes of collation and comparison before the printing of the *Histoire* was undertaken. Whatever may have been the Cardinal's intentions it was not he, but his nephew, who supervised the publication of the *Histoire du Vicomte de Turenne*, in which the known documents relating to the life of Marshal Turenne were printed. By 1705 the Cardinal was in serious political difficulties; in 1710 he was exiled. The *Histoire*, published in 1735, included a section entitled 'Les Memoires du Duc d'Yorck, depuis Jacques II. Roi de la Grande-Bretagne,' which is based on the present manuscript.

There are numerous omissions, however, sometimes marked by a row of dots, sometimes not. Generally speaking the printed text is confined to the description of Turenne's campaigns in France and the Low Countries. But the narration of events at the time that James changed sides at the order of his brother Charles and

---

[4] This seems extraordinary, if we are to suppose that the original Memoirs were in the third person. But Thomas Inesse's testimony is suspect (Editor).

joined his erstwhile enemies, the Spaniards, against Turenne is suppressed. The most important omissions in the *Histoire*'s text are the detailed and interesting accounts toward the end of the Memoirs portraying the negotiations for and ending with the Restoration of Charles II. The *Histoire* ends James's Memoirs in 1658.

Therefore it is clear that these Memoirs have never been printed in their entirety or verbatim. Their discovery makes it possible for the first time to check the accuracy of Dicconson, Carte, Macpherson, and all those scholars and historians who have relied upon them.

Takeley, Bishop's Stortford   Percy Muir
and
Bloomington, Indiana   David A. Randall

TRANSLATOR'S INTRODUCTION

IN the foregoing pages, Mr. David Randall has reconstructed the history of the various manuscripts and printed works that contain records of the life of James II. The present writer's task has been not simply to translate those portions of the French manuscript, *Campagnes* . . . *de Jacques Stuart*, which are of value or importance to history, but also, by comparing the text it contains with those contained in the *Histoire du Vicomte de Turenne* (1735) and in *The Life of James II* (1816), to assess the relative value of these works and also, by comparison and analysis, to propose tentative conclusions regarding the text of the autograph memoirs of James II.

If then we leave aside those works which are of inferior value, such as Macpherson's *Original Papers* (1775); or which have disappeared and perhaps been destroyed, such as Charles Dryden's revision of James's memoirs, and the second translation of the military memoirs to which the heads of the Scottish College allude in the certificate preceding our manuscript—if we leave these aside, we have four documents to consider:

I. James's autograph memoirs (in English).

II. The French MS. entitled *Campagnes*. . . .

III. (*a*) *The Mémoires du Duc d'Yorck* printed by A. M. Ramsay as an appendix to Vol. II of his *Histoire du Vicomte de Turenne* (Paris, 1735).

(*b*) The English translation of the above (London, 1735).

IV. *The Life of James II collected out of Memoirs writ of his own hand*. Edited by the Rev. J. S. Clarke (London, 1816).

I. JAMES'S AUTOGRAPH MEMOIRS. On the testimony of Thomas Innes, Vice-Principal of the Collège des Ecossais in Paris, testimony conveyed in a letter of 1740 to the secretary of James Francis Edward Stuart,[1] it has been supposed that these memoirs related the story of his life down to the Restoration in 1660, and that they were written in the third person. They were preserved

[1] The so-called 'Old Pretender'.

for many years at the above college, but were destroyed about 1793 during the Revolution. Andrew Michael Ramsay speaks of them in the 'Avertissement' he placed at the beginning of his *Histoire du Vicomte de Turenne*,[2] where he lists the original sources to which he has had recourse. Of these the third is James's memoirs:

Les Mémoires du Duc d'Yorck, depuis Jacques II. Roi de la Grande Bretagne, qui servit quatre ans avec le Vicomte pendant les guerres civiles, & deux ans avec le Prince de Condé dans l'armée Espagnole: l'un & l'autre de ces deux grands Capitaines admirerent toujours la valeur & la capacité du duc d'Yorck. Le Prince Anglois écrivoit dans sa langue le soir ou le lendemain de chaque action, ce qui s'étoit passé sous ses yeux, & le communiquoit ensuite au Général. Le manuscrit original a été déposé au College des Ecossois à Paris. En 1696. ce Prince devenu Roi d'Angleterre,[3] fit faire une Traduction Françoise de tout ce qui regardoit le Vicomte de Turenne, & la donna au feu Cardinal de Bouillon:[4] huit ans après, la Reine sa femme envoya au même Cardinal une autre Traduction des mêmes Mémoires, signée de sa main, scellée de son grand Sceau & contresignée par Mylord Caryll, Secrétaire d'Etat.[5]

It emerges from the above that, in Ramsay's belief, the military part of the memoirs, that is, the part that covered the years 1652 to 1658 inclusive, had been composed as a day-to-day journal. This would not apply to the period prior to 1652, nor to the sometimes lengthy passages that describe diplomatic movements and court intrigues. The latter, by the way, are partly omitted or abbreviated in the French translation. One cannot but wonder whether a day-to-day journal would have been written in the third person. It is not clear, from Ramsay's statement, that he had consulted the original memoirs; what he unquestionably utilised was our manuscript translation.

II. 'CAMPAGNES ... DE JACQUES STUART.' This MS., entirely in French, contains 290 folio pages of narrative (145 sheets written on both sides), with an entry for each year from 1652 to

---

[2] Paris, 1735, 2 vols. in folio. Vol. I (the introductory matter is not paginated. The pages in question would be x–xi).
[3] He had not been king *de facto* after 1688.
[4] This is our MS.
[5] This has disappeared.

1659–60 inclusive.* The entry for 1652 is very long (85 pages); that for 1659 (which includes 1660) very short (14 pages). There are nine pages of preliminary matter: the Cardinal's preface (8 pages) and the Certificate from the Collège des Ecossais (1 page). The narrative of the *Campagnes* is in the third person throughout. The certificate affirms that the text of *Campagnes* is conformable ('conforme') to the late king's autograph memoirs. It is certain that the translation was made under James's direction and supervision and it is not impossible that he dictated it himself, translating from his own memoirs, while Dempster took it down. James was no writer – his letters are often very obscure – and the literary deficiencies which are here and there apparent in the French MS., so that it is not always at once clear whom 'he' or 'they' refer to, and which 'armée', the French or the Spanish, is in question, are in keeping with what we know of his way of writing. One can be sure that he read or reread, and corrected, the MS. because a few of the corrections are in a hand different from, and inferior to, that of the MS. as a whole. I think also that a few remarks or statements, such as the pious moralising, à propos of the Frondeurs, on the just doom that befalls rebels (MS. p. 47) and the record of James's first meeting with Anne Hyde (MS. pp. 195–196) were inserted when the translation was made, and were not in the original memoirs. They are certainly not in the *Life* (ed. Clarke). But these considerations go to establish the authenticity of the MS., if indeed further evidence of this were needed.

IV. I turn next, for convenience, to *The Life of James II collected out of Memoirs writ of his own hand*. This work can with some certainty be ascribed to a 'M. Dicconson'[6] who was entrusted with the task by James's son and heir, Prince James Francis Edward. His identity is still not widely known, although it was brought to light by Mr. Malcolm Hay[7] as recently as

---

* James used New Style dates throughout his MS.

[6] According to the statement of Thomas Innes in the letter of 1740 referred to above. Sir Winston Churchill, who quotes this letter in vol. I of *Marlborough, his Life and Times* (London, 1933) takes the same view, and he regards the last part of the *Life* as an unreliable document (see vol. I, 356, 357, 363, 364).

[7] M. V. Hay, *Winston Churchill and James II* (London, 1934), pp. 9–10.

1934. William Dicconson (1655–1743) was the eldest son of Hugh Dicconson, of Wrightington Hall in Lancashire.[8] As a Catholic and Royalist he was devoted to the Stuart cause and he served as treasurer to the exiled Court at Saint-Germain. He was a layman and should not be confused with his younger brother Edward,[9] who in later years was Vicar Apostolic for the northern district of England. When William Dicconson came to edit the memoirs and other records of the life of James II, he certainly wrote from a Jacobite standpoint, and he can scarcely be expected to have spoken impartially about the adversaries of the House of Stuart and particularly about John Churchill. That he handled those records which concerned the Restoration, and especially the critical years after about 1671, in such a way as to present James in the most favourable light, seems more than probable. But for the period of James's soldiering in France, he would have fewer motives for omitting any important circumstance, and here at least I have discovered no evidence to suggest that he falsified James's own memoirs.

However that may be, the MS. *Life of James II* which he prepared, or a copy of it, subsequently came into the hands of the English Benedictines in Italy. From them it was acquired by the future George IV and was printed in two folio volumes by the Rev. J. S. Clarke in 1816. Now it is generally supposed, again on the testimony of Thomas Innes, that James's own memoirs ceased with the Restoration, that is, at the same point as the French MS. *Campagnes*. It would follow that by far the greater part of the *Life* (Vol. I, 385–750 and all Vol. II) is the work of secretaries or others. I have reason to believe, on the contrary, that James continued to record his doings. The question is important for the historian of the reigns of Charles II, James II, and William and Mary; but it is of no moment for a study of James's campaigns in France.

For this earlier period (1652–1659) and for his still earlier life, he certainly left memoirs. Although they have been lost, we can

    [8] J. Gillow, *Bibliographical Dictionary of the English Catholics* (London, 1855), vol. II, 60–62. Cited by Hay.
    [9] Edward Dicconson (1670–1752) was the third son of Hugh. He was educated at the English College at Douai, where he subsequently held professorships of Syntax, Poetry, and Philosophy, and of which he was Vice-President in 1713–14. He was later sent to Rome as agent of the secular clergy of England (*D.N.B.*).

infer certain things about them by analysing the corresponding portions in the *Life* and in the *Campagnes*: by comparing the *Life* and the *Campagnes*; and by taking account of the testimony contained in the Certificate from the Scottish College (1734) and in a letter from Thomas Innes to the secretary of Prince James Francis Edward (1740). Of this, more later.

To return to J. S. Clarke's edition: this ostensibly includes a copy of James's autograph memoirs, probably edited and narrated partly in the third, partly in the first person. For the years prior to 1652 the narrative is in the third person; but for the years covered by the French MS. an unusual procedure has been adopted by the copyist or editor (presumably Dicconson). Sometimes the narrative is in the third person; but at other times the editor writes, for example, as follows: 'Of this Campagne his R. Highness gives the following Account in the Memoires written in his own hand' (Clarke, Vol. I, 159); and the section that follows is in the first person. Here is the arrangement: 1652: third person; 1653, 1654, 1655: first person; 1656: third person; 1657 (a) Introductory portion (Clarke I, 288–296): third person; (b) narrative of the campaign (pp. 297–329): first person; 1658: first person; 1659–60: third person. In all the instances of first person narrative, on pp. 159 (for 1653), 192 (for 1654), 244 (for 1655), and 296 (for 1657 and 1658), the editor states that the account is from James's own memoirs, and there seems no reason to suppose that he is not copying them textually. As regards the other years, namely 1652, 1656, introduction to 1657, and 1659–60, he is frankly editing the memoirs, at any rate to the extent of putting them into the third person. Thus, a study of the Clarke edition, which is invaluable for this and other reasons, has come near to convincing me that the original memoirs were in the first person throughout. One must here mention another document, which has also been lost: a version of the original memoirs which is said to have been made by 'Dryden' (presumably Charles Dryden, son of the dramatist) and which is described as an improvement on them. Now in the letter of 1740, referred to above, Thomas Innes says there were differences between the original version and Dryden's, although James supervised the latter. One may assume that the differences were mainly literary. Innes further states that Dryden's version was in the first person, while the original was in the third. This last statement is extraordinary. The text published by Clarke casts the greatest doubt on it; one would be astonished indeed if James, after writing his own memoirs in the third person, employed Dryden to rewrite them in the first. May we not assume that Innes had confused in his memory the original memoirs with the *Life* as edited by Dicconson?

Finally, I see no reason to regard this version of Dicconson's, which was to be published by Clarke, as containing anything but an honest edition, sometimes a copy, sometimes an arrangement, of James's own memoirs down to 1660.[9a] Where the editor interpolates a remark of his own, the thing is fairly clear. As, however, we have no absolute proof of the above, we cannot be certain of its authenticity, still less of its reliability. For my own part, I believe it to be authentic as regards the sections that are in the first person.

With the MS. we are on firm ground. We can now compare it with the *Life*. The entries in the MS. for the years 1652, 1653, 1654, 1655, and 1658 do not differ materially from the corresponding sections in the Clarke edition. The entries for 1656 are similar for the first few pages (MS. pp. 195–199: Clarke, I, 267–271), except that in the MS. James has inserted, at the top of p. 196, an account of his first meeting with Anne Hyde. This took place in February 1656, between Péronne and Cambrai, and is nowhere else recorded. The account of Dr. Frazer's mission, on p. 271 of Clarke, is followed by a narrative of court intrigues (pp. 271–275) which is omitted in the MS., as is a part of pp. 276–277. The encounter with Lockhart at Clermont is in both texts.

There next follow in Clarke, still under the heading 1656, several pages about James's doings in the Netherlands and Lord Bristol's machinations (pp. 279–287). Under 1657 we have a further account of James, now in Holland, of the efforts to make him join the Spanish army, and a good deal more about Lord Bristol (pp. 289–299). These parts (pp. 279–287, and 287–299) are omitted from the MS., where the account of the campaign of 1657 (beginning on MS. p. 202) corresponds with the passage beginning on p. 299 of Clarke. Thus some 25 pages which were

---

[9a] And also of memoirs, possibly not complete, which he wrote for many years after 1660, and probably until 1684. See his remarks to the Cardinal (p. 52 below): 'even confiding to me that, as he had already written pretty exactly year by year in English the memoirs of his own life, he would....'

presumably in the original memoirs, and were mainly of personal and diplomatic interest, do not figure in the MS. Apart from this, the entries in the two works for 1657 are similar. The story of how, during the siege of Mardyck, the French officers identified James by reason of the greyhound they had previously seen with him in France, is in both narratives; likewise the fraternising between the officers and the interview with Reynolds who, according to James, hinted that he might one day render him service (MS. pp. 229–230: Clarke, p. 327). James appears later to have had doubts about this, because in the MS. he interpolated the following remark: 'On ne scait point quelle intention Reynold (sic) pouvoit avoir.' We do not know, either; and we also have doubts.[10] The entries for 1658 are virtually identical and those for 1659 and the early months of 1660 are very similar. The narrative in the MS. is slightly abbreviated in one or two places (for 1659–60) and no attempt is made to translate 'the Select Knott' which is simply described as a 'conjuration' (MS. p. 279: Clarke p. 371).

Such are the main differences between the MS. and the text printed by Clarke; these, and minor differences, are indicated in footnotes to the translation.

III (a). The *Mémoires du Duc d'Yorck* published by Andrew Michael Ramsay among the 'pièces justificatives' at the end of Vol. II of his *Histoire du Vicomte de Turenne* (Paris, 1735, i–cl),[11] were obviously transcribed from the MS. now at Indiana University. This MS. must have belonged to the then Duc de Bouillon, and we know for a certainty that Ramsay had been for the past three or four years intendant and tutor to the Duke's son, the little Vicomte de Turenne. The whole work is dedicated to this little boy, and is designed to inspire him to emulate the virtues of his great-uncle (or rather, great-great-uncle).

The Cardinal's preface is here (p. ii) and the certificate from the Collège des Ecossais (p. cl). The text as a whole has been carefully copied, the paragraphs slightly modified; but a large number of passages, some of them substantial, have been omitted, and although omissions are often indicated by a row of dots, they are

[10] See Maurice Ashley, *Cromwell's Generals*. London, 1954, pp. 190, 234.
[11] But this is a pagination relevant only to this 'pièce'.

not always so indicated, as for example on p. cxlviii (relating to 1659 but placed under the heading of 1658) where seven pages (pp. 277–284) of our MS. are simply passed over, the 'loose ends' being joined by a few words of paraphrase. Some of these omissions are trifling, others fairly important. Here is a summary:[12]

1654. MS. p. 118 : there are a few minor omissions in Ramsay, p. lxxv.
   MS. p. 123 line 9 to p. 124 line 5 are omitted in Ramsay p. lxxviii.
   MS. p. 140 line 5 to p. 141 line 25 are omitted in Ramsay p. lxxxvii.
   MS. p. 163 line 21 to p. 164 line 4 are omitted in Ramsay p. xcix.
1655. MS. p. 181 line 14 to the bottom of the page (line 29) are omitted in Ramsay p. cviii.
   MS. p. 195 (relating to 1656). The opening lines (1–10) are omitted in Ramsay, p. cxv (How Mazarin and the Queen explained to James the difficulty arising out of the treaty with Cromwell).
1656. MS. p. 195 line 28 to p. 196 line 6. This passage, which describes James's first meeting with Mistress Hyde, is omitted in Ramsay p. cxv.
   MS. p. 196 line 25 to p. 198 line 9 are omitted in Ramsay p. cxvi.
   MS. p. 199 line 18 to end of p. 121 are omitted in Ramsay (this includes the encounter with Lockhart).
1657. MS. p. 212 line 14 to bottom of page (16 lines) are omitted in Ramsay p. cxxii. Ramsay slightly rewords the first four lines of p. 213.
   MS. p. 219 line 28 (at bottom), all pages 220 and 221 to p. 222 line 17 are omitted in Ramsay p. cxxvi.
   MS. p. 228 from line 7, all p. 229 and to p. 230 line 23 (the anecdote about Reynolds), are omitted in Ramsay p. cxxix.
1658. MS. pp. 232–236 inclusive and to p. 237 line 5 (Lord Bristol's plan for the invasion of England and advice to James regarding his policy towards the Spaniards). All this is omitted by Ramsay, middle of p. cxxix. R. resumes at MS. p. 237, line 7.
1659. MS. p. 277 line 11 to p. 284 line 16 (Hopes of a Royalist insurrection in England; disappointment; Charles II's journey to the Spanish frontier). These portions, about 7 pages, are omitted in Ramsay p. cxlviii, where we read: 'Tous ces projets échouèrent. Le Roi Charles alla *incognito* en Espagne, où l'on travailloit à la Paix des Pyrénnées (*sic*). Le Duc d'Yorck se retira à Boulogne sur mer.' And from this point the MS. is reproduced.

[12] See also the accompanying Concordance.

CONCORDANCE FOR THE
CAMPAIGNS OF THE DUKE OF YORK

Year	MS. *Campagnes* (1696)	Ramsay, *Histoire de Turenne*. Vol. II (1735)	Eng. trans. *History of Turenne* Vol. II (1735)	*Life*, ed. J. S. Clarke (1816) Vol. I
1652	pp. 1–85 (events in 1653 begin on p. 81)	pp. iii–lvii (events in 1653 begin on p. lv)	pp. 343–404	pp. 54–157
1653	87–115	lviii–lxxiii	404–426	159–191
1654	116–172	lxxiv–ciii	427–461 ("1653" is printed in error at the head of certain pages.)	192–244
1655	173–194	ciii–cxv	461–475	245–266
1656	195–201	cxv–cxvi (A great deal omitted, including the meeting with Anne Hyde and the encounter with Lockhart.)	475–477	267–287 (A full account, containing material not in the MS., but *not* the meeting with Anne Hyde.)
1657	202–231	cxvi–cxxix	477–492	288–329 (A fuller account than in the MS.)
1658	232–276	cxxix–cxlviii (On p. cxxxv Condé's remark to the Duke of Gloucester is altered and "improved.")	492–513	330–368
1659 (and 1660)	277–290 The entry for 1660 begins on p. 289.	cxlviii–cl Beginning on p. cxlviii, 7 pages of the MS. (277–284) are omitted and all this part is headed 1658, although it really belongs to 1659. Pp. 288–290 of the MS. are omitted. Nothing for 1660	514–516 Nothing for 1660	369–380 [1660] 381–382

MS. p. 286 lines 3 to 12 (choice of an English port at which to land). Omitted in Ramsay, p. cxlix.

MS. p. 286, last line, and all of pp. 288, 289, and 290 are omitted by Ramsay, who concludes his edition of James's memoirs at the point where Turenne advises James to take patience and wait, gives him 300 pistoles and a passport (MS. p. 287, Ramsay pp. cxlix, cl). In brief, the offer to James of a naval command under the Spaniards, his preparation to go to Spain, and finally the events leading up to the Restoration do not figure in Ramsay.

To sum up: Ramsay generally leaves out of his edition all passages not of military interest; passages that concern James's private life or encounters with compatriots; and those that relate to Bristol's intrigues. His edition is therefore less valuable than our MS. and of course much less compendious than the *Life* (ed. Clarke). It has, however, been valuable as an historical source and was used for this purpose by the editor of Turenne's *Mémoires* and by others. In transcribing the MS. Ramsay took a liberty in two instances. At the top of p. 6 where James says that in the spring of 1652 the Spanish army crossed the Seine at Mantes with a view to joining the Princes' army 'qui estoit alors assemblée aux environs de . . .', he left the place a blank. Ramsay inserted 'Montargis', which may be correct. The other instance seems to have hitherto escaped everyone's notice, perhaps because it concerned the critical hour preceding the battle of the Dunes (1658) and because Ramsay's text has been considered authentic—as indeed it seems to be in other respects. On the evening prior to the battle Condé had warned the Spanish generals that Turenne and the English would certainly fight them. The Spaniards remained slightly incredulous. About 5 a.m. next morning the Anglo-French army was seen to be advancing. Condé who, all along, had been aware of the extreme peril of the situation, was now on horseback near Prince James and Prince Henry. James writes (MS. pp. 249–250): '. . . et voiant le Duc de Glocester [Henry], il [Condé] luy demanda s'il s'estoit jamais trouvé à une battaille. Il respondit que non et le Prince luy dit dans une demie heure vous en verrez une.' This was so evident that one wonders whether Condé did not really say something better. Ramsay seems to have thought so, because he boldly altered it (one wonders on what authority) so that on p. cxxxv of his edition we read: '& le Prince lui dit: *dans une demie heure vous verrez comment nous en perdrons une.*' (The italics are Ramsay's.) This is much better, and there is little doubt that it is what Condé was *thinking*; but it is not in the MS., or in Clarke. Some of the best historians have gleefully seized on it and perpetuated it; and it has come as a shock to the present writer to discover that, if Ramsay had any authority for taking such a liberty with James's MS.—for, in other words, so brilliantly improving upon history—he does not cite it. But he lived in an age of wits.

III (b). The contemporary English translation of Ramsay's *Histoire de Turenne* is the work of a man well conversant with French and master of an English style that is concise, vigorous, masculine. I doubt whether it could be equalled today, and I see no mistake in it, except possibly in the rendering in one place of the difficult word 'insulte'. The translator knew that 'insulter' not only meant 'to insult' in the modern sense, but 'to deliver a physical attack', 'to assault'. Thus, he translates the phrase: 'dans le dessein d'insulter un ouvrage avancé . . .' (MS. p. 20, Ramsay, p. xiv) by: 'with a view to batter an advanced work' (English version, p. 356). In the place where the members of the English court, then lodged in the Louvre, dared not even look out of the windows, 'de peur de s'attirer quelque insulte, ou au moins quelques injures', on account of the animosity of the Parisians (MS. p. 33, Ramsay p. 23), the translation reads: 'for fear of some insult, or at least some abusive language' (p. 366). The word 'insult' could still mean 'to leap upon' (cf. the sense in Latin), and this meaning, which is very near that of the French text, is given by Dr. Johnson in his *Dictionary* (1783).

The passage about Anne Hyde is of course absent from the English translation, and the probably apocryphal remark that Ramsay attributed to Condé is naturally and in good faith reproduced on p. 499: 'in half an hour's time you will see how we shall lose one [a battle].' The translator made one slip in connection with the movements of the French and English to blockade Dunkirk. The French having invested the place by land, the Spaniards could not relieve it from the sea, 'parce que', as we read in the MS., p. 241, and in Ramsay, p. cxxxi, 'la flotte Angloise commandée par le Général Montaigu, fermoit l'entrée du port'. The English version (p. 494) reads 'General Montaigne', a curious error. Sir Edward Montagu, a very prominent man, had been joint-commander of the Commonwealth navy since 1655. Less than two years after the siege of Dunkirk, he was to bring a fleet over to Holland to transport Charles II and the Royal family to Dover. Charles created him Earl of Sandwich. It was through him that Samuel Pepys, who was his cousin, became Secretary to the Navy Board.

In view of the consideration that, as the above analysis has shown, the greater part of the French manuscript appears to be a close translation of a text identical with the text printed by Clarke —always allowing for occasional paraphrase, abbreviation, and omission—it has been thought impracticable to translate the whole of it back into English. The gain to scholarship would have been negligible. It was therefore decided to translate the entry for 1652, which is the longest, while keeping an eye on the corresponding pages in the *Life* and inserting in square brackets those passages from the *Life* of which the French text is a *literal* translation. For the years 1656 and 1657 the differences were sufficiently marked to justify a complete retranslation. While it would have been vain to attempt an absolute reconstruction, the translator has tried to use language not too far remote from what the original must have been.

The entries for the other years have been reprinted from the Clarke edition; so that the reader now has before him a complete English version of James's military memoirs, a version based on the Bouillon MS., which is the only record of the period that we can regard as authentic.

James writes plainly and conscientiously, though without much distinction. His comments are of the driest; he has none of the good-natured and cynical wit of his elder brother. What a relief to turn from his pages to the shrewd and brilliant memoirs of Mademoiselle de Montpensier, and Retz, and Bussy-Rabutin, or to the random and vivid jottings of Aubrey, or to the sparkling diary of the incomparable Pepys! But this is to compare James with some of the most brilliant prosateurs who have ever lived. One is reminded, in reading him, of a witty Frenchman's description of Simonides' dilemma when he was asked to compose an epigram on a great athlete: 'Il trouvait son sujet plein de détails tout nus.' James's 'campaigns' are indeed full of details innocent of adornment. Add to this a complete lack of verve in the syntax, and it requires much self-denial to leave his language alone: that is, to put it back into the kind of English he habitually wrote. Of style, he had nothing; and this is why he conveys so little sensation of reality. If the spirit of the time ever breathes in these pages, it is only on rare occasions when he relates an anecdote or speaks of the 'civilities' that were exchanged between officers of opposing armies. One would never guess, from James's record, that life in those days was extraordinarily varied, picturesque, and entertaining, that men and women spoke and acted with a license, an *insouciance*, almost unknown today. The human spirit was still, to use modern jargon, 'uninhibited'. War was occasionally far more amusing than we should gather from James's memoirs, but it was usually far more terrible, too. Yet all this is plain enough from other records, and these we must consult if we are to see James's memoirs in their true focus and draw a picture of the age in which he lived.

To turn the leaves of the old records, to compare and collate them, is neither dull nor tedious. These men and women were like ourselves, or rather like our great contemporaries—creatures animated by hope or fear, by ambition or love of money, by love of glory or love of God. If they were not cast in a bigger mould than the men of today, they were apparently less cramped by timidity and convention.

Take the Cardinal de Bouillon, for whom and for the sake of whose family James arranged for his memoirs to be translated. To read the Cardinal's preface, one would take him for a timid, even subservient and conventional ecclesiastic. On the contrary, he had been haughty, imprudent, and ambitious, and he was still, at the age of fifty-two (he had been born in 1644), one of the most independent-minded and rebellious spirits of the age. But it is appropriate that at this point we should say something about his forebears and relations, something about a troubled career which, in the years that followed, was to agitate the French court and the court of Rome even more than it had agitated them in the past.

The family of La Tour d'Auvergne, which had possessed a fief in the Limousin (whence the name of Turenne), had risen to greatness in the sixteenth century, partly by their alliance with the house of Montmorency, still more by the marriage in 1594 of Henri de la Tour d'Auvergne, Vicomte de Turenne (1555–1623), with Charlotte de la Marck. Charlotte was the last survivor and heiress of those semi-independent princes who had been rulers of the Ardennes.[13] It was through this marriage that the Vicomte became Duc de Bouillon and Prince de Sedan, master of these great fortresses and of a principality which the Papacy was later to recognise as sovereign. He was a Calvinist, a companion-in-arms of Henri IV, and a Marshal of France. When Henri IV turned Catholic, the Duke remained faithful to the reformed religion. He was recognised in later years as head of the Huguenot party and, by his foundation of a Protestant Academy at Sedan, as 'père et protecteur des lettres'.

By his wife, Elisabeth of Nassau, a daughter of William of Orange, he had two sons: Frédéric-Maurice, Duc de Bouillon (1605–1652), and Henri, Vicomte de Turenne (1611–1675). Both were brought up as Calvinists. In 1623, at the age of fourteen, Frédéric-Maurice succeeded his father as Duke. He learned the profession of arms from his uncle, Prince Maurice, in Holland; he then entered the French service, was promoted to the rank of Lieutenant-General in 1642 and appointed to command the French forces in Italy. But, being implicated in the conspiracy of Cinq-Mars, he was arrested by order of Richelieu and would probably have shared the fate of the others, if his wife—a woman of character and resolution—had not at once threatened to hand over Sedan to the Spaniards unless her husband were pardoned. To avert what would have been a catastrophe, the Cardinal released the Duke (1644); but, as usually happened, the former 'won in the exchange'. Bouillon abjured the Protestant faith, was received with open arms in Rome and placed in command of the Papal army. But Richelieu remained master in France.

The Vicomte de Turenne had in the meantime risen rapidly in the French service. He had fought in the Rhineland and Italy; towards 1639 he was a general officer and in 1643 Marshal of

[13] The personality of William de la Marck, 'wild boar of the Ardennes,' will be familiar to readers of *Quentin Durward*.

France. Between 1643 and 1648, Turenne and the Duc d'Enghien (Condé) were joint-commanders in Germany. Turenne was victorious at Nordlingen in 1645, at Zusmarhausen in 1648. But in 1649 his elder brother came back from Italy (Richelieu being dead) and joined the Fronde in opposition to Mazarin. Turenne also joined the Fronde.

For several years the possession of Sedan was in dispute between the French government and the Turenne family. The government seized it in the end, and in 1650, when Duke Frédéric-Maurice submitted to Mazarin, he was given titles and extensive possessions, including the Duchy of Albret, by way of compensation. He was soon to become a trusted counsellor of the Court; but he died in 1652.

He left two sons: Godefroid-Maurice, sometimes called Godefroy-Marie (1641–1721), and Emmanuel-Théodose (1644–1715). Towards 1678 Louis XIV reinstated Godefroid-Maurice in the title and possession of the Duchy of Bouillon. This duke had a son, Emmanuel-Théodose (1667–1730), who became Grand Chambellan du Roi and Governor of Auvergne. This Emmanuel-Théodose was therefore a nephew of the Cardinal, and our MS. must have passed into his possession in 1715. He had a son, Charles-Godefroid (1706–1772), and the latter had a son, Godefroid-Charles-Henri, who must have been born about 1726 or 1727 and who died without issue in 1791. It was for this, the last of the Dukes of Bouillon, as a little boy, that the Chevalier de Ramsay composed the *Histoire de Turenne*.

We may now return to the Cardinal. Born on 24 August 1644 he was brought up as a Catholic and embarked, while still young, on an ecclesiastical career. The 'abbé Duc d'Albret', son of a Prince and nephew of a Marshal of France, might look to the most brilliant future. In 1658 he was a canon of Liége; in 1667 docteur en Sorbonne. Thanks to the influence of his uncle, Turenne, he now became chaplain to Louis XIV, and received the Cardinal's hat. But in the years that followed, he was handicapped by the haughtiness of his character and the imprudence of his conduct. He found occasion to ask, on behalf of a nephew, for part of the county of Auvergne which had been assigned to the Duke of Orleans. The request was refused, and the Cardinal made no secret of his vexation. He did not realise that Louvois was a potential, if not actual enemy, and he had not learned that a wise man should never, even in a private and confidential letter, express views that may give offence in high quarters. The Cardinal wrote a letter in which he attacked the government and criticised Louis' conduct; the minister intercepted it; and the punishment was exile.

Emmanuel-Théodose was not deprived of his benefices; but he had lost the chaplaincy and the road to further advancement was closed. When in 1694 he had hopes of becoming Prince-Bishop of Liége, Louvois prevented his elevation to the see. What exactly was the Cardinal's theological position is hard to determine; but it seems to have been independent. The religious situation in France was, moreover, quite different from the situation in Spain, and even from the conditions prevailing in Italy, where there was more tolerance than in France and much more than in Spain. The Gallican Church was marked by certain *national* traits and, while fairly respectful of Rome, presented some of the features of a national church. Louis XIV had recently acted in defiance of the Papacy· Innocent XI knew, and said, that one does not win souls by violence. Then, too, there were dissident elements among French Catholics. The Jansenist group was learned, saintly, and influential. The king might destroy Port-Royal-des-Champs, but he could not destroy its adherents. And he had not—as he hoped—crushed this heresy before another began to raise its head.

This was the Quietist movement. It too was learned and saintly, and it was supported by a great prince of the Church, François de la Mothe-Fénelon, Archbishop of Cambrai. Bossuet, who was spokesman of the Gallican party, attempted to rebut Fénelon; the King and the Court also opposed the Archbishop; and in 1697 or early 1698 the Cardinal de Bouillon, who had now been taken back into favour, was sent to Rome as the government's emissary. The credit he enjoyed at the Papal court may have had something to do with the king's choice of him: he had been bishop of Albano since 1689 and was now sub-dean of the College of Cardinals. His orders were to defend the Gallican position and press for the condemnation of Fénelon; but he was a great friend of the Archbishop and in the event, instead of attacking him, he appears surreptitiously to have worked in his favour.[14] He failed, it is true, to prevent the condemnation of the Quietists,[15] but this apparently did him no harm in Rome. He had become Bishop of Ostia in December 1698, and was now Dean of the Sacred College.

In Paris it was another story; and one can understand the consternation his procedure had provoked there. He was ordered to return, but now demurred to obeying. As Dean of the College his duties, he alleged, required his remaining in Rome. Paris took a different view; and when Louis ordered the seizure of his benefices, the Cardinal felt obliged to comply. He was exiled to his abbey at Tournus. But by this time, it may be supposed, the highhanded policy of Louis XIV had alienated a man who, whatever his faults of character, had inherited from his ancestors a sense of personal dignity and a great spirit of independence. He began to correspond with foreign powers and in 1710 took refuge in Flanders and wrote a personal letter to the king. The Parlement de Paris immediately ordered his arrest, and his estates were sequestrated. For some time he appears to have wandered abroad; but Clement XI interceded for him and obtained the restitution of his revenues, the Cardinal being permitted to go into retirement in Rome. He was now an old man and in no condition to give further trouble.

It was in Rome on 16 February 1715 (I infer he had recently arrived) that he found the MS. translation of the Duke of York's military memoirs—a MS. he had thought he would never see again. It was a document that bore witness to the greatness of his

---

[14] Alfred Rébelliau, one of the great authorities on the religious history of the age, points out that Bouillon was 'très mécontent du Roi' as well as 'fier et indépendant'; also that he was in close relations with the Italian Jesuits who were freer than the French to support Fénelon (see Lavisse, *Histoire de France*, VIII, Part I, 307–308).

[15] Innocent XII had appointed a committee of ten Cardinals to examine the question whether Fénelon's *Explication des Maximes des Saints* (1697) should be condemned or not. They discussed the problem at length and when at last the matter came to a vote, five were for and five against. The Pope, greatly embarrassed, opined that 'the Archbishop of Cambrai has sinned through excessive love of God, the Bishop of Meaux [Bossuet] has sinned through lack of love of his neighbour'. Rome was clearly then in favour of Fénelon; but Louis wrote urgently and imperiously to the effect that Fénelon must be condemned. The question was therefore re-examined, and after several weeks a brief (not a bull) was promulgated in which his Holiness censured the book, but did not call it heretical and did not name Fénelon; moreover the brief was drafted by the Cardinals who were favourable to Fénelon (P. Janet, *Fénelon*, Paris, 1892, pp. 97–98).

uncle—and of the princely house to which he belonged. Rapidly, anxiously, and in a large hand that becomes almost illegible in the last few lines, he wrote a preface explaining the circumstances in which the translation had been made for him. A fortnight later, on 2 March 1715, he passed away.

The reader may be surprised at the terms of reverence in which he speaks of James. Was he ignorant of the late king's character, of his incontinence and ineptitude, and of the low opinion the French had formed of him? It is hard to suppose so. What seems likely is that he had respected in James, on the one hand the gallantry of his behaviour in the French army and on the other 'the divinity that doth hedge a king'. In the seventeenth century the doctrine of divine right had a serious meaning and a certain validity. It strengthened, in times of disorder, the principle of legitimacy in government and offered some guarantee against anarchy. A king reigns, even if he does not govern, by the grace of God. Those who clung to this doctrine were wiser than they perhaps realised. Thanks largely to it, the era of violence was still hidden in the future.

It would be interesting to learn whether, in the course of his sojourn in Flanders (1710-?), the Cardinal de Bouillon had ever met the future Chevalier de Ramsay; whether, even, it was through the Cardinal that Ramsay entered the service of the Duc de Bouillon. A common association with Fénelon lends point to the question—one dare hardly say the conjecture.

Andrew Michael Ramsay[16] (1686–1743), some of whose ancestors may have been gentlefolk,[17] was a graduate of Edinburgh University. In 1706, when about twenty years of age, he was with the British army in the Netherlands and here—possibly in Holland—in a milieu where a free, mystical speculation in matters religious was rife, he began to find himself detached from the Protestant orthodoxy of his childhood. Aware, at least, of serious difficulties,

---

[16] See A. Chérel, *Un Aventurier religieux au XVIIIe siècle: André-Michel Ramsay*, Paris, 1926.

[17] In the *Histoire de Fénelon*, he is described as 'chevalier baronnet en Ecosse, issu d'une ancienne famille de ce royaume' (*Œuvres complètes de Fénelon*, Paris, 1852, vol. X [second part], p. 205).

he corresponded with theologians in different countries; and finally went over to the Catholic church.[18] He visited Fénelon at Cambrai in 1709, had with him many conversations which he has recorded, and became his literary confidant. It may have been through this connection that Ramsay afterwards entered the family of La Tour d'Auvergne as a tutor and was made a knight of the Order of Saint-Lazare. In 1724 he went to Rome as tutor to Prince Charles Edward (the 'Young Pretender') and Prince Henry, the future Cardinal of York. His subsequent resignation of this post can be ascribed to the lack of harmony in the family and the intrigues that were current in the Stuart entourage. But Ramsay continued to benefit from his association with Fénelon,[19] and the great name of the Archbishop continued to 'protect'[20] his protégé long after the former had been laid to rest. It was this that certainly facilitated his visit to Great Britain in 1730, a visit expressly permitted by George II. Fénelon in fact enjoyed immense prestige in Protestant circles as well as in Catholic. Ramsay was elected a Fellow of the Royal Society, while Oxford conferred on him the degree of LL.D. *honoris causa*.[21]

Returning to France after these triumphs, Ramsay was appointed tutor to the Vicomte de Turenne, Godefroid-Charles-Henri, son of the Duc de Bouillon. The Vicomte was still very young, probably not more than five when Ramsay became his governor (*c.* 1731). Writing towards the beginning of 1735 he urges his pupil: 'Hâtez-vous de sortir de l'Enfance, & montrez de bonne heure que vous serez un jour digne des Héros dont le sang coule dans vos veines'—words that could scarcely have been addressed to a boy over nine or ten years of age. It was on behalf of his patrons that Ramsay had collected or consulted all the documents he could find relative to the life of the great Marshal. The outcome was a magnificent work of scholarship, the first volume containing a biography of Turenne (pp. 1–597), while in the second Ramsay printed Turenne's own *Mémoires* (pp. iii–

---

[18] *Ibid.*, pp. 205–206, but see H. G. Martin, *Fénelon en Hollande*, Amsterdam, 1928, p. 140.

[19] He had published a *Vie de Fénelon* in 1723.

[20] *Histoire de Fénelon*, ed. cited, p. 206.

[21] There was some opposition which, however, Dr. King overcame when, leading Ramsay forward, he declared: 'quod instar omnium est, Fenelonii magni archipraesulis Cameracensis alumnum praesento vobis.'

clxxxvii); the *Relation de la Campagne de Fribourg*, by the Marquis de la Moussaye (pp. clxxxviii–ccix), and various 'Pièces justificatives', which include a selection of letters, Fléchier's *Oraison funèbre*, and the military memoirs of the Duke of York. This work, which Ramsay dedicated to his young pupil, appeared in Paris, 'Chez la Veuve Mazières & J. B. Garnier, Imprimeurs et Libraires de la Reine, ruë Saint-Jacques, à la Providence'. It was immediately, as we have seen, translated into English and published in London.[22] It has been only through this book and its French original that scholars have hitherto had knowledge of the *Campagnes de Jacques Stuart* (our MS.), and that only in a form that is truncated and in one place inaccurate. Not that this remark should be taken as disparaging to the distinguished author of the *Histoire de Turenne*. Ramsay was justly admired for the importance of his works and the excellence of his prose style. For the rest, he was fairly typical of his age: a friend of Louis Racine and Jean Baptiste Rousseau, a deist in Catholic clothing, and also a freemason.[23]

Of his pupil less seems to be known. He succeeded his father in the Dukedom in 1772 and died in 1791. With him expired the senior branch of the family. The Duchy of Bouillon had meanwhile become part of the French domain. The question of how to dispose of it came up in the peace negotiations of 1814 and 1815. At this moment a claimant to the Duchy appeared in the person of Philippe d'Auvergne, who appears to have been the cousin and adopted son of Ramsay's pupil. He was an officer in the British navy; but whether he had been a Royalist refugee in England or (which seems more likely) was descended from the junior branch of the family who came from Jersey and were British subjects,[24] I have not been able to discover. The population of the Duchy

---

[22] 'Printed by James Bettenham: and sold by A. Bettesworth and C. Hitch at the *Red-Lion* in *Pater-noster* Row; and T. Woodward at the *Half Moon* in Fleet Street. MDCCXXXV.'

[23] He died at Saint-Germain-en-Laye in 1743.

[24] This family derived from Edward d'Auvergne (1660–1737), who claimed descent from a junior member of the Bouillon family, probably back in the 16th century. This Edward d'Auvergne (M.A. Oxford) was chaplain to the Scots Guards; he went through the campaigns in Flanders between 1691 and 1698, and chronicled them in seven volumes. In 1701 he became rector of a parish in Essex and in 1729 married a daughter of Philip le Geyt, of Jersey. Their son, Philip d'Auvergne, had a large family, one of whom, a midshipman in the navy, died at Spithead in 1782. It

44

fully accepted his claim, and Louis XVIII supported it; but the Congress of Vienna assigned the Duchy to the Netherlands.

The period of James's life covered by our manuscript is particularly rich in memoirs and correspondence, much of which we owe to the principal actors in the drama. Turenne enables us to appreciate the intellectual character of tactics and strategy. He is no writer, and his language is often clumsy, though his brevity has its advantages. He is not vainglorious, and is never consciously unjust to his great adversary; but he sometimes passes over or ignores the exploits of his generals (*Mémoires du Maréchal de Turenne*, ed. Paul Marichal, Paris, Laurens, 1914).

Jacques de Chastenet, Marquis de Puységur, is one of the most reliable memorialists of the age. He is far more of a writer than Turenne and his pages are often brightened by a quiet sense of humour (*Mémoires*, ed. Tamizey de Larroque, 2 vols., Paris, 1883).

Roger de Rabutin, Comte de Bussy, gives a clear and businesslike account of the operations in which he was engaged. He systematically records the dates which are so often missing in Turenne's memoirs, and thus enables us to check the dates given by James, Puységur, and Montglas. His occasional outbursts of levity should not deceive one as to the solid historical value of his narrative. It seems evident that he kept a day-to-day diary. His faults of character were grave and the many people whom he offended saw to it that he received the minimum of recognition for his services. But the virtues, the wit, and even the peccadilloes which amused his amiable cousin, Madame de Sévigné, have also endeared him to posterity (*Mémoires de Roger de Rabutin*, ed. Ludovic Lalanne, 2 vols., Paris, 1857).

For the Prince de Condé, whose career stands in a class apart, the documentation is immense: his personal correspondence with Lenet and others, in the Condé archives at Chantilly and in the Bibliothèque Nationale; La Moussaye's *Relation*; Woerden's *Biographie*; Désormeaux' *Histoire de Louis de Bourbon*; Le Père Bergier's *Actions mémorables*, etc.; and vols. IV, V, and VI of the Duc d'Aumale's *Histoire des Princes de Condé* (Paris, 1889–96).

seems not unlikely that the Philippe d'Auvergne, who was an adopted son of the last Duc de Bouillon, was a child of the Philip d'Auvergne just mentioned.

45

The best recent works are by the Honourable Eveline Godley, *The Great Condé* (London, 1915), an admirable biography; and by Georges Mongrédien, *Le Grand Condé* (Paris, 1959). The *Mémoires* of François VI, Duc de la Rochefoucauld, one of the great writers of France, cover the period 1624–1652, and only the last year or two of them really concern us (ed. Gilbert and Gourdault, in vol. II of the *Œuvres complètes*, Paris, 1874).

The *Mémoires* of the Cardinal de Retz are invaluable for the political history of France from about 1638 (although they begin earlier) to 1653. His 'Remontrance au Roi', written late in 1657 to protest against the handing over of Mardyck to the English, reveals for all its one-sidedness extraordinary political prescience. As an observer of men and affairs he is shrewd and penetrating, and he is a wonderful portraitist (see *Œuvres complètes*, ed. Feillet, Gourdault, and Chantelauze; also ed. Allem and Thomas, Paris, 1955).

Anne-Marie-Louise d'Orléans, 'la Grande Mademoiselle', wrote what is virtually an autobiography, rich in observations on the social and political life of her times. It is less informative regarding the war, except for the year 1652 when she alone, in the affair at the Porte Saint-Antoine, saved Condé's army from destruction. (*Mémoires*, ed. Chéruel, 4 vols., 1891. See Arvède Barine, *La Jeunesse de la Grande Mademoiselle*, Paris, 1909, and Philippe Amiguet, *La Grande Mademoiselle et son siècle*, Paris, 1957.)

There are of course many other sources: the military memoirs of Montglas, La Trémoïlle, and Tavannes; the civilian memoirs of Omer Talon, Conrart, and others; the correspondence of Turenne, Mazarin, and Condé; the official *Gazette*; La Mesnardière's *Relations guerrières*, etc., etc.

For the nature and principles of war as conducted in the campaigns described by the Duke of York, see Commandant Julien Brossé's commentary which is published in Marichal's edition of the *Mémoires de Turenne* (1914), vol. II, xxvii–xxxiv. The primary object of a commander was not to destroy the enemy's forces but to wear him down by a process of attrition. Hence there were few decisive victories. The main purpose was to secure possession of fortified towns in hostile territory. These enabled one not only to live off the country but to deprive the enemy of food and forage, exhaust his supplies, and thus after a few years compel him to sign peace. We therefore find that sieges play a more conspicuous part than pitched battles. If in 1658 Turenne decided to offer battle to the Spaniards, this was because the exigencies of the political situation, and the massive reinforcements he had received from England, rendered the move advisable. The result was an overwhelming victory; and if it did not actually end the war, it brought the end within sight.

It is a pleasure to acknowledge the support and assistance I have received in preparing this edition. My wife first pointed out to me the interest and importance of the manuscript which Mr. Randall had discovered; and the Director and the Faculty Committee of the Indiana University Press did me the honour of entrusting me with the work. In handling the long entry for 1652 I received most helpful secretarial assistance from Mr. Stanley Gray; while for the rest, and indeed a large part, of the secretarial work, I have been indebted to Mrs. Gray and Mrs. Margaret Lauer, both of whom took a personal interest in a project which has been necessarily complex. My sincere thanks go also to Professor Leo Solt for comparing the French manuscript with the English translation of Ramsay's *Vie de Turenne*; to Sir Arthur Bryant for the introduction which he has so kindly contributed; and to the staff of the Indiana University Press for their encouragement and advice.

Bloomington, Indiana   A.L.S.
January 1961

THE MILITARY MEMOIRS OF
THE DUKE OF YORK

Campaigns

Extracted word for word from the
memoirs of James Stuart Then Duke of York,
and since
King of England, James Second:
from 1652 inclusively till 1660, the year
in which The King of England Charles Second
his brother was re-established
On the throne of Great Britain:
These Memoirs
written by Him self in English, and Translated
into French in his presence,
The Translation Corrected by Him self,
were given by the very hand of this sacred King
at St Germain en Laye the 27th of January, 1696,
to
Emmanuel Théodose de la Tour d'Auvergne,
Cardinal de Bouillon Nephew of
Henry de la Tour d'Auvergne, Vicomte de Turenne,
of whom His Majesty speaks so honourably in the
whole course of these nine years, and especially
in the course of the Campaigns which this
great Prince waged under the Vicomte de Turenne
in 1652, 1653, 1654, 1655, who even did him the
honour until he was made Lieutenant General
in 1654,
of having no other quarters, or lodging,
than those which were assigned for the General

*Preface of the Cardinal Bouillon**

THE King of England James II having done me the honour
of relating to me, in the year 1695, several particulars, and a
few considerable actions in the life of the late Monsieur de
Turenne, my uncle, which were unknown to me, not being reported in the memoirs I have of him, written in his own hand:
I took confidence to testify to this Prince that I was very sorry my
profound respect for him did not permit me to beg him very
humbly to be kind enough, by the friendship he retained for the
late Monsieur de Turenne, to set down in writing, at the hours
that would be least inconvenient to him, the particulars and
actions of which I had no knowledge; and I added that I should[1]
take the liberty of asking this favour of any one but his Majesty,
whom I must respect even more than the memory of the late Monsieur de Turenne which I had regarded until that moment as the
thing that was most dear to me in the world. Whereupon his
Majesty, by a quite particular act of a goodness and generosity
without equal, told me that he would do me this favour with joy,
as soon as it should be possible, even confiding to me that, as he
had already written pretty exactly year by year in English the
memoirs of his own life, he would extract and put into French all
that concerned the campaigns in which he had served in the
French Army commanded by Monsieur de Turenne and those in
which he had next served in the Spanish Army, in the Netherlands, until the declaration of the Peace of the Pyrenees and the
re-establishment of King Charles II his brother on the throne of
Great Britain. I was agreeably surprised on the twenty-seventh of
the month of January of the following year, 1696, when having
gone to St. Germain-en-Laye to pay my respects to this great and
sacred King, he led me into his cabinet where he told me he had
brought me, in order to keep the promise he had made the pre-

---

* This preface is found at the beginning of the Duke of York's Memoirs, and it is
written in the Cardinal de Bouillon's own hand.

[1] '..., et je lui adjoutay que je prendrais la liberte de demander cette faveur a tout
autre qu'a sa Mte, que je devois encore plus respecter, etc.' He was not venturing to
ask, but only to hint that he would like to ask.

vious year, and at the same time put into my hands the present book, in which he assured me he had collected all that he had observed in his Memoirs regarding the late Monsieur de Turenne from the year 1652 inclusively to 1660; and that he made me a gift of it, as much in respect to the memory of the late Monsieur de Turenne which he told me must, all his life, be very dear and very precious to him, because he regarded him as the greatest and most perfect man he had ever known and the best friend he had ever had;[2] as in respect to the friendship with which he honoured me in particular, charging me in the meanwhile never, during his lifetime, to permit anyone to read these memoirs.[3] After rendering his Majesty very humble thanks[4] for this benefit, I promised to execute what he had just ordered me, and I have very faithfully observed it as long as he lived. This gift from the hand of so great a King appears to me so considerable and so honourable for the memory of the late Monsieur de Turenne and for the whole of our house, that from that day, as I had the honour to tell his Majesty on receiving from him this precious gift, I made the resolution to bequeath[5] it one day in perpetuity to the eldest son of our house: and this is what I do today, being at Rome the sixteenth of the month of February of the year one thousand seven hundred and fifteen, having by an act[6] of Divine Providence once more found this precious book which I believed I should never see again.[7]

Le Cardinal de Bouillon, Den du Sre colge.[8]

[2] This passage strikingly confirms the affection and admiration which James elsewhere expresses for Turenne.

[3] '. . . me recommandant cependant de ne donner jamais a qui que ce soit, durant son vivant la lecture de ces memoires.'

[4] 'de tres humbles actions de graces'—strictly, 'thanksgiving', a term appropriate to the person of a sacred Majesty.

[5] 'le substituer', in the legal sense, to bequeath or entail.

[6] 'par un *effet* de la Providence Divine.' (Cf. above 'par un effet tout particulier d'une bonte . . . etc.'.) 'Effet' was commonly used in the sense of 'act' in the 17th century. Corneille has: 'Les effets de César valent bien ses paroles' (*Pompée*, Act V, v. 150).

[7] This suggests that he had left the book in some lodging or with a friend in Rome and that, being aware of his approaching end, had feared he would not see it again. He however found it in time to bequeath it to his family; and his death took place on 2 March, that is, a fortnight after he had written these words.

[8] The signature is hard to read, except for the words 'Bouillon' and 'Den du Sre colge'='Doyen du Sacré Collège.' He had been Dean of the College of Cardinals since December 1698.

Certificate from the Administrators of the Scottish College of Paris

W E the undersigned, Priests and Administrators of the Scottish College in the University of Paris, to wit, Louis Inesse, formerly first Chaplain to the late Queen of Great Britain and former Principal of the College, Charles Whytford, Principal, Thomas Inesse, Vice-Principal, George Inesse, Procurator and Alexander Smith, Prefect of Studies in the same College, certify to all those whom it may concern that the accompanying Memoirs of the late King James II of Great Britain are conformable to the original English Memoirs, written by the hand of his Majesty and preserved, by virtue of a certificate signed by his hand, in the Archives of our College. And we, the above named, certify more-over that the accompanying manuscript, revised and corrected by the above named King James, translated by his order, given by his hand to his late Highness and Eminence the Cardinal de Bouillon, on the twenty-seventh of the month of January, 1696, and written by the hand of Mr. Dempster, one of His Majesty's secretaries, is conformable for the facts, details, circumstances, reflections and generally everything, except for the style only and the order of the relation, to a second translation of the same original English Memoirs made by the order of the late Queen of Great Britain, signed by her hand, sealed with the Seal of her arms, counter-signed by My Lord Caryll, Secretary of State, on the fourteenth of November, 1704, and given on the fifteenth of January, 1705, by the above named Louis Inesse to his Highness and Excellence the Cardinal de Bouillon to serve for the history of the Vicomte de Turenne. In testimony whereof we have signed these presents and have affixed thereto the Seal of the College. Done in Paris this twenty-fourth of December, One Thousand Seven Hundred and Thirty Four.

L. Inesse   *Geo: Inesse*
Ch: Whytford   *Al: Smith*
Tho: Inesse

MEMOIRS
OF THE
DUKE OF YORK

BOOK I

Of The Civil Wars In France 1652*

THE Duke of York was in France in 1652 with the Queen his mother, when the return of Cardinal Mazarin had made it impossible for that Minister's enemies to reconcile themselves with the Court. The Duke judged that the flames of war would be rekindled with great violence; and being very desirous of making himself fit one day to serve the King his brother in a useful capacity, he resolved that, if he could obtain his and the Queen's permission, he would go on campaign as a volunteer in the King of France's army.[1] Sir [John] Berkley was the only person who did not oppose this design when it was first proposed; but by dint of the Duke's insisting, consent was given. However, there remained a much greater difficulty to overcome than the first. Nothing was so rare as money. The French Court was then at Angers, and in very great straits, so much so that, but for the help of three hundred pistoles that were lent him by a Gascon gentleman named Gautier who had served in England, he would have found it impossible to go on campaign. With this small sum his equipage was

* The entry for 1652 has been translated in extenso from the Bouillon manuscript. I have placed between square brackets the passages where the text of the French MS. is a *literal* translation of the original English text as reproduced in the *Life* (ed. Clarke): these passages, in brackets, are taken from the *Life*. It seems clear, however, that both the MS. and the text of the *Life* are based on the same original, and that the French MS. is a somewhat abbreviated version—as I indicate in footnotes.

[1] In place of this sentence, the *Life* (I, 54) reads: 'This being considered by the Duke who was very desirous to improve himself that he might one day be fitt to serve in the French King's Army as a volunteer, And tho when he made . . .'—which makes no sense, as J. S. Clarke saw. He appended the following note: 'Here some words appear to have been omitted by the Secretary, who probably intended to have written: "That he might one day be fitt *to command, he resolved* to serve," & C.— Editor.' A sound emendation. The French text shows what these words were. This supports the view that the MS. *Campagnes* were either translated directly from James's own memoirs, or dictated by him to a secretary.

got ready. The King his brother gave him a set of six horses which the Lord Crofts had brought from Poland. They were too small for the coach, but served to mount two or three footmen and as many grooms. Two mules were hired to carry the camp bed and his small baggage to the army. The Duke was to be accompanied only by Sir [John] Berkley and Colonel Woerden, and he had no led horse, to change mounts in case of need.

These few preparations were easily made with the secrecy that was needed in order not to be stopped, as he would have run the risk, if his intention of going to the King's army had been discovered; besides which he could not fittingly take leave of the Duke of Orleans, his uncle, in order to go and serve in the party opposed to his. To avoid this inconvenience the Duke went with the King his brother to Saint-Germain-en-Laye under pretext of hunting, and after staying there two or three days he set out on the 21st of April to go and join the army.

He passed through the Faubourg St. Antoine and could go no further than Charenton the first night. The next day he travelled to Corbeil. On arriving in the suburbs he found a few companies of the regiment of Guards against whom the inhabitants of the town had closed the gates in the resolution of not letting them enter. Being very uncertain whether he would be received himself, he risked presenting himself; they made many difficulties, but he used persuasive words and they permitted him to enter on foot on condition that he should leave his horses in the suburb. Then, having represented to the magistrates the dangers to which they were exposing themselves by continuing to refuse admission to the King's troops, they at last let themselves be persuaded, although it was clear that if they had persisted, the Court, which was then at Melun, would have had great difficulty in taking possession of the place, both because of its strong situation and its nearness to Paris; [and had not the King by this unexpected means gott possession of that Town, it had much prejudiced his affairs, as on the contrary it prov'd afterwards a very advantageous post, and was very usefull to him on Severall occasions].

As soon as the Court was informed that its troops had entered Corbeil, the Court left Melun to go there. The Duke of York had remained to await it and its arrival procured him a little assistance in money, of which he had great need, as on arrival in that town he had not twenty pistoles remaining for himself and his retinue. His equipage was increased by one horse and two mules. He left the same evening for Châtres with several volunteers from the Court who accompanied him; [and there he found the Army, which arriued at that Town but some few hours before him].

But before beginning to relate [the actions of] this Campaign and of those that followed, it is necessary to go back some years to explain the state of affairs [as they then stood in France].

[The Crown was reduced to a most deplorable condition in the beginning of this year; Few there were who preserved their loyalty to the King, and even they whose interest] should have attached them to the safety of the State, [were the chief instruments] of those troubles which distracted it; [grounding themselves on that common and plausible pretence which has occasion'd So many Rebellions in all ages,—namely, The removing evill Counsellors from about the person of the King; to make which Argument the more popular, they farther urged, how great a disreputation it was to France to be govern'd by a Stranger; when so many Princes of the blood were both more capable, and more proper to undertake the Ministry] than the Cardinal. These Princes were at the head of the malcontents and were followed by the greater part of the lords and the most qualified persons in the kingdom; the most considerable towns and the greater number of the Parlements had declared for them; and although the Duc de Longueville had not openly taken sides it was well known that with the whole of Normandy he inclined to the party of the Princes, and that he only affected neutrality in order without peril to take sides with the stronger party. Whatever overtures were made him from the King's side, he always found excuses to elude them and to dispense himself from receiving the King in Rouen, when none of the most considerable towns would open its gates to him, and when the smallest, as witness the affair of Corbeil, followed the same example, so generally was the poison spread through the whole kingdom.

The Spaniards, who were always eager to profit by the disorders in France, neglected nothing in order to foment them in the hope of regaining in a short time from the French Crown the places which had been taken from them and which had cost so many years, so much toil, and blood and money. It even seems very likely that they had vaster designs; that they flattered themselves on entirely overwhelming that monarchy, or at least on weakening it to such a point that it would be incapable of attacking them for a long time. But they took the wrong measures, and their precautions, which were always excessive, caused them to fail in both objects.

[The affaires of France being in this posture, the Spaniards besides their large promises and making distribution of mony to severall of the cheif Malcontents, sent some Troopes from Flanders into France under the conduct of the Duke of Nemours, to strengthen the Army of the Princes; he having been sent purposly to Brussels to demand their assistance. This Army of Spaniards which he led, enter'd France in the beginning of the spring; their numbers were about seven thousand men in horse and foot, and they pass'd the Seine at Mantes; of which place the Duke de Sully was then Governour], who could, if he wished to refuse them passage, have greatly retarded their junction with the Princes' Army which was then assembled near [Montargis].[2]

After this junction, and the taking of Angers by the King's troops, nothing important happened until the affair at Bléneau, except that Monsieur de Turenne, whom these memoirs particularly concern, anticipated the enemy's intention of possessing themselves of Gerveau. They had already seized a bridgehead and would have lost no time in taking possession of the place, which was only defended by a gate and a very small number of soldiers, if Monsieur de Turenne had not by chance arrived with enough troops to prevent the execution of this plan, the success of which they would have found very advantageous. They were obliged to retire with some loss, the most considerable of which was that of Sirot, a Lieutenant-General, and one of their best officers. The Court then went to Gien, where the army passed the Loire and took up its quarters near Bléneau. The Princes' army advanced to Lorris. In the meantime, the Prince de Condé[3] had

[2] There is a blank here in the MS. (p. 6) and also in the *Life* (p. 58). Ramsay, probably on good authority, supplies 'Montargis' (*Mémoires du Duc d'Yorck*, p. v, in *Histoire du Vicomte de Turenne*, Paris, 1735, vol. II).

[3] Louis II de Bourbon (1621–1686), a prince of the Blood Royal and one of the most brilliant commanders of the age. After serving his apprenticeship as a soldier in 1640 and 1641, he in May 1643 defeated a supposedly invincible Spanish army at Rocroi. In 1644 and 1645 he co-operated with Turenne in Germany, where they

secretly started from Guyenne, where his affairs were in a bad
state, to come to Paris where his presence was more necessary. On
this dangerous journey he was accompanied only by four or five
persons. Scarcely had he arrived than he was obliged to set out
again and place himself at the head of the Princes' army; and
having been apprised of the way in which the King's troops were
posted, he resolved to attack them in their quarters, which they
had been forced to extend widely for the purpose of obtaining
forage. Monsieur de Turenne had his quarters at Briare and Marshal d'Hocquincourt's[4] were at Bléneau. The latter, having had
warning that the Princes' army was marching against him, ordered

overcame a Bavarian and Imperialist army at Freiburg and won an overwhelming
victory at Nordlingen. In 1648, after a campaign in Catalonia, Condé was again victorious at Lens. During the troubles of the Fronde his overbearing manner at Court
led the Queen Mother and Mazarin in 1650 to have him arrested. Released in 1651,
he went into open rebellion and threw in his lot with the Spaniards. In the years that
followed, the latter owed much of their success to his genius. He was however rarely
given a free hand and, being matched against Turenne, was unable to win any such
brilliant successes as marked his earlier and later campaigns. He was moreover handicapped not only by the behaviour of the Spanish generals who were hidebound by
convention and by the preposterous habit of taking a siesta every afternoon, even in
the presence of the enemy, but also by the fact that he himself was subject to attacks
of intermittent fever. In 1657 he was completely prostrated and at one moment his
life was despaired of. Yet the manner in which he struggled to remain on his feet, and
wrote letter after letter to the Spanish generals to urge them to pay his troops and
make adequate provision for them, inspires the highest opinion of his heroism. His
fortunes were at their lowest ebb, yet no one was more universally admired.

By the terms of the Treaty of the Pyrenees (1660) Condé was pardoned by Louis
XIV and restored to possession of his estates. He was able to recondition and inhabit
Chantilly; and here he entertained a number of the great writers and theologians of
France. But he lived mainly for war. In 1672 he and Turenne led the French armies
against the Dutch, and in 1674 he defeated the Prince of Orange at Seneffe. Turenne
was at this time in command of the army in Alsace, where he was matched against
Montecuccoli, the Emperor's most brilliant general. Fortune favoured now one side
now the other; but in the winter of 1674–75 Turenne drove Montecuccoli back into
Baden, followed him, and defeated him at Salzbach in July. He was himself killed in
the battle; and so great was the consternation that the Imperialists would probably
have been able to invade France if Condé had not been brought from the north to
replace Turenne and if he had not succeeded in retrieving the situation.

The remaining years of his life were spent mostly at Chantilly.

[4] Charles de Monchy, marquis d'Hocquincourt, came of a Picard family. Born in
1599, he had served in Italy, Roussillon, and Germany. He had just (1651) been
made a Marshal of France. His character was impulsive. Once, during the Fronde,
he suggested to the Queen that they should have Condé killed in the street. 'Il avoit
fort peu d'esprit,' according to Bussy-Rabutin: very brave, but not a good general. He
was a connoisseur of women and horses, especially the latter: circumstances which,
together with his slow, sententious manner, made him a butt for ridicule.

his troops in case of alarm to march to the rendezvous which he had fixed for them between his quarters and Monsieur de Turenne's. He at the same time sent advance guards towards the enemy, and posted Dragoons at the place by which in all likelihood they would come. Monsieur de Turenne, having also been informed of this plan, went himself to meet and warn Monsieur d'Hocquincourt, who was the more exposed.

The Dragoons on whom he had depended and who, he thought, could stop the enemy on the way, supported him as badly as his own opinion of them had been good, for, whether out of cowardice or treachery, they were no sooner attacked than they abandoned their post. Monsieur le Prince, pursuing his advantage, fell upon the quarters of Monsieur d'Hocquincourt, who did not resist long and was driven out,[5] but with little loss on either side. The beaten troops escaped under cover of night and lost all their baggage; and their terror was so great that they forgot the rendezvous which had been given them. Night prevented the enemy from pursuing them. But the enemy knew that Monsieur de Turenne was near and they counted on beating him as soon as it was day, if he did not retire. And indeed both he and the whole kingdom were in the greatest peril. If this little army had been routed, the King and the whole Court would have had difficulty in not falling into the hands of the Princes, and everything was to be feared at a time when the ambition of a few great lords knew no bounds.

As soon as Monsieur de Turenne was advised of the enemy's approach, he came out of his quarters and marched to the rendezvous; at the same time sending out small parties which very soon informed him that Monsieur d'Hocquincourt's quarters had been beaten up. The night was so dark that he could not know what position he had taken up. It was dangerous to advance, the enemy being so near, and retreat was no less hazardous, because he was insufficiently acquainted with the country. He was afraid of intimidating his troops and throwing them into confusion. He decided to remain where he was, in the hope of giving those of his men who were scattered time to rejoin him. When at early dawn

---

[5] 'et fut forcé,' i.e., worsted and driven out. The *Life* (I, 60) has: 'the Enemy . . . beat them up.' The term was then used commonly in this sense. Cf. Lovelace, 'The Falcon': 'The dogs have beat his quarters up,' meaning that they have started a heron and forced him to take wing.

he caught sight of the enemy, he observed very joyfully that he could occupy a most advantageous position, where they could only attack him by passing through a very narrow defile.

Behind this defile he drew up his little army in battle order, having a wood on one flank and a large pond on the other. Some of the officers suggested that he should post small parties of infantry along the wood, so as better to defend the pass. He did not follow this advice because, as he afterwards told the Duke of York, the enemy's infantry was half as numerous again as his own, and they would have had no great difficulty in driving his men from the wood. This would force him to go to their help and have involved him so deeply that he would have been unable to avoid having his whole army defeated. He thought it better to leave the wood unoccupied and he drew back more than a musket shot between the wood and the defile, and in this position awaited the enemy who, seeing him take measures that were so sound, durst not attack him. Both sides remained in battle order, contenting themselves with watching each other and firing with their cannon; until Monsieur de Turenne making as if to withdraw, the enemy thought this a good opportunity for attacking him and marched in battle order to the defile. Fifteen or twenty squadrons had already passed through, when Monsieur de Turenne suddenly turned round, marched upon them and forced them to retreat in a disorder and haste that were the greater because they had no other choice if they were to avoid being entirely cut to pieces; and as most of their army had advanced near to the defile, the King's army now took up its former position and with its cannon wrought terrible execution upon the enemy who were crowded together, one upon the other. This cannonade went on for the rest of the day.

Towards evening [the troopes of Mareschall d'Hocquincourt came up and joyn'd with Monsr. de Turenne, while they were yet in presence of the Enemy, so that the party was not now so unequall as before]. It is not known which withdrew first. However that may be, it is certain that by his conduct and firmness on this important occasion Monsieur de Turenne saved the State; for, had this little army been defeated, it had no other resource and would at least have suffered shocks from which it could scarcely have recovered.

[After this action the Prince of Condé left the Army and went to

Paris, where he was received with great applause; his party mag-
nifying the advantage he had got, above what really it was. But in
the mean time his absence from his Army prov'd very prejudicial]
to the interests of the Cabal; [for there was no Commander left in
cheif: Monsr. de Tavannes[6] commanding the Princes' troopes,
Monsr. de Valon[7] those of the Duke of Orleans, and Monsr. de
Clinchamp[8]] the Spaniards. Although all three were men of
courage and capacity, none of them had enough brains to lead an
army; and so it turned out as it always does when there is no
recognised General whom all the troops obey. Although they had
a common interest, their views were different and jealousy ruined
everything. Monsieur de Turenne was too skilful not to profit
from this lack of understanding between them: [for notwithstanding that they lay not far distant from one another, he amus'd[9]
them so, that by taking great and well order'd marches ('The
Court moving at the same time) he gave them the slip, and got
betwixt them and Paris; and though he was to take a great compass, and as it were to march round them, yet his diligence was
such, that he arrived at] Châtres[10] [on the 14th of Aprill, when
they were got no farther then Etampes: and hereby gave an opportunity to the Court of getting to Paris], as had been resolved.
The most important members of the King's party in that city and
even the Cardinal de Retz favoured that course. But whether the
Court was lacking in resolution or whether the artifices of Cardinal Mazarin's enemies, who wanted to frighten him, prevailed,
the Court remained at Melun and came to Corbeil about the same
time that Monsieur de Turenne arrived with the army at Châtres,
where the Duke of York joined him.

[6] Jacques de Saulx, Comte de Tavannes (1620–1683) had been one of Condé's
friends at the 'Académie Royale' in 1636. Here they had studied fencing, horseman-
ship, general history, military science, and political conditions in modern Europe. The
Academy, in short, provided a training both for war and diplomacy. He had been
with Condé in the campaign that culminated at Rocroi (1643), and in that which culminated at Nordlingen (1645).

[7] François de la Baume, Comte de Valon, was, with Tavannes and Clinchamp, to
be one of Condé's Lieutenant-Generals at the battle of the Faubourg Saint-Antoine.

[8] Bernardin de Bourgueville, Baron de Clinchamp, was one of 'The Lorrainers'.
He had served under the Archduke Leopold in 1648, the campaign in which the
Archduke was defeated by Condé at Lens.

[9] Beguiled.

[10] Not Chartres, as in the *Life*.

A few days passed without anything important happening. The parties that were sent out towards Etampes often brought in horses which they took at forage and prisoners who reported that the whole of the enemy's army was quartered in the city and the suburb.

Mademoiselle[11] sent a trumpet to Monsieur de Turenne asking for a passport to go to Paris. She was coming from Orléans, [which Town by her presence and credit there, she had caus'd to declare for the Princes], and could not return to Paris without passing through both armies. Monsieur de Turenne made some difficulties about granting the passport without permission from the Court, to which he dispatched an express messenger; [but, before his return, having consider'd that probably he might make some advantage of her request, and knowing on what day she would be at Etampes], he sent the passport. [Having understood by his partys, that the Enemy had not been out at forage for two or three days], [he conjectur'd that on that day, which was the 3d of May, Madmoiselle would see the Army, and that on the next she wou'd go away for Paris, so that he reckon'd they would not go out to forage till the 4th; that the forage having been so long deferr'd would be great;] that, as most of the General Officers would not fail to accompany Mademoiselle a part of the way, this forage would not be carried out with great precaution: [So that weighing all these Circumstances, he and Monsieur d'Hocquincourt resolv'd to march away all night with the whole Army, leaving only an hundred horse and a small regiment of foot to guard the bagage, which was left at Châtres.] In an hour's time the whole army was in movement; it began to march at eight in the evening in great silence and good order. The design was to take up a position between the enemy's army and Orléans so as to cut off the foragers whom it was thought to find in the country in that direction.

They passed the defiles before sunrise. Monsieur d'Hocquincourt was leading the van as it was his turn. They had to make a little circuit in order to get between Etampes and Orléans, and the army, on arrival, was beginning to draw up in battle order, when scouts who had been sent out in advance reported that,

11 Anne-Marie-Louise d'Orléans, demoiselle de Montpensier (1627–1693), daughter of Monsieur, the King's uncle.

instead of being at forage, the enemy's army was in battle order a league distant, in a plain above Etampes. It was immediately decided to march against them with the intention of fighting; but as soon as the enemy perceived the King's army on the heights, their advance having been hitherto unknown, they began to withdraw into the town. The cavalry were sent forward at full trot in the hope of charging their rear guard before it could get under cover, and the infantry and cannon were ordered to follow with all possible diligence.

Instead of having gone to forage that day, as had been expected, the enemy had brought out their army in order to show it to Mademoiselle, who was to leave in the morning. When their Generals saw the King's army, they asked for her advice. She replied that they had to follow the orders of Monsieur, the Duke of Orleans, and of the Prince de Condé, and immediately set out on her journey. [They drew back into the Town and Suburbs with so much expedition, that before the two Mareschalls Turenne and Hocquincourt had gain'd the heigth above the City, all the troopes of the Enemy were already in security.] In view of this hasty retreat, it was now decided to attack the suburbs, and orders were sent to the infantry to prepare for this while marching, and to form detachments.

Etampes is situated in a hollow; a little river flows under the walls and falls into the Seine at Corbeil. [All that side of the Town and suburbs, which is on the right hand as you come from Châtres], is commanded by a low height, and, from the top of a very high round tower,[12] the whole plain can be discovered. [The Town-wall is flank'd with small round towers, not cannon proof, and incompass'd only with a dry ditch on the side towards Châtres]. The suburb towards Orléans is covered by the river and by a stream which join at the Porte d'Orléans, by which gate alone the town has communication with the suburb. In that quarter the enemy had nine regiments of infantry, among others those of Condé, of Conti and of Burgundy, the auxiliary troops from the Netherlands, namely those of Berlo, Pleure, Vange, La Motte,[13] Pelnitz, etc., and about five hundred horse. They had entrenched

[12] This tower was *in* the town, a fact that appears later.
[13] The *Life* (I, 66) reads 'Vangè la Motte.' Vangè and La Motte were really separate persons.

themselves, being protected by the stream, which covered all one side except for a small space near the gate where they had raised a line of earthworks. [As soon as the King's foot came up, they fell on immediately, scarse staying till their cañon had fir'd two or three shott at the Enemys retrenchments, which was rather done to let them see they had cannon, then for any execution they expected from them. Monsieur d'Hocquincourt's foot had the right hand, so that their attack was made where the brooke was]. They marched to the edge of the brook under fire of the enemy; but the officers having sounded it with their pikes and found it deeper than was supposed, they retired in good order and marched a little higher up towards the mill.

Monsieur de Turenne ordered Monsieur de Gadagne,[14] Lieutenant-Colonel of the Régiment de la Marine, to attack that side of the town on the left which, being defended only by a line of trenches, was carried without much resistance. [This was the only part that was ill maintain'd and yet was the place of the greatest consequence, for by losing it] the enemy had no more communication between the town and the suburb. Gadagne's soldiers immediately afterwards raised barricades across the street opposite the gate. [At the same time Monsr. de Turenne enter'd at this place all his foot, which instantly made way also for the horse; at the head of which Mareschall d'Hocquincourt came in, but with such eager hast, that he forgott to give order to the rest of his wing what they should next perform, so that they were all following him into the suburb, which being perceiv'd by Monsieur de Turenne, he came up to them, and stopt them all but two or three of the former squadrons,] which had already entered [and order'd them to draw off to the top of the hill where all his own horse were posted, because more then enow were already enter'd to second the foot]; and had a greater number entered, the enemy who were in the town would have been able to take advantage of it by coming out through the other gate and falling upon the cavalry which was outside, for without counting their troops in the suburb, they had in the town as many cavalry and infantry as there were in the whole of the King's army.

[14] Charles-Félix de Galléan, Comte de Gadagne (1620–1700), was a Provençal. He led the French infantry with great success at the battle of the Dunes (1658). His lordship, in the Vaucluse, was raised to the rank of a Duchy in 1669. In 1675 he took service under the Venetian Republic.

[In the mean time the regiment of Picardy and the rest of Monsr. de Hocquincourts foot] passed the brook at the mill and vigorously attacked the enemy, who defended themselves with equal vigour and, even after being forced back, resisted bravely from wall to wall and from post to post. In another quarter Monsieur de Turenne's infantry having [secured the traverse against the Town, turn'd immediatly to the right hand, and fell on the flanks of] the Regiment of Burgundy which was defending the line. They had made breaches in it so that six men could pass abreast when marching along this line. Here the enemy's resist-ance was so vigorous that they drove back the attackers from the walls they had gained and chased them so far and put them into so great a disorder that, but for the Régiment de Turenne which stopped their impetuosity and gave the others time to rally, there was risk of losing all the advantage which had just been won. But the enemy's efforts having now been arrested, they were once again driven back from wall to wall until the last was reached. Here they recovered strength and for a second time repelled the attackers in a near-by enclosure, and wrought great carnage.

They had been pursued this last time too hotly and in so little order that riders and foot soldiers were mingled pell mell. [The Enemy did not pursue their advantage, contenting themselves to have made good their last wall, whilst the King's men rallyd be-hind the covert of the next, so that there was the space of an in-closure between the two partys]. They contented themselves for a time with firing briskly at each other. The Duke of York who was present at this hot attack saw an officer of the enemy named Du Mont, a major of Condé's, undertake an action which, had he been supported, might have stopped the course of victory. He came out, pike in hand, and advancing twenty paces, which was the breadth of the enclosure, exposed himself to the full fire of the attackers; [but not being follow'd by any of his men, was con-strain'd to return.] He repeated this dangerous manoeuvre three times, without receiving the least wound. This act inspired emu-lation in the King's troops. It was dangerous to go straight to the breach or opening, which was defended by so many brave men. But an officer whose name has been forgotten went out from the opening in the wall on the attackers' side and, in full view of the enemy, advanced against the breach they were defending. He was followed by as many of his men as could get cover from the fire. The enclosure, as already observed, was narrow and there was only one wall between the two parties. A singular kind of battle was fought there. The wall being composed of great stones, the men heaved[15] them at each other, and the wall was diminishing notably when the King's troops, seeing a small height from which they could attack the enemy from the rear, fired on them to such good purpose that, finding themselves attacked both on the flank and in front, and the place being now untenable, they abandoned their last wall. They retired into a neighbouring Church where the Regiment of Picardy had also driven those it had attacked. They could not defend themselves and asked for quarter, which was granted them. Their cavalry crossed the brook and escaped, after losing the Baron de Briole who was in command and the Comte de Furstemberg, both of whom were killed.

While fighting was going on in the suburb, the enemy in the town made sorties to force the barricade and pressed the King's troops so vigorously that, had not Monsieur de Turenne himself advanced with a squadron of cavalry to within a pistol's shot of the town, to support his men, the barricade would have run great risk of being carried. Everything depended on this position; its loss would have entailed the utter defeat of the troops which were then fighting in the suburb. But the very timely support which Monsieur de Turenne brought them, the munitions he distributed and the firmness of Monsieur de Gadagne rendered the enemy's efforts quite useless. They made two more sorties, which were beaten back with loss.

Of the nine regiments of infantry which the enemy had in that suburb, scarcely a man escaped. Nine hundred were killed and 1700 taken prisoner.[16] The principal officers captured were Briole, Maréchal de Camp, Montal who commanded Condé's regiment, Du Mont or Damon, a major in the same regiment, whom the Duke of York recognised as the same man who had distinguished himself with such bravery at the attack on the last wall; Baron de Berlo, Maréchal de Bataille, Vange, Pleur, La Motte. The King's

---

[15] 'On se les rouloit les uns sur les autres.' But they could scarcely have *rolled* them at each other.

[16] The text of the *Life* is less specific. 'They kill'd above a thousand of the Enemy upon the place, and took a considerable number of prisoners.'

army lost at least five hundred men, but no one of special note. The young Comte de Quincé had a musket ball through his body and Comte Carlo de Broglio[17] one in the arm; but both recovered.[18]

This action was as bold as it was fortunate. The Generals would not have undertaken it, had they known the weakness of their infantry which did not amount to two thousand men, whereas it should have been at least 5000. The march having taken place suddenly and in darkness, the soldiers engaged in skirmishing could only join the army when the attack was over. The enemy had 3000 foot in the town and a similar number in the suburb, not counting the cavalry: but the disorder among them which was observed [when the King's forces] reached the high ground [which overlooks the suburbs],[19] the confusion in which they withdrew, and the absence of concerted action which is generally the trouble under a divided command,[20] probably decided the Generals to attack them.

Had the enemy been as watchful for the mistakes made by the King's army, they might have taken advantage of the opportunity to defeat it when it was withdrawing. Monsieur d'Hocquincourt did not trouble to find out whether Monsieur de Turenne was following him with the rear guard, which it took him a long time to reassemble, as a great number of the soldiers were amusing themselves by pillaging the suburb. Monsieur d'Hocquincourt, however, marched with the van straight to Etréchy and made no halt. The enemy, by coming out of the Porte de Paris, might have

---

[17] 'Carlo de Brole.' This was François-Marie, Comte de Broglie. He later came over to the King's side and fought under Turenne. He was Governor of La Bassée in 1654.

[18] At this point in the *Life* (I, 71–72), the person who made a copy of James's memoirs, inserted the following paragraph, which does not of course appear in the French manuscript:

'By the exact account which the Duke gives in his Memoires written in his own hand of every particular circumstance of this great Action, it may be observed that his Royall Highness (thõ he never mentions his own danger) was present in the places where the Service was hottest, which demonstrably appears by his remembring Monsr. Dumont when he was taken prisoner, to be the same person whom he had seen performing that bold action above mention'd at the last wall in the suburbs of Etampes.'

[19] 'le désordre qu'on remarqua parmy eux en arrivant sur la hauteur,' which is not perhaps very clear. I have supplemented the text at this point by insertions from the *Life* (I, 72) which is fuller and clearer.

[20] The *Life* is here far more detailed and explanatory.

got between the two forces and beaten them both. But they contented themselves with attacking the rear as it was retiring near the barricade and pressed it so hard that Monsieur de Turenne[21] [was forced to advance with som horse to disingage] it. [When they had gain'd the top of the hill, My Lord Berkley] [told Monsr. de Turenne, that the Van was march'd away; to which he reply'd, shrugging up his shoulders, that it was now too late to remedy it]. The danger was so much greater as the army was embarrassed with the prisoners they were taking away. They marched with all possible diligence and their fear ceased only on arrival at Etréchy. The next day the whole army returned to Châtres.

This success greatly improved the outlook for the King and revived the courage of the Cardinal who sent orders to Monsieur de Turenne to blockade the enemy in Etampes, where they were beginning to be short of forage. Before everything was ready, and as the forage round Châtres was all consumed, the army had to march to Palaiseau, where it remained until the 26th, when it went and camped near Etréchy and the next day advanced to within a league of Etampes. Then, on the ridge of the hill and within musket shot of the town, they began work on a line of contravallation. As soon as the enemy perceived it, they made frequent sorties to interrupt the work. [At one of which attempts they cutt off above a hundred of the King's workmen, before the guard could get a horseback, but then they were very vigorously repulsed by the Marquis de Richelieu[22] who commanded the guard]. The next day the lines were nearly finished. They could not but be poor ones, on account of the soil which was very stony and the lack of tools to work with, and of wood, of which there was none at all in the vicinity. The infantry were lodged in the ruins of the suburb, which had been burned down by the enemy when they knew that the army was returning to attack them. The [Royall] army was camped within less than a cannon shot of the town, but this did not trouble it because the town lies in a hollow. However, from the top of the very high tower which has already been spoken of, [the Enemy could discern with ease all that was

---

[21] 'The Duke being with him' (*Life*, I, 73).

[22] J.-B.-A. de Vignerot du Plessis, marquis de Richelieu. He commanded the cavalry reserve at Dunkirk in 1658.

doing in the Camp, which was of great advantage to them]. A bridge was thrown over the river to prevent their going for forage and preparations were in hand to make several others which would have confined them and starved them out in a short time, when the Duc de Lorraine[23] came and upset all these measures.

[This Prince had given the Cardinall such assurances of his being in his interests, that he had sent orders to the Mareschall de la Ferté[24] then Governour of Lorraine to permitt the Duke to joyn togather his divided troopes; which he had no sooner got into a body, but he march'd immediatly into France, and declared for the Princes, having had an underhand correspondence with them during all the time that he was treating with the Cardinall].

This setback obliged Monsieur de Turenne to change his plan and to attack Etampes with all his strength, foreseeing that, if he did not take it promptly, the Duc de Lorraine would come to its aid. Considering this, the army worked with all possible diligence to raise batteries; [some upon the Line, and others in the bottom, close to the Orléans-Gate]. They fired on this and at the same time on the wall between the gate and the high tower with the intention of making a surprise attack[25] on an outwork[26] that the enemy had established a little nearer the gate than the tower. On the night of the * * * to the * * *[27] Monsieur de Gadagne with a thousand men attacked the place, and [after some dispute he master'd it and lodged upon it without any considerable loss, thō it was distant from the wall of the Town but pistoll-shott]. Cavalry had been sent out of the camp and placed between the town and the lines on the side of the hill. To prevent Monsieur de Gadagne from being surprised in the rear, it was brought back at early dawn; but as

[23] Charles IV, duc de Lorraine (1604–1675). Deprived of his territories by Richelieu, he had raised a private army which was very efficient, and taken service under the Emperor. He was a man of indifferent character. La Ferté compelled him in 1663 to come to terms with Louis XIV.

[24] Henry, duc de la Ferté-Saint-Nectaire (1600–1681). He had taken part in the war against the Huguenots (1627–1629), and fought later in Flanders. Commanded the left wing in Condé's great victory at Rocroi. Lieutenant-General 1643, Marshal of France 1651. Loyal to the Court but not a very good general.

[25] 'dans le dessein d'insulter un ouvrage avancé . . .' Richelet defines 'insulter' as 'attaquer par un coup de main, en parlant d'une place de guerre et de fortifications'. It retained the sense of Latin 'insultare'.

[26] This outwork was 'une grande demi-lune'. (See Turenne, *Mémoires*, ed. Marichal, Paris, 1909, I, 193–194).

[27] Blanks in the manuscript.

soon as the sun was up, the enemy sallied out along the ditch to attack the outwork in the rear while from the town they attacked in front; and although Monsieur de Gadagne did all that could be expected of a good officer, he was driven off and only with great difficulty made good his retreat along the ditch towards a barricade which he had raised in front of the Porte d'Orléans. He was believed lost because he did not at once return with his men, and indeed he only escaped by great good fortune, having become engaged in the midst of the enemy's cavalry, with only two or three sergeants and as many musketeers who did not abandon him and who, very bravely, helped him to free himself. He [came off unhurt, thō he had above twenty thrusts of swords, and some of pikes in his buff coat], the quality of which preserved him. Monsieur de Turenne had gone to the camp when all this happened, having been all night in the lines. As soon as he heard the alarm he sent forward all the infantry in his quarter and, his regiment arriving the first, [he commanded them to regain the outwork]. He immediately marched within sight of both armies; and without the slightest diversion being made or a single cannon fired to support the attack, he advanced, preceded only by a few soldiers from among those who had been driven from the outwork. But a captain of Picardy, who was leading them, having been killed, they fled and carried with them the part of the musketeers on the left wing of the regiment. This accident was not enough to discourage him. The captains took the colours in their hands and went at the head of their men without firing a shot until they reached the foot of the outwork, which was crowded with as many of the enemy as it could contain. Then the attackers opened fire with all their musketeers and, having advanced to a pike's length, they charged the enemy so bravely and resolutely that they carried the outwork and lodged themselves in it. They lost only one captain of their regiment, one or two subaltern officers and a few soldiers, although for a long time they had been under the fire of the enemy whom nothing prevented from taking good aim since, during the whole of this action, not a single cannon or musket-shot was fired from the side of the King's army; and as the soil was dry, one could, from the lines, see the dust which the balls, which were falling like hail, raised under the feet of the attackers.

All those who witnessed this action confessed that they had

73

never seen a bolder or livelier one. Monsieur de Turenne himself and the most experienced officers thought that it would have been impossible to push bravery so far, if the colours had not continually been carried before the soldiers' eyes; and it was partly this which decided the regiments to obtain new ones, as the old corps and also the others had hitherto affected the ill-advised glory of having their colours so tattered that generally only the staff remained. The Regiment of Turenne was the only one which then had fairly complete colours, not excepting the French Guards, for there were no Swiss in that army.

After this action it seemed as though the army would have rest for the remainder of the day. But the enemy, remembering the ease with which they had recovered the outwork in the morning, and considering its importance, resolved to attack it again and at the same time to storm the lines. About three o'clock in the afternoon they sallied out with twenty squadrons and five battalions. Monsieur de Turenne, who was fortunately in the lines, commanded the troops to march to their posts and sent orders to all the infantry in the camp to come and join him. Meanwhile, to gain time, he sent out from the lines three squadrons under the Comte de Renel, to charge the first body of the enemy that was approaching. This he did with great firmness until, being unable to bear up against such uneven odds, he was pushed right back into the lines. The ditch was so shallow that the enemy's horsemen, who could not enter by the avenue, jumped over it, and very few horses fell in. The Comte de Schomberg,[28] who was then only

[28] Armand-Frédéric, Vicomte de Schomberg (1608–1690), was the son of Johann Meinhardt von Schomberg, Grand Marshal of the Palatinate. His mother was English. The ancestral estates had been lost as a consequence of the Elector Frederick's adventure in Bohemia, and the young Schomberg grew up as an exile in Holland. He fought in the French army at Nordlingen, and later, after the death of the Stadtholder William II, he and his family emigrated to France. In 1652 he purchased a company in the Gardes Ecossaises, and in July 1653 was made a Lieutenant-General. He continued to serve under Turenne with the greatest distinction, particularly at the moment of the setback at Valenciennes and the difficult retreat to Le Quénoi (1656). In 1661 he went to Portugal to reorganise the Portuguese army, and lead it in the war against Spain; and in the course of brilliant operations he assured the independence of Portugal.

Louis XIV conferred a dukedom upon him and made him a Marshal of France, and he took part in the campaigns of 1677 and 1678 in Flanders.

Owing, however, to the persecution of his co-religionists—for Schomberg was a lifelong Calvinist—he decided to leave France. How he organised the Huguenot

a volunteer, was wounded in the right arm as he was standing his ground in the avenue, for which there was no barrier, because not enough wood had been found in the country to make one. At the time when he sent out the Comte de Renel, Monsieur de Turenne himself had advanced with the two squadrons he still had towards the avenue, as he believed the enemy would make his principal attack there. Things were now in a very sad state. No troops were coming up to help, the enemy was approaching with three battalions and several squadrons, of which some were only a pistol shot away, waiting for the infantry which was only a half musket shot distant. To defend the lines there only remained two squadrons of cavalry and a few sentinels at intervals, who instead of impeding the enemy, displayed great weakness. There were no cannoneers in the batteries, no hope of any considerable reinforcement of infantry that might arrive in time, at a moment of such urgent necessity, most of the foot having been sent to the Orléans-suburb on account of the morning's action. An attack was believed so imminent that the Duke of York who was on an ambling horse[29] did not think he had time to change his mount, although a war horse had been brought for him, or to put on armour. This they put on him while he was still mounted. There arrived at the same moment two hundred musketeers of the Regiment of Guards, which was all that could be collected in the camp. Monsieur de Turenne recommended them not to amuse themselves by firing all together but [to take good aime, which accordingly they did, and to so good purpose that it was beleev'd never so small a body of men did so great execution]. At the first volley they shot down so many officers and horsemen and so thinned out the ranks of the three squadrons that the latter thought well to withdraw. They next fired on the infantry, which was still advancing; but, fortunately, as they advanced they found a low ridge that covered them up to their heads, and this shelter seemed to them so agreeable that neither exhortations, nor blows, nor threats were able to make them go further. They were content to keep up a heavy fire upon the Lines, until the Cavalry from the other quarters came up

regiments in Holland; how he accompanied William III to London in 1688; how in 1689 he was appointed commander-in-chief of the English army, led the operations in Ireland, and was killed at the crossing of the Boyne—all this is well-known to historians.

[29] 'a pad' (*Life*, I, 79).

to relieve the Lines, and the enemy then thought of retiring.

The enemy were no more fortunate in their attack on the out-work, for, as they had further to go, the men defending it had time to prepare to receive them. [Monsr. de Tracy,[30] who commanded the German horse which were in the seruice of the King of France], having been warned in his quarter of what was happening, [thought it better to go between the line and the Town;] [he met those of the Enemy who were going to attack the outwork: and thō he had but four squadrons with him, and consequently was much outnumber'd by them, yet he charg'd them so vigorously that he put them to a stand, which gave time to more troopes to come up to his assistance, commanded by the Marquis de Richelieu]. With the help of this reinforcement, the enemy were charged a second time and forced to draw back in great disorder, but as they were near the town it would have been dangerous to push them further. As most of the King's troops were now arriving in the Lines, while the enemy were retiring, several officers urged Monsieur de Turenne to pursue them; to which he replied that as they were too near their own walls, one could do them no great damage and also one would be exposed to the danger of losing too many men and being forced to retire in disorder.

The enemy were so roughly handled in this engagement, in which they lost great numbers of men and more than 60 officers, that they had no stomach to commit themselves further. They were hard pressed at the Porte d'Orléans and from the outwork that had been captured, and the miner was already lodged in the wall when it was learned that Monsieur de Lorraine was marching with all possible diligence towards Paris and that a bridge of boats was being made ready for him a little above Charenton.

This news obliged Monsieur de Turenne to raise the siege, in order to avoid the risk of being caught between two of the enemy's armies. His men first withdrew the cannon from the batteries nearest the town. But they were so ill-furnished with teams, that, although the Court had sent all the coach-horses that were there, even those of the King and Queen, it was only possible to move half the artillery on the day before the army broke camp, and they

[30] Alexandre de Prouville, marquis de Tracy, had been maréchal-de-camp. He had been one of the negotiators for the Treaty of Ulm. Was also serving under Turenne in 1654.

had to wait for the return of the horses to take away the other half.

On the 7th of June, the army being in battle order, they began to withdraw the troops that were in the outwork. Monsieur de Navailles,[31] who commanded them, retreated in good order, although the enemy was pressing him vigorously. Then the army began to march after setting fire to the huts. While the first line was halting, the second advanced about five hundred steps, after which it turned about and faced the town. Then the first line moved off and marched in halt step until it had gained a distance five hundred steps beyond. It then halted and turned round to face the enemy, as had the second line which now began the same movement. In this way the army withdrew for the space of a league, and it was a very fine sight. The enemy followed the first line in its first movement, skirmishing in great numbers, but after that they undertook nothing that could give anxiety. Having arrived at Etréchy, the army remained two or three days, then went to camp at Ytterville, and from there to Ballincour, where Monsieur de Turenne learned that the Duc de Lorraine had arrived at Villeneuve-Saint-Georges. He marched promptly with the intention of attacking him before he could be joined by the enemy who had been left in Etampes. On the 14th the army passed the Seine at Corbeil and made such speed that it surprised the enemy when he least expected it. It was about two o'clock in the afternoon when they came face to face, but the army could not fight because there was a brook between them which, coming from Brie, falls into the Seine. They marched upstream without losing any time until they found a crossing. The army marched all night and, leaving the forests on the left, the van reached Grosbois at dawn. Beaujeu, who was the Cardinal's emissary to the Duc de Lorraine, came with d'Agecourt, captain of that Prince's Guards, to find Monsieur de Turenne and make proposals. The principal and most urgent proposal was that Turenne should not advance. But he did not let himself be surprised by the Duke's artifices. He continued his march and, learning that the King of England had reached the Duke's army the same night to

[31] Philippe de Montaut de Bénac, Duc de Navailles (1619–1684). He was at this time a Lieutenant-General and cavalry leader. Continued to serve under Turenne, notably in the sieges of Sainte-Ménéhould and Valenciennes. Served under Condé at Seneff (1674). Marshal of France, 1675.

assist in the negotiations that were on foot between the Duke and the Cardinal, he asked the Duke of York to go and meet the King. This he accepted the more willingly as the King his brother had sent him word that he would be very glad to speak with him and that he had Monsieur de Lorraine's *parole* for his safe return.

The reason for the King of England's coming to the Duc de Lorraine's army was the request which the Duke[32] had made to his Majesty to mediate between him and the Court of France, to be the guarantor of the treaty which was on the point of being made. For this purpose he wished the King to do him the honour of coming to his army so that, when the affair was concluded, he could take him to the Court which was at Melun. The King had been in Paris when he received Monsieur de Lorraine's letter making these proposals. He immediately went and communicated them to the Queen his mother, who was at Chaillot.

As she knew that this Duke rarely acted in good faith, she did not think that the King should be his cautioner. But his great desire to contribute to an affair which might be so advantageous to the Court overrode all other considerations in his mind. He set off instantly, taking in his coach Lords Rochester, Jermyn, and Crofts. On arriving at Charenton, he heard that the two armies were face to face, and it is believed that he found there an express from the Duke asking him to make haste. On reaching Villeneuve-Saint-Georges, he found the Duc de Lorraine much perplexed and disquieted by the importunate vicinity of Monsieur de Turenne. It was then that Monsieur de Beaujeu and the Captain of the Guards were sent with proposals. [But it not being yet certain what might be the issue of the Treaty], Monsieur de Lorraine prepared to fight. He posted himself [with all the advantages which the ground affoorded him;] [working very hard all night on five redouts with which he cover'd his front.] [His Army consisted of about 5000 horse and 3000 foot, with a small train of Artillery]; [he placed the greatest part of his foot in those redouts above mention'd, keeping one great battalion for a reserve behind the midlemost redout, having most of his cañon placed upon a height by the gallows just above the Town; his horse was drawen up in two lines behind the redouts, his right hand was cover'd by a great wood, and his left by the Town]. He could not be attacked

32 i.e., the Duc de Lorraine.

on this side because there was a very steep hill. He had shown great experience and skill in choosing this position. Thus posted he awaited the fight or the conclusion of the treaty.

On arriving at Villeneuve-Saint-Georges, the Duke of York went to find the King his brother, who told him what had brought him there [and then desir'd him to use his best endeavours that the Treaty might succeed] in such a way that he might come off with honour from so ticklish an affair; he was in fact much embarrassed as to the attitude he should adopt in case the two armies came to blows. It was not befitting him, on the eve of a battle, [to withdraw without having his share in the honour of it].³³ The Duc de Lorraine had invited him to help him to make his treaty with France; he was also under special obligations to him; he was now in his camp and had lodged for a night in his quarters. [On the other side, he was at that very time under the protection of the King of France, and,] [in his Country]. [He had a pension from him, which in that juncture was the only visible support he had: But the consideration which press'd him most was, that in fighting for the Duke of Lorraine, he manifestly appear'd in the quarrell of Rebells against their Lawfull Soveraign]; for that very reason he only remained in the camp with great repugnance, well knowing what a bad impression this would create in the public mind. However, he did not see how he could honourably withdraw. In this state of perplexity he asked the Duke of York what propositions he was bringing. The latter told him in a few words that Monsieur de Turenne required Monsieur de Lorraine immediately to cease working on the bridge which he was having built over the Seine; to engage to leave French territory within fifteen days, and at the same time to give his word never again to furnish any help to the Princes: that, with regard to the first article, Monsieur de Varenne, who had come expressly with him, had orders to see to the execution of it himself and that, without this preliminary, Monsieur de Turenne would hear of no other proposals. The King, knowing what engagements Monsieur de Lorraine had with the Princes, answered that he greatly feared that the Duke

---

³³ The *Life* (I, 86) adds at this point: 'but which side he was to take, was a matter of no slight consideration.' It is hard to suppose that a cynical realist like Charles II could have been troubled by any such dilemma; also, one sees no evidence to suggest that either party expected him to fight.

would never sign such hard conditions. The Duke of York replied that Monsieur de Turenne would certainly not relinquish his terms.[34] Monsieur de Lorraine came into the room at that moment. The Duke of York immediately presented him the draft of the treaty. He received it with the mocking air which was usual with him but which was a little forced on this occasion. He at once agreed to the first article and sent an officer with Monsieur de Varenne to stop the work on the bridge; but as for the other articles he protested that nothing could oblige him to submit to such shameful conditions. The Duke of York asked whether he wished him to take back this reply; he replied that he could give no other, and, imagining that this young Prince's hands were itching and that he felt more inclination for a battle than for an agreement, he asked the King to send Lord Jermyn with him in order to try and obtain from Monsieur de Turenne terms that were more endurable.

In the meanwhile Monsieur de Turenne was losing no time, but advancing with so much diligence that the Duke of York and Lord Jermyn found his army still marching in battle order, only a league distant from the Lorrainers. The Duke reported Monsieur de Lorraine's reply and Lord Jermyn omitted nothing that he thought might persuade Turenne to desist from what appeared too severe in his proposals, but the Marshal would abate nothing, and Jermyn returned to let the Duc de Lorraine know the result of his negotiations. He had urged the Duke of York to return with him, in the hope that he would gain time and that Monsieur de Turenne would not attack until he had come back with a final answer. But the Duke of York absolutely refused. He was sure that the Marshal was incapable of wasting his time because he knew that the army from Etampes was following him so closely that at any moment it might appear on the other side of the river. So he did not doubt that the French army and the Lorrainers would be fighting before he could return. He added with a smile that his own presence would not make the Duc de Lorraine conclude the affair any sooner and that Monsieur de Turenne's approach would much rather decide him on coming to terms.

[34] '. . . que Mr. de Turenne n'en demordroit assurément pas'–'would not loosen his grip,' strictly 'would not get his teeth out of it'; but the metaphor was probably a well-worn one.

Lord Jermyn set out and the Army, which continued to march, was not further than a cannon shot from the enemy, [when the King him-self came to Monsieur de Turenne to make the last attempt on his resolution but M. de Turenne begg'd his pardon for insisting still on the same conditions which he had sent, and added, that he knew his Maty had so much concernment for his King, as not to press him on any change of his proposalls].

[The Armys were then so very near that every moment of time was precious, and therfore the King desired Monsr. de Turenne that he would send for the last time to the Duke of Lorraine; to which he consented, and Monsr. de Gadagne was commission'd] to take him the terms in writing and tell him that he would have to sign or fight. He found Monsieur de Lorraine on the hill near the gallows where he had set up batteries. On reading the paper that was presented to him, Monsieur de Lorraine [call'd out to the cannoneers to fire]. But it appeared that they had previously been forbidden to obey. Monsieur de Gadagne told him clearly that they durst not and repeated what he had said at the outset, [that he must either sign, or expect instantly to be attack'd. Wherupon Monsr. de Lorraine sign'd the Treaty, and Mr. de Gadagne brought it back]. [So soon as Monsr. de Turenne receiv'd it, he commanded his Army to make a halt, and sent to demand hostages] and also that the Duke should march off his troops. The latter gave Monsieur de Ligneville and Monsieur d'Agecourt, the Captain of his Guards, as pledges for the execution of the Treaty, [who were to be return'd so soon as Monsr. de Vaubecourt], who had orders to follow the Lorrainers, [should send word that he was out of the French Dominions].

After the ratification of the treaty, the King of England came to see Monsieur de Turenne's army; he then went to take leave of the Duc de Lorraine, and returned to Paris. Scarcely had he left when the two Generals had a meeting; but after exchanging a few cold compliments they separated. Monsieur de Lorraine immediately set his army in motion, while Monsieur de Turenne's remained in battle order. In full view, the Lorrainers entered a long and very narrow defile where they were at the discretion of the French. But Monsieur de Turenne was a more religious observer of his word than Monsieur de Lorraine, whose troops were no sooner in the defile than the Princes' army appeared on the other side of the Seine; but, having been informed of what had just happened, this army marched off to Paris.

Monsieur de Turenne remained a few days at Villeneuve-Saint-Georges [and departing thence the 21 of June, by small marches he came to Lagny, and there past the Marne on the 1st of July[35]], and camped at la Chevrette, a league distant from Saint-Denis where the Court was. Marshal de La Ferté had joined the Army at Garges with three or four regiments of cavalry and two of infantry, one of which was his and the other Wall's;[36] he had brought these troops from Lorraine.

The Duc de Beaufort,[37] a great favourite of the populace in Paris, had come with five hundred Parisians on horseback to join Monsieur de Lorraine at Villeneuve-Saint-Georges. They were permitted by the treaty to withdraw, but as no mention was made of their general, [he doubted of his own security], and not wishing

[35] James's memory is at fault here. The treaty had been signed on 16 June, and Turenne probably left Villeneuve-St.-G. on the 17th and had crossed the Marne by the 18th. Lagny is barely sixteen miles from Villeneuve-St.-G. Moreover 1 July was the date of the battle of the Porte Saint-Antoine (Turenne, *Mémoires*, I, 200–201 and notes).

[36] This was the 'Régiment de Wall-Irlandais', composed of Irish mercenaries commanded by Robert Wall. It had come into prominence when fighting on the right wing of the French army at Nordlingen in 1645 (see Hon. E. Godley, *The Great Condé*, London, 1915, p. 132).

Henri de Senneterre, marquis (later maréchal-duc) de la Ferté (1600–1681) had previously served under Condé at Rocroi (1643) and Lens (1648). He seems to have been, not unnaturally, averse to taking advice from colleagues junior in years or rank; this weakness was to lead to his being taken prisoner at Valenciennes in 1656. A brave and loyal officer, but apparently deficient in alertness and imagination.

[37] François de Vendôme, duc de Beaufort (1616–1669), a grandson of Henri IV and Gabrielle d'Estrées. He figures prominently in the memoirs of Retz, who makes no secret of his disdain for

Monsieur de Beaufort
Ce Duc si grand, si haut, si fort,
Et de prestance si blondine,

as Loret describes him. He had fought well at Hesdin and Arras (1642) and in 1643 dominated the Queen's council. But his influence derived from his good looks and his enormous popularity with the market women of Paris whose language he spoke perfectly–an unusual accomplishment among Henry IV's descendants (Retz). He was known as 'le roi des Halles', and his self-assurance led to his party's being called 'La Cabale des Importants'. But he had no political sense. 'In conversation,' says Miss Godley, 'he showed a reassuring slowness of intellect' (*The Great Condé*, p. 78), and before long his behaviour scandalised the Queen. Mazarin, who supplanted him, imprisoned him in the fortress at Vincennes. He escaped in 1648 and joined the Spaniards–hence the part he was now playing in the Fronde.

to make trial of Monsieur de Turenne's generosity, he took a trumpet with him, passed the Seine and rode to Paris where, to irritate the people against the King of England, he spread the malicious rumour that the Duc de Lorraine had signed the treaty on the King's persuasion. If his Majesty had a hand in it, as it was his interest to have, he was not the original cause of it, because Monsieur de Lorraine had urged him to come and help in its conclusion. The report however made such an impression on the multitude that neither the King nor the Queen nor any English-man of their Court dared to leave the Louvre for several days, or even to look out of the windows for fear of provoking some assault[38] or at least some insults; and the people's animosity increased to such a point that their Majesties were compelled to leave the city in secret and to retire to Saint-Germain until it was appeased.

After failing to join up with the Lorrainers, the Princes' army could no longer hold the field against the King's, so it went to camp near Saint-Cloud behind the Seine. Monsieur de Turenne, having no other enemies on his hands, decided to attack them openly, and began work on a bridge of boats on the same day that he arrived at La Chevrette. As the Seine there is very wide he needed time to make the bridge, [and least the Enemy should in-terrupt the work, the two regiments of la Ferté's foot were com-manded over into an Island, at the point of which it was intended to pass the Army] over the river. The enemy durst undertake nothing. The King's army had the advantage of the ground which was higher than on the other side. The enemy opposed neither the building of the bridge nor the passage. It is true that they at first made some movement as if they intended to do so: they lodged about a hundred soldiers behind a little ridge and ad-vanced a few squadrons to support them, but these were quickly driven off by the cannon. The soldiers, thinking themselves safe, remained in their post and fired upon the workmen. La Fuitte, a Major in La Ferté's cavalry regiment, found a place which was not deep and having swum across with fifty horsemen, intercepted the retreat of the hundred foot soldiers, cut most of them to pieces,

---

[38] '. . . de peur de s'attirer quelqu' *insulte* ou au moins quelques injures.' Furetière (*Dictionnaire universel,* 1690) defines 'insulte' as 'assaut qu'on donne à une place brusquement et à découvert' and gives as example, 'Valenciennes a été prise d'insulte.' Cf. 'insulter un ouvrage' above.

embarked the remainder whom he had taken prisoner in a boat, and swam back without losing a single man before the enemy's squadrons, whom the cannon had driven off to a good distance, could come to the help of their people. After this enterprise the enemy did not think fit to make others, and to discourage any such desire a reinforcement of foot with a few fieldpieces was sent over onto the island.

Monsieur le Prince despaired of being able to prevent the passage of the King's army, whose bridge might probably be finished the next day. He therefore resolved to march to Charenton and take up a position behind the Marne. While his horse were passing over the bridge at Saint-Cloud, his foot passed over a bridge of boats which he had had made so as to proceed more quickly. He marched through the Bois de Boulogne, but on his arrival at the Porte de la Conférence,[39] the Parisians refused him entry, and he was obliged to march round the city, as he had intended if he were not allowed to go through.

Monsieur de Turenne had been promptly informed of all things by a messenger whom the King's friends sent from Paris and whom they let down in a basket over the walls because the gates were closed. He set the King's army in motion and went to find the Cardinal at Saint Denis, with whom it was decided that the army should continue to march with all possible diligence and attack Monsieur le Prince before he could reach Charenton. It was not thought fitting to wait for the cannon or for Monsieur de la Ferté's infantry who were in the island, as the least delay might make them lose so good an opportunity. On reaching La Chapelle [they perceived the Rear Guard of the Enemy]. Monsieur de Turenne advanced to reconnoitre, [and finding that to favour their retreat, they had to put] some infantry [into certain wind mills, and other litle houses which were at the entry of the fauxbourg St. Denis], he advanced musketeers who drove them out in a moment, [and made way for the King's horse to charge their Rearguard in the very street of the fauxbourg. The Enemy] at first defended themselves [with resolution enough, but at length were routed]. Most of the officers were killed or taken prisoner, among others Des Marais, Maréchal de Camp, who had received some wounds, and the Comte de Choiseuil, captain of cavalry. The losses

[39] On 30 June.

in the King's army were so slight that the only one worthy of mention was Lisbourg, Lieutenant-Colonel of Streff, who had a musket ball through his body.

After the success of this first attack the King's men pressed the enemy so vigorously that, on reaching the remainder of their rearguard, which numbered 200 or 300 horse near the Hôpital de Saint-Louis, they cut the greater number of them to pieces [before they could reach the body of their Army, which was then retiring into the fauxbourg St. Antoine]. The Prince de Condé was obliged to make this move as, in view of the vigour with which he was being pressed, he saw no likelihood of being able to reach Charenton. He was fortunate indeed in this extremity to find some good entrenchments in the faubourg: these had been dug by the inhabitants for their own security during the Civil War. But for this his army [had infallibly been lost]. He had only just time to post his men, so closely was he followed by the King's troops, whose ardour was only arrested by the barricades that were already there; and as the infantry had not yet arrived, the enemy had leisure to draw up in battle order in the Grande Rue.[40]

In the meantime the King, the Cardinal, and the whole Court arrived on the heights of Charonne, whence as from an amphitheatre they were spectators of what followed this scene of carnage. As soon as they saw that the infantry had arrived they sent orders to Monsieur de Turenne to attack, though neither Monsieur de la Ferté's infantry nor the cannon had come up, and though the army lacked all the tools needed to destroy the walls, fill in the trenches and break down the barricades. It was in vain that Monsieur de Turenne begged them to be patient, pointing out that the enemy could not escape him if the Parisians, regarding whom one felt assured, did not open their gates; that the time needed to have the cannon would not give the Prince de Condé enough leisure to fortify himself further; that by attacking without the necessary tools there was the risk of receiving a check which would cause the enterprise to miscarry, for otherwise it could not fail as soon as they had received the cannon, the pick-axes and other tools for

[40] James's memoirs call this 'the Great Street'. From the market place, which was just outside the Porte Saint-Antoine, the Grande Rue ran straight east and out into the country. The Rue de Charonne ran northeast, and the Rue de Charenton southeast, past the Jardin de Rambouillet.

moving the earth, which could not be delayed much longer. But the impatience of the Court overbore all these reasons. Even Monsieur de Bouillon,[41] who had but recently made his peace with the Cardinal, urged Monsieur de Turenne his brother more than anyone. He felt it was better blindly to follow the orders of the Court than to risk being censured by certain courtiers who might put into the King's mind the suspicion that the Marshal wished to spare the Prince, however irreconcilable at bottom they might be after what had happened. Monsieur de Turenne was not yet well enough established in the King's mind and in that reputation for probity which he afterwards acquired, to dare to refuse obedience to orders which were not to his taste; and he did not yet trust his own capacity and experience as much as he was to do later on several occasions.

The French Guards and the Régiment de la Marine, supported by the King's Gendarmes and Light Horse on the extreme right, attacked the barricade of the street which led to the Grande Rue of the faubourg where the market is. Success rewarded the bravery of the attackers. Although the walls were lined to right and left with defenders and the houses full of soldiers, the King's men carried the barricade and were driving the enemy from house to house when the imprudent ambition of the Marquis de Saint-Maigrin,[42] who commanded the Gendarmes and the Light Horse, lost the benefit of this first advantage. He wanted to share the glory of the infantry, and fearing that he would win none, [press'd on with great precipitation through the midst of the foot, in that strait passage of the street], without giving them time [to finish their work of dislodging the Enemy], [but still pursuing those who fled even almost to the market place]. Monsieur le Prince, who was here in person, [observing the fault committed by the King's horse], placed himself at the head of twenty-five officers or volunteers who were near him and charged them so vio-

[41] Frédéric-Maurice de la Tour d'Auvergne, Prince de Sedan (1605–1652), a Catholic, was one of the great feudal lords. He had declared openly for the Princes in 1650, and as he was the head of the family, his adherence to the Fronde probably accounts for Turenne's defection from the Court party about the same time. Emmanuel-Théodose, the future Cardinal de Bouillon (1644–1715) for whom James II caused the translation of his memoirs to be made, was one of his children.

[42] Jacques d'Estuert de Caussade, marquis de Saint-Maigrin. He was buried at Saint-Denis.

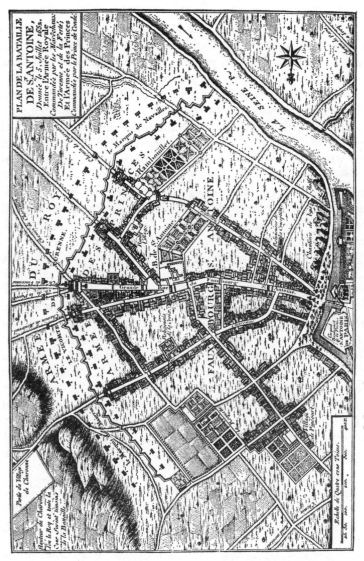

PLAN DE LA BATAILLE
DE S. ANTOINE,
Donné le 3. Juillet 1652.
Entre l'Armée Royale
Commandée par les Maréchaux
De Turenne et de la Ferté;
Et l'Armée des Princes
Commandée par le Prince de Condé

Map of the Battle of St. Antoine, July 1, 1652

87

lently that they were thrown into disorder, fell back upon the infantry and were exposed to all the fire that the enemy directed from the windows. Those of the King's troops who had got into the first houses saw this disorder and abandoned them; and the enemy, regaining courage, pursued the King's men as far as the first barricade. It was only the presence of Monsieur de Turenne that prevented this from being retaken as all the others had been.

Saint-Maigrin was not the only one who paid for his temerity with his life; the Marquis de Nantouillet and several men of quality were also killed upon the spot, and many others [dyd of their wounds afterwards, amongst whom was Monsr. de Manchini[43] the Cardinal's nephew], a man of great promise, [and Fouillou ensigne of the Queen's guards]. The two infantry regiments had been so roughly handled that [all that could be expected from them] was that they should hold the first barricade, which they had taken.

Turenne's infantry regiment was employed in attacking some houses and gardens which the enemy occupied on the left. The two regiments of Uxelles and Carignan which made up only one battalion assaulted a garden wall that abutted on the Grande Rue, a little further off, still on the left; and on the extreme left the rest of the infantry, commanded by Monsieur de Navailles and consisting of the regiments of Picardy, Plessis-Praslin,[44] Douglas and Belle Cense, attacked a barricade which was down towards the river near the garden of Rambouillet.[45]

The enemy were first driven from several posts by the regiment of Turenne, but the failure of the right prevented it from pushing further and it was satisfied with holding what it had won. A squadron composed of the regiments of Clere and Richelieu

---

[43] Paul Mancini (1638–1652). There had been a question of marrying him to Mlle de Retz in order to reconcile Gondi (Retz) with the Cardinal. Retz, who hated Mazarin, says that Paul Mancini 'had courage and merit'. He was only fourteen when he was killed.

[44] This appears to have been the regiment belonging to César de Choiseul, Comte du Plessis-Praslin (1599–1675). He had been a Marshal of France since 1645. Whether he was the same person as the 'Comte de Choiseuil, captain of cavalry' who had been captured an hour or two earlier, I do not know. The captain may have been his son.

[45] This record of Navailles' movements is, in the *Life* (I, 99–100), separated by nearly two pages from the preceding narrative; and the whole narrative is more condensed in the French manuscript than in the *Life*.

Campagnes

Tirées mot pour mot des memoires de Jacques Stuart

Pour lors Duc d'Yorck, et depuis Roy d'Angleterre Jacques Second :

depuis 1652 inclusivement, iusqu'en 1660, année dans laquelle

Le Roy d'Angleterre Charles Second son frere, fut rétabli

Sur le trosne de La Grande Bretagne :

Ces Memoires écrits par luy même en Anglois, et Traduits en François

en sa présence, la Traduction Corrigée par luy même, furent donner

de la propre main de ce Saint Roy a St. Germain en Laye le 27.e de Janvier 1696.

à

Emmanuel Theodose de La Tour d'Auvergne, Cardinal de Bouillon

Neveu

de Henry de La Tour d'Auvergne, Vicomte de Turenne, duquel

Sa Majesté parle si honnorablement dans tout le Cours de ces neuf années,

et surtout dans celuy des Campagnes que ce grand Prince

fit sous le vicomte de Turenne en 1652 · 1653 · 1654 · 1655.

Luy fesant même l'honneur iusqu'a ce qu'il fut fait Lieutenant General

en 1654 ·

de n'avoir d'autre quartier, ny d'autre Logement que celuy qui estoit

marqué pour Ce General · 1·

1. TITLE PAGE OF THE BOUILLON MANUSCRIPT

Preface du Cardinal de Bouillon.

(a) Le Roy d'Angleterre Jacques II m'ay
=ant fait l'honneur de me ra
conter dans l'an mil 1695 plu
sieurs particularités, et quelques
actions considerables de la
vie de feu Mr. de Turenne
mon oncle, qui m'etoient In=
=connues, n'estant pas appo
=tees dans les memoires que
J'ay de luy ecrit toute de ma
main. Je pris la confiance
de temoigner a ce prince
que J'etois bien fache que
mon profond respect pour
luy, ne me permit pas de
le supplier tres humblement
de vouloir par l'amitié
qu'il conservoit pour feu
Mr. de Turenne... estre par

(a) Cette preface trouvee au commencement des memoires
du d. d'York, et elle est ecrite de la propre main du Card.
de Bouillon.

2. PREFACE BY THE CARDINAL DE BOUILLON

which was to have supported it, was surprised by a hail of musketry fire from the enemy who, from a near-by wall, took it in the flank and killed a great many. The squadron was thrown into disorder and fled, but the officers, running after the fugitives, stopped them and immediately brought them back to their posts in good order. Here during the rest of the action they conducted themselves with extreme bravery, and this was all the more extraordinary since it very rarely happens that troops who have once been seized with fear cut a good figure for the rest of the day. This squadron was so roughly handled that there was not a captain who was not killed or wounded; of the regiment of Richelieu the only one remaining alive was La Loge, a Captain-Lieutenant, who had a musket ball through his body, from which he recovered.

The regiments of Uxelles and Carignan attacked on their side about the same time as the other attacks were being made. The two Lieutenant-Colonels were killed at once, but this did not prevent the men from advancing straight to the wall despite the heavy fire that was opened on them. They placed themselves between the holes through which the enemy were firing. The fighting here was rather like the fighting behind the last wall in the suburb gardens of Etampes. As the muskets could do no great execution, the men heaved stones at each other, fired pistols and thrust their swords through the holes; but the lack of tools for demolishing the wall explains why the action did not go on for long. Meanwhile the cavalry which was supporting this attack stood facing the Grande Rue out of musket shot, to prevent the enemy's sallying from the barricade which they had in order to charge the infantry who were attacking the wall. It was not thought fitting to undertake anything against this barricade because it was defended by the neighbouring houses which the enemy occupied. It was difficult and in fact useless to take it until these troops had first been driven out.

Monsieur de Navailles on his side carried the barricade opposed to him. He met with no great resistance and dislodged the enemy from the houses in the neighbourhood. He had at first been content to maintain his position without pushing further, because he had found that the enemy had posted some of their cavalry in a rather large open place opposite and that behind him there were gardens and houses defended by infantry. The enemy

89

also judged that it would be rash to attack the King's troops and decided to retire behind the houses and gardens occupied by their foot. But Monsieur d'Eclinvilliers, Maréchal de Camp, took their retreat for a flight and rode in pursuit of them with the cavalry he commanded, through the barricade that had been won. At the same time the enemy turned about and, knowing that only two horsemen could attack them at a time, they charged him before he could form up his squadron and when only half of his men had passed through. They beat him, made him prisoner, killed several officers and horsemen and, after pursuing the rest as far as the barricade, retired at a round trot under a fairly heavy fire from the King's troops who had taken possession of the houses.

The cannon and Monsieur de la Ferté's infantry came up about the same time. The two regiments were immediately ordered to relieve the French Guards and the Marine regiment which had been so roughly handled, and to hold the posts which had been won on that side. The cannon, six fieldpieces in all, were dragged to the windmills which were a little less than a musket shot distant from the entrance to the Grande Rue; and they began to fire very successfully on the soldiers and baggage with which it was crowded and which disappeared in an instant; then they battered [the houses which commanded the passage to the Barricade]. As these were lightly built, every shot went through; nevertheless the enemy stood their ground so obstinately that they could not then be dislodged and they kept up a heavy fire from the windows and holes that the cannon had pierced.

During this cannonade, a great rattle of musketry was suddenly heard coming from the attack commanded by Monsieur de Navailles. Monsieur de Turenne rode there but the action was over before he could arrive. Never was there a more eager or violent one for the time it lasted. See how it had arisen.

Monsieur de Beaufort had [been almost all the morning in harangueing of the people of Paris, and endeavouring to perswad them to open their gates to the Prince of Condé and his troopes]. His eloquence had been useless; he came out and, on reaching the faubourg, he could not listen to what had happened—the heat of the action in which Saint-Maigrin had been killed, the bravery with which Monsieur le Prince and the men of quality who accompanied him had distinguished themselves—without being filled

with noble emulation, [and resolv'd on doing something as remarkable. He therfore propos'd to Monsr. de Nemours[46] (with
whom he had a quarell then depending) that they shou'd endeavour to regain the Barricade gain'd by Mr. de Navailles, as an
action of the greatest importance to their party]. Monsieur de
Nemours accepted the proposal and they immediately set about
executing it. All the men of quality who were still able to fight
followed them. [These two then putting themselves at the head of
a good body of foot march'd on with great resolution and bravery
to attack the Barricade]. The Regiment of Picardy was posted behind it. There was a house on each side of the passage by which
the enemy had to come: the Regiment of Du Plessis-Praslin was in
one house and Douglas's in the other. Between these two fires
which were violent and continual they none the less made their
way with great intrepidity and courage, not stopping until they
had reached the barricade. But [there they found so vigourous a
resistance, that it was impossible for them to master it; they were
beaten off with considerable loss]. [Monsr. de Nemours was
wounded in severall places, and one of his fingers shott from his
hand as it was upon the Barricade, Monsr. de la Rochefoucault
was shott in at the corner of one eye, the bullet coming out under
the other, so that he was in danger of loosing both[47]]; Monsieur de
Guitaut[48] had a musket ball in his body and there were several
other men of quality wounded or killed, though their names have
been forgotten. Monsieur de Flamarin[49] was one of the latter and

[46] Charles-Amédée de Savoie (1622–1652) had succeeded his brother, Louis de
Savoie, as Duc de Nemours in 1641. He had married Elisabeth de Vendôme,
Beaufort's sister, but he did not get on with his brother-in-law, for whom he seems to
have entertained an excessive dislike.

[47] Mlle. de Montpensier describes this in some detail. See *Mémoires de Mademoiselle de Montpensier, fille de Gaston d'Orléans* in *Nouvelle Collection des Mémoires
pour servir à l'Histoire de France* (Paris, 1838), IV, 32–37, 83, 85.

[48] Guillaume de Peychepérou, known as 'le petit Guitaut', to distinguish him from
the Comte de Comminges-Guitaut ('le vieux Guitaut') who was Captain of the
Queen's Guards. 'Le petit Guitaut' was one of Condé's adherents and with Boutteville and Coligny fought under him at the battle of the Dunes. Louis subsequently
pardoned him and invested him, at the same time (1662) as Condé, with the Order of
the Holy Ghost.

[49] Antoine-Agésilan de Grossolles, marquis de Flammarans. He appears to have
been attached to Monsieur and dependent on the Abbé de la Rivière; in 1649 he had
been acting as intermediary between La Rivière and La Rochefoucauld. Retz, who
gives these details, mentions him about eight times in his *Mémoires* (ed. Allem et
Thomas, Paris, 1956, 194–195 ff.).

his adventure was too remarkable to be forgotten. Fortune-tellers had predicted that he would die with a rope round his neck, a thing contrary to custom in France, where gentlemen condemned to death are beheaded. But he had the misfortune to fulfil the prophecy, if one can so describe the ridiculous stories put out by such people; although indeed God may sometimes make use of them in order to punish these kinds of curiosity which are always criminal.[50] This gentleman had fallen under a musket ball and had been left for dead near one of the houses that the King's troops were occupying. The soldiers, judging from the richness of his clothes that his purse was proportionately well garnished, were very desirous of going to strip him, but the enemy, who were in the near-by houses, not permitting them to do this without too much peril, they bethought them of fastening a rope to the end of a pike; and making a running knot, they passed it round his head [and so drag'd him into the house then just expiring].

Monsieur de Turenne found on arrival that the enemy had been repulsed and that the post was in good condition. He returned to the battery by the windmills in spite of the fire which the enemy still directed on him from the houses to the left of the barricade. His men however discovered a place not guarded, by which these houses could be attacked from the rear. As all the infantry were employed in the main attack, Monsieur de Turenne made the horsemen alight, and they delivered such a timely and valiant assault on the houses that, of more than a hundred of the enemy who had so long defended them, not one was not killed or taken.

[Just when the King's horsemen began this attack, the two Regiments] of Uxelles[51] and Carignan[52] which had continued to fight by the garden walls in so strange a manner [began to get the mastery of some of those holes which the Enemy had defended with so much obstinacy]. [They had now made them wider] with no help but that of their hands which had had to supply the lack of levers and other tools. Whereupon the enemy, judging that the

[50] This last remark appears to be an afterthought, as it does not figure in the *Life*.

[51] Louis-Chalon du Blé, marquis d'Huxelles. He appears to have been one of La Ferté's officers. At the siege of Valenciennes in 1654 the good work he carried out at Turenne's bidding was undone by La Ferté—who was to suffer in consequence.

[52] Thomas-François de Savoie, Prince de Carignan (1596–1656), son of the Duke of Savoy and grandfather of Marlborough's colleague, Prince Eugène.

King's men intended to force the position through these openings, [abandoned the whole wall thō they had a squadron of horse to second them in the garden]. The attackers, seeing this, [plyd them so hard, that the horse following the example of the foot began to run]; but having only a very narrow space through which to retreat, and every man striving with the others to escape the first, they blocked up the passage and for some time remained in a confused mass of horse and foot. A heavy fire was directed upon them, the wall was beaten down, they suffered great losses. As to those who were posted at the great barricade at the entrance to the Grande Rue, they were surprised at the same time to see that the gardens on their left had been taken, and as they were being fired on from the houses on their right, they took fright and abandoned the barricade which the King's troops now occupied.

It was not thought fitting to pursue them at once, [for it was then resolved to make a generall attack on all sides. In order to which all necessary preparations were making]. The troops were given time to breathe and to recover a little from the fatigue of so much fighting which the stifling heat that prevailed that day rendered in every respect more heated.

All was now disposed in good order, and, at the signal of three cannon shots, the attack began. Monsieur de la Ferté commanded the right and Monsieur de Turenne the left. The latter, advancing with a big body of horse and foot, had resolved to march a little to the left in the direction of the Bastille and to attack a place where he hoped not to find strong barricades. But as he was about to attack, the Bastille opened fire on the King's troops to the great amazement of those who had flattered themselves that Paris would remain neutral and would give no shelter to the enemy. It was already suspected and immediately after found to be true, that the Parisians had opened their gates to the Princes; [for when their Barricades were attacked, they made no countenance of defending them, but only retreated in good order from their Severall posts, leaving only some few men at each of them]. The latter abandoned them as the King's men advanced, and followed their own people into the city. The remnant were pursued up to the gates; and the Generals, seeing nothing more to be done, decided to return to La Chevrette where they had left their baggage, and to rest their troops and carry up the wounded.

One cannot say exactly how many men were lost in this action, but it is believed that in addition to the wounded, who were in great numbers, from eight to nine hundred men were killed. Apart from the persons of quality already mentioned, several others were killed or wounded whose names have been forgotten.[53] Comte d'Estrées, maréchal de camp, Pertuys, Lieutenant in Monsieur de Turenne's Guards, Colonel Woerden, a Gentlemen of the Duke of York's, Lisbourg, Lieutenant-Colonel of Streff, the Chevalier de Neuville and many others recovered from their wounds.[54]

It has been calculated that more than a thousand of the enemy were killed on the spot, [amongst whom were great numbers of Officers and men of quality]: of the latter, apart from Monsieur le Prince, the Duc de Beaufort, and the Prince de Tarante,[55] not one was not killed or wounded.

The Prince de Condé had never better fulfilled the duties of a great captain and dauntless soldier than on this occasion, never had he exposed himself to such great perils, [And truely it was his only vigour which preserv'd his Army from utter ruine in the very beginning of it]. He afterwards admitted to the Duke of York that he had never been in danger for so long. But what added lustre to his glory was that he had to deal with Monsieur de Turenne who, everyone agrees, was the greatest captain of his age and who can justly be compared with the most famous who preceded him.

What decided the Parisians on refusing entrance to Monsieur le Prince's troops when they presented themselves at the Porte de La Conférence, were the following reasons, which the King's loyal subjects propagated all over the city: [That thō they were indeed against the Cardinal, and wish'd his ruine, yet it was unworthy] of

[53] In place of these two sentences, the *Life* simply states that about 800 or 900 Royalists were killed. But it then mentions Mancini, Fouillou and M. de Mespas, 'an old Mareschall de Camp', as having died later of their wounds.

[54] These details are also in the *Life* (I, 106) which, however, adds the following: 'Monsieur de Turenne himself was very much expos'd that day, and so was consequently his R. Highness the Duke who accompanied this great Generall all along, and hazarded his person where ever he was.'

[55] Henri-Charles de la Trémoïlle, prince de Tarante and, later, Duc de la Trémoïlle (1621–1672). A great friend of Condé, for whom he was to deputise during the Prince's illness at the siege of Rocroi in 1653. The Archduke Leopold made things so difficult on that occasion that La Trémoïlle resigned from his post, though he remained on good terms with Condé.

94

their pride in being good Frenchmen [to suffer an Army, partly compos'd of Spanish troopes] [to enter within their walls]; that it would be an odious spectacle which might well excite dangerous sedition among the people if the Crosses of Burgundy which were usually seen only in Notre Dame were carried in triumph through the midst of their city; [That it would look as if they had already submitted to the Spanish Yoke] if they should see every where only the red scarves which would recall the shameful memory of having endured them during the rebellion that had been disguised under the specious name of a Holy League;[56] that in short it was contrary to the interests of the capital to receive an army under any pretext whatever.

When the fighting began in the Faubourg Saint-Antoine, Monsieur de Beaufort's harangues met with no success. Monsieur le Duc d'Orléans, believing that all was lost, had shut himself up in his palace and was remaining behind his gardens, his coaches being ready to take him to Orléans. But Mademoiselle,[57] full of courage and resolution, considered that the defeat of Monsieur le Prince would involve the whole party in ruin. She went to the Hôtel de Ville and spoke so vigorously to the Magistrates that her reasons, joined to the clamour and threats of the populace who had followed her, wrested from Marshal de l'Hôpital[58]

[56] The Catholic League in the time of Henri III and Henri IV had resisted the Crown which was then supported by the 'Politiques' and the Huguenots.

[57] Mademoiselle de Montpensier, whose memoirs gives the fullest and best account of what was taking place that day in Paris.

Anne-Marie-Louise d'Orléans (1627–1693), the elder daughter of Gaston d'Orléans, brother of Louis XIII, was a conspicuously romantic figure in an age of warlike princesses and intriguing amazons. Charles II, after his escape from the battle of Worcester, had paid court to her without success. She really wanted to marry Louis XIV, who however disapproved of her. For her exploits in 1652 she was punished by five years of 'exile' in her château on the Loing; but after this was allowed to return to the Luxembourg, where her literary salon became the most distinguished and influential in Paris. In 1670 she fell in love with the so-called Duc de Lauzun, 'one of the smallest men God ever made,' and yet a man who carried himself with incredible 'hauteur'. The King gave his assent to the marriage, then withdrew it, and then had Lauzun incarcerated in the fortress at Pinerolo. It was believed that he and Mademoiselle de Montpensier had been secretly married. Lauzun was released after ten years, but he and Anne-Marie-Louise did not get on together and they parted in 1684. (See Philippe Amiguet, *La Grande Mademoiselle et son siècle*, Paris, 1957).

[58] François du Hallier, comte de Rosnay (1583–1660). An old and trusted, though not a brilliant, officer. He had been, though already a Marshal of France, Condé's Lieutenant-General in the campaign of 1643, and had been severely wounded at Rocroi, a battle in which the carnage was great on both sides.

and the Provost of the Merchants[59] an order to the bourgeois guard at the Porte Saint-Antoine to open it and let Monsieur le Prince's army enter the city. She carried this order herself and saw it executed; she then went into the Bastille and had the cannon fired on the King's troops. In this way her courage saved the Prince de Condé and his army. Two days after this affair a great disorder broke out in Paris. It was on the occasion of a solemn council that was held in the Hôtel de Ville to have the Duc d'Orléans declared Lieutenant-General of the Kingdom, to effect a union which should be indissoluble until the Cardinal was banished from France, to appoint the Duc de Beaufort in place of Marshal de l'Hôpital as Governor of Paris, and to depose Le Fèvre from the post of Provost of the Merchants and give it to Broussel.[60]

But what they thought would establish their faction was one of the principal causes of its ruin. There suddenly arose an emotion so violent that it nearly exterminated the assembly. A multitude composed of every sort and condition of persons burst impetuously into the Place de Grève, crying out that they wanted the business terminated according to the Prince de Condé's wishes and all Cardinal Mazarin's partisans killed. But as they saw that little regard was paid to their request, they set about forcing the Hôtel de Ville; and Marshal de l'Hôpital, seconded by a few resolute men, having forbidden them to enter, the populace set fire to the doors. The fire quickly spread. The mob then shot at all those who appeared at the windows and killed several of them. Others, being less apprehensive of the popular fury than of the flames with which they were threatened, abandoned themselves to the mercy of the mob and were pitilessly massacred without distinction of party. The populace confused *Frondeurs* and Royalists, and by a fitting judgment of God there perished many more of the former than of the latter.[61] All those who have been suspected of provoking this sedition have denied it and thrown the blame on each other; and although the Prince de Condé has always maintained that he had

[59] Antoine Le Fèvre.

[60] Pierre Broussel, Dean of the Counsellors in the Grand' Chambre, and one of the most influential members of the Parlement.

[61] This remark is not in the *Life*. I suspect it occurred to James in 1695 when he was dictating and probably translating his Memoirs (with slight alterations) to the secretary who was taking them down.

no hand in it, the hatred it inspired fell upon him and his partisans; no one thought Monsieur le Duc d'Orléans capable of having had any share in it. This disorder was followed by another
accident which was also very prejudicial to the *Fronde*. The Duc de
Nemours was killed in a duel by the Duc de Beaufort, for the ties
of blood[62] had not sufficed to appease the mortal hatred they had
borne each other for so long.

While these tragic scenes were being enacted in the centre of
the kingdom, the Spaniards took the opportunity of recovering in
a short time several towns they had lost in previous years. They
took the field early, and not finding any troops able to arrest their
progress, they advanced without much difficulty.

The Court, which remained some time at Saint-Denis, was
exceedingly alarmed on hearing that the Archduke[63] at the solici-
tation of the Princes was preparing to march into France at the
beginning of July with an army of more than twenty-five thousand
men. After deliberating for some time on this pressing danger it
was decided towards the 15th of July that the Court and the Army,
which was too weak to resist such considerable forces, should
march in two days and retire to Lyons. The Duke of York and
Monsieur de Turenne came to Saint-Denis on the same day [that
this resolution had been taken in Council]. Before going to the
Court they went to see the Duc de Bouillon in order to learn from
him what had been decided. He told Monsieur de Turenne it was
his opinion that the Court could seek safety nowhere but in Lyons;
that the reasons which had brought about this decision were that
there was no other city where the King could be in safety, since it

---

[62] They were brothers-in-law. Every effort had been made to reconcile them and
Beaufort would have agreed to a reconciliation, but Nemours appears to have been
unwilling. The wounds Nemours had received in the battle kept him quiet for a time,
but on 29 July he sent an implacable challenge to Beaufort, who was compelled to
meet him. Condé, hearing of the affair, made all haste to the spot, but arrived just too
late. As Nemours was still weak, they had fought with pistols. Beaufort had protested
to the last moment, but when Nemours rushed furiously upon him, he fired—apparently in self-defence—and shot Nemours dead. Beaufort was overcome with horror,
and so apparently was Condé who, 'looking more dead than alive,' immediately went
to offer his condolences to Nemours' young widow (Godley, *The Great Condé*,
398–400).

[63] Léopold, Archduke of Austria and son of Ferdinand II. He was Viceroy and
commander-in-chief in the Spanish Netherlands between 1647 and 1656. Condé was
to find him a rather trying ally, though less so than his successor, Don Juan.

was the only great city that would receive them;[64] that they were not in a condition to resist the Spanish army which was marching into France, and there was a danger that the Court and the Army would be trapped between the Spaniards and Paris; [That so long as the person of the King was safe] there was every hope, but there was everything to fear [if he shou'd once fall into the hands of the Spaniards, or the Princes]; and that Lyons was the one place in France from which one could best make head against the enemy, since the whole region was devoted to the King's interest.

Monsieur de Turenne, on the contrary, considered this the most dangerous expedient of all. He said that the Court's withdrawing would infallibly mean the loss of all the frontier towns in Picardy, Champagne, and Lorraine, which were held for the King; that seeing themselves abandoned each one would think only of coming to terms with the Spaniards or the Princes; that the Spaniards and the Princes would have leisure to get from this all the advantage they pleased; that there was great danger of such a situation's inspiring in people's minds the thought of dividing France, or at least that part of it which they would be in possession of; that after the Princes were established in that quarter, their reputation increasing with their forces, the Court would lose both and would be on the verge of being entirely driven from the kingdom. After advancing several other reasons, he concluded that the surest and most prudent decision was for the King to retire to Pontoise with the Guard that usually accompanied him and which would suffice for the purpose. The position was easy to defend against any enterprise of the Parisians who would probably not push things to such a point, because there was a certain decency in their behaviour which still showed a kind of respect. He said that the Court being thus secured, [he with the Army wou'd advance towards Compiegne to observe the motion of the Spaniard, and hop'd by the favour of that Town and the Rivers which were near it] at least to delay their progress if he did not stop them altogether. He added that he was sure the Spaniards, who were naturally suspicious and subject to taking exaggerated precautions, when they saw him advancing upon them would not fail with the ordinary refinements of their prudence to imagine there was some mystery in his move and to believe that he would not

[64] Rouen had refused.

dare risk it [without good grounds]; finally that their opinion of the French temperament would make them fear that the Princes might be negotiating some secret treaty of which they would be the victims.

Monsieur de Turenne easily brought round his brother to his point of view. They went together to the Cardinal who, after weighing and considering the solidity of their argument, also agreed. The journey to Lyons was abandoned [And on the 17th of July the Court mov'd to Pontoise]. The Army marched in three days to Compiègne and camped under the walls. The Spanish army had advanced as far as Chauny where the Duc d'Elbeuf very unfortunately let himself be caught [with seven or eight hundred horse, which he gather'd out of his government of Picardy]; so that when on the enemy's approach he thought he could withdraw, they cut off his escape and, the place being weak, he was obliged to capitulate after two days of siege on condition that his horsemen should march out on foot and should leave their horses for the Spaniards.

Monsieur de Turenne had wisely foreseen that his own move would stop the enemy. [After they had taken Chauny, they did not so much as put a garrison into it, nor lay Seige to any other Town in those quarters, where no opposition could haue been made], and contented themselves with eating up the country. It was believed they thought it much more to their interest to recover the places they had lost in Flanders than to make any conquests so far into France. They considered that the Princes would be strong enough with the help they could send them to make head against the King, whereas if they gave the Princes means of overwhelming him, the King would be compelled to place himself in the Princes' hands or in those of the Rebels, which, by uniting the forces of both parties, would oblige the Spaniards to loose their hold and to restore everything they might have conquered, which would be too far from the Low Countries to be succoured. They were afraid of taking the shadow for the substance. If these were not their views their conduct at least gave ground for supposing so. They returned to Flanders, took several towns and left the Duc de Lorraine on the frontier with his troops and a detachment of their own commanded by the Duke of Wirtemberg to be near enough to help the Princes when it should be judged fitting.

99

As soon as the Spaniards had returned to their territory, Monsieur de Turenne came back to the neighbourhood of Paris. The army of the Princes was camping under the walls; it was not strong enough to risk a battle and it feared that if it went away, the King's party which was daily increasing in strength, might soon prevail. The Parisians' animosity was cooling down and they were beginning to open their eyes and recognise that they had been misled. But what contributed most to bring them back to the path of duty was the Cardinal's leaving the kingdom. He had made ready for this retreat on arriving at Pontoise, as he judged it necessary for the King's interest and for his own. By this means he removed all pretext for rebellion. His re-establishment was certain if his Majesty's affairs were once again in the ascendant. He counted also on the Queen's firmness, which nothing could shake. He knew how everyone was persuaded that her word was inviolable. Never had princess shown more greatness of soul and more constancy, and such was her resolution in moments of greatest peril that history does not record any more heroic. It was nevertheless believed [that the Cardinal had run a great hazard of not being recall'd, if Monsr. de Bouillon had liv'd longer]. His great capacity, joined to that of Monsieur de Turenne who was at the head of the army, might have paved the way to the Ministry. It is not certain that they had this design but it is sure that they alone were capable of bearing the weight of office in so difficult a conjuncture. [However it were, the death of the Duke of Bouillon put an end both to those discourses, and to the apprehension] or the hope[65] of such a change.

The King's army arrived at Thillay a league distant from Gonesse towards the beginning of August and remained there until the end of the month. Monsieur de Turenne considered this an advantageous post for observing the Princes' army which was still near Paris and to prevent their being joined by the help which the Spaniards might send. He was at last advised that the Duc de Lorraine was returning a second time with his troops and with the Spanish detachment under the command of the Duke of Wirtemberg, and that he had taken the road through Champagne and Brie in order to join the Princes' army. Monsieur de Turenne at

[65] 'ou l'espérance'—an afterthought, which is inserted above the line in the manuscript.

once marched towards the Marne and, having learned on the way that the Lorrainers were advancing, his army passed the river at Lagny and advanced to the little village of Saint-Germain near Cressy-en-Brie. Monsieur de Turenne there received an order from the Court to remain until further instruction and to undertake nothing against Monsieur de Lorraine unless the latter undertook to march towards Paris and broke camp from where he was; in that case the Marshal was to do his best to prevent his joining the Princes. The reason for this order was that the Court was negotiating with Monsieur de Lorraine, who had sent his secretary for the purpose and had at the same time promised that he would remain where he was and would not advance until terms were agreed upon or the negotiations broken off. He was hoping to beguile the Court, to deceive it by his artifices and to find the opportunity [either to get into Paris, or to meet the Princes in his way to it, without hazarding a battell]. Monsieur de Turenne, who knew him better than did the Court, did not, like the Court, fall into the trap. Monsieur de Lorraine's secretary who was on his way to report to his master on the state of the negotiations, himself brought the order in question; but Monsieur de Turenne told him [That the promises of Monsieur de Lorraine, and just nothing, were the same thing to him]. And in fact to prove his good opinion of those promises, [he resolved to march the very next day, which was the 5th of September, to Brie-Comte-Robert] so as to be in a position to intercept him in the event of his wanting to march, as the Marshal thought he would, and that, following his custom, he would break his word. The Marshal told the Duke of York in confidence [That tho his orders from Court were positive not to leave his post, yet being morally certain that the Duke of Lorraine intended to deceive them, and knowing that it was for his Master's interests that he shou'd march, he thought it better to venture his head by disobeying] than to give Monsieur de Lorraine the chance of reaching his goal and duping him. The army broke camp in the morning and the Quartermasters on arriving at Brie-Comte-Robert found the enemy's Quartermasters who were coming to pitch camp, as their army was already on the march and intending to camp there the same night. The former returned at once to advise Monsieur de Turenne who, with the van of the army, had passed through a defile. He immediately sent to warn

Monsieur de la Ferté, who was bringing up the rear guard, with the request that he should come and meet him to consult together as to what was to be done; and as he did not come quickly enough, Monsieur de Turenne went to meet him and found him at the defile. They decided, instead of going to Brie-Comte-Robert, to march straight to Villeneuve-Saint-Georges. Monsieur de Turenne went in advance with all his cavalry, ordered the infantry and the cannon to follow him with all diligence and asked Monsieur de la Ferté to do the same. He rightly feared that [the Duke of Lorraine, who knew as well as himself the advantages of that post, shou'd get there before him] and he did not doubt that the latter's Quartermasters, warning him of their meeting with his own, would decide him on taking the same course. His conjecture proved to be sound. Whatever haste he made, the Duke's van arrived before his at Villeneuve-Saint-Georges, and he[66] [thought himself so secure of that post, that he wrote a letter to the Prince of Condé, and dated it from thence], to inform him that he had taken possession of it. The Duke of York heard of this afterwards from the officer who had carried the letter, for the Duke was with Monsieur de Turenne when a party which had made this officer prisoner brought him into Villeneuve-Saint-Georges; and the man was so surprised at finding the King's army there that he could not understand how it was possible.

Although the Lorrainers had gained the lead and were masters of the town and although a part of their troops had passed the Yerre, Monsieur de Turenne, arriving with his van on the heights which command the town and the rivers, drove them off and seized the bridge. Their army was already so near the other side of this little stream that its cannon fired on the first squadrons of the King's troops when they arrived on the hilltop; but the advantage of being on high ground served the King's men better than any speed they had made. Monsieur de la Ferté arrived in the evening with the rest of the army, and the enemy having failed to seize this position retired a league higher up the stream over against the Château d'Ablon, where Monsieur le Prince joined them a few days later, having passed over his troops [in two or three large boats which he found accidentally on the River].

It was then that the enemy, being stronger by a half than Mon-

[66] The Duc de Lorraine.

sieur de Turenne, counted on a certain victory: they held him as it were in a cul-de-sac between the Seine and the Yerre, whence they did not think he could escape them. They knew that he had only four or five days' supply of bread at most in his waggons; he had no forage and could get none from anywhere, as all the surrounding country was devastated; and they hoped to finish the war without striking a blow. But the very night he had arrived at Villeneuve-Saint-Georges Monsieur de Turenne had had the good fortune to stop twenty-four or twenty-five boats, which proved the salvation of the army, because they served to make bridges over the Seine.

No time was lost. The first bridge was finished in two or three days; defences were built on the other side of the Seine to cover it, and the second bridge was finished a few days later. The difficulties appeared insurmountable and yet they were overcome. At first there was neither wood nor money; but the enterprise of the artillery officers and the liberality of the gamesters supplied the lack of both. The latter lent three hundred pistoles, a small enough sum, though even the Paymaster could not provide as much; the former demolished houses in the town and took the beams and planks from them. The communications that were thus established with the other side of the Seine provided forage for the cavalry which had been without any from the first days. In order to put itself in a better position to maintain this post, the army entrenched itself towards Limay, which was the only quarter from which the enemy could attack it. It was covered by a wood on the right, it had the Seine on the left and the Yerre protected its rear. Thus having to protect only its front, which was over against Limay and Grosbois, it had only to build lines between the five redoubts which the Duc de Lorraine had raised there and which were still intact.

While the men were digging the trenches and building the bridges, the enemy's army broke camp after putting a garrison in Ablon, and marched towards Brie with the intention of passing the Yerre and completely surrounding the King's army. When the enemy made this move Monsieur de Turenne thought it well to attack the Château d'Ablon in order to assure communication by water with Corbeil, a town from which he hoped to get every kind of provisions. [In order to this design, Monsr. de Renneville was commanded out with a party of horse and foot, and two pieces of ordinance]. But before he had reached the château Monsieur de Turenne, who had seen him pass over the bridge, was warned that some squadrons of the enemy had been observed between the wood and Limay. He immediately ordered Renneville to return to the camp and he himself went to the hilltop to reconnoitre the enemy, believing at first that they were marching upon him. On arriving [he saw their foot beginning to appear; and that he might be inabled to make a true judgment, whither or no they intended immediatly to attack him], he and the Duke of York put themselves among the skirmishers who drove off the enemy's skirmishers and enabled him to observe their movements more closely. [Mr. de Turenne who saw not clearly at a distance, would not trust his own eyesight, he therefore desired the Duke to observe] what they were doing. The Duke was the first to advise him that they were entrenching themselves, which having been confirmed by several other witnesses, he returned to the camp well satisfied that the enemy were not going to attack his lines which indeed were not yet quite finished. He made his men work unremittingly on the trenches and put up palisades, and this having been completed in six hours, it was judged fitting to open the redoubts on the rear side because, from the way in which the Lorrainers had built them, it would have been difficult to recover them if the enemy had once taken possession.

At the same time as the Prince de Condé marched to Limay, the Duc de Lorraine advanced further up the Yerre between Brie and the King's army. The enemy thought they had the latter blocked, so that it could not quickly escape them; and they did not doubt that they would either starve it out or reduce it to undertaking some desperate action. After Monsieur le Prince had finished his trenches which were very deep and within a cannon shot of Monsieur de Turenne's, his principal care was to build a bridge of boats a league below the Marshal's in order to interrupt his foragers and prevent his communicating with Corbeil on the far side of the Seine; at the same time Monsieur de Lorraine had parties continually out in the country to prevent communications on the Brie side of the river. But before the enemy's bridge was finished, the King's troops captured the Château d'Ablon, which rendered useless all the enemy's precautions and assured communication by water with Corbeil. They also brought in a good supply of forage which they had found some way off, between Juvisy and Paris.

The enemy's bridge being finished, the foragers were only able to go out with large escorts of infantry and cavalry, which was the more difficult as they had to go so far that they could not return the same day. But the Generals at last thought of an expedient that was both easier and less hazardous. Two hundred horse[67] which had come to Corbeil after the taking of Montrond[68] were ordered to remain there. From this force little parties were detached every day[69] to go roaming downstream on both sides of the Seine. They met parties from the camp who were doing the same thing as they went upstream. After communicating what they had discovered, each party would return to its own post, and when the men from the Marshal's camp reported that there was no danger, the foragers were sent out; they would then push beyond Corbeil and pass the river Essonne, after which they foraged at their ease, let their horses browse at night, then came back to the town and returned to the camp on one side of the Seine or the other, according as they were advised that there was no danger.

This method was pursued with such system and good fortune that no accident befell any of the convoys, and one can truly say that the French Monarchy was reduced to such an extremity that its salvation depended on each of these convoys; the loss of a single one might have caused the loss of the whole army.

During this blockade little parties of the King's army pushed their forays very far in the direction of Orléans and sometimes went up to the gates of Paris, which greatly incommoded that

[67] The *Life* says 300. Turenne (I, 216) gives a clearer account. He had sent Vaubecourt (Nicolas d'Haussonville, comte de Vaubecourt) with troops from the main army to join the cavalry from Montrond, and this made up a force of about 2000 men to hold Corbeil.

[68] This was one of Condé's castles and is in Berry. Condé had spent part of his childhood here. It was here that, in September 1651 in response to the urgings of his sister, of La Rochefoucauld, of Nemours and others, Condé had agreed, apparently against his better judgment, to make war on the Court. As early as February 1652 the Royalists had prepared to besiege it. The siege operations were left in the hands of 'M. de Palluau' (Philippe de Clairambault, comte de Palluau), and the fortress had apparently surrendered in August. Bussy-Rabutin had distinguished himself during this siege.

[69] Between *c.* 8 and 20 September 1652 (Turenne, I, 217, note 1).

great city whose commerce was interrupted on this side while on the other side the Princes' troops pillaged it as much. For some time the Parisians endured these importunities with a good deal of patience; the Prince de Condé was promising to rid them of the trouble before long and to end the war by forcing Monsieur de Turenne and his troops to submit. But when the results did not answer to the hopes with which they were daily entertained, they inclined more than ever to the side of the Court and returned to sentiments more in harmony with their duty. They reflected seriously on the blindness with which they had allowed themselves [to be devoured by Strangers, with no prospect of benefit accruing to their City or of advantage to the French Nation, but that they were only to be made the stalking horses of some ambitious spirits], whose only object was to engage them in their design of usurping the royal authority.

The partisans of the Court took advantage of this better frame of mind and skilfully fomented [the misunderstandings which began to kindle betwixt the Parisians and the Princes]. The Cardinal de Retz[70] omitted nothing on his side that could increase them. People still remembered the massacre at the Hôtel de Ville and several other outbreaks which revealed the inclination of the populace. The firebrands who had so often set them in movement against the King's interest lost all credit, and this revived the courage of his faithful subjects who now showed the others the abyss into which the Princes' ambition would hurl them.

As the Generals' prudence had assured forage for the King's army and as the entrenchments were such that it would have been dangerous for the enemy to try to force them, [there happened] during the blockade only [frequent Skirmishes, which were not to be avoided on either side by reason of the nearness of the Lines] of the two armies. There was among others a considerable skirmish which nearly engaged the armies in spite of their Generals. The Duc d'Orléans having come to see the Princes' army, the young men of quality who had accompanied him wanted to show their bravery and came out of the lines to fire their pistols at the King's troops. The latter saw them coming in great numbers and sallied out to fight them. The horse were skirmishing in the plain

[70] Retz also went to interview the King and Queen-Mother at Compiègne (*Mémoires*, ed. Thomas, 718–723).

and the foot soldiers were doing the same thing in the vineyards which stretched from the bottom of the slope to the top of the hill. The affair grew so serious and the volunteers on both sides came so near each other [that Monsr. de Turenne was forced to send out Mr. le Marquis de Richelieu[71] with severall small bodies of horse] [to disengage them; which the Prince observing, did the like on his side]. There were several killed or wounded in both armies. A captain of the Regiment of Douglas named Tiry, who was captured, escaped a few days later and brought Monsieur de Turenne the news that the Prince de Condé had fallen sick and had been taken to Paris; and that the [leaders of the Faction were still endeavouring to keep up the hearts] of that party by encouraging the hope that the King's army was lost. If they thought so they were grossly deceiving themselves, [for the longer the Army stayd at Villeneuve St. Georges, the better they were supplyd, being furnish'd very plentifully] from Corbeil.

Meanwhile a very notable action was performed by Le Sieur Seguin, Captain of Horse in the Regiment of Beaunaux.[72] He often led out parties. He had gone out this time with a hundred men [and having put himself in ambush to fall on the foragers of the Enemy], he let them arrive and set about their work. He then came out to capture them when, discovering a squadron on a hill nearby, he went to charge it, thinking it was the only escort they had. But on approaching he found four other squadrons. He immediately made up his mind and told his men in a few words that [It was now too late to think of a retreat, and that they must instantly resolve to work out their safety with their swords]. He divided them into five small bodies each in two ranks [and they attack'd the Enemy so vigourously that they routed them, killing sixty on the place] [and taking fifty prisoners]. Thus, despite a great inequality in numbers, he defeated the old Regiment of Wirtemberg whose Major and two Captains were among those captured.

[The Court was all this while either at Pontoise, or at St. Germain's, and maintain'd their intelligence at Paris], from which place they were well informed of what was happening and of the

---

[71] Jean-Baptiste-Amador de Vignerot du Plessis, not to be confused with Armand-Jean du Plessis, duc de Richelieu.
[72] This is an error for 'Beauveau'.

discontent of the Parisians with the Princes for keeping up the war at their gates; and negotiations being now well on foot, the Court went to ask the two Generals [to know whither (sic) they thought it possible for them to bring off the Army from their post] without risking anything and to find means of rejoining the King in order to promote the treaty which was being discussed with the Parisians.

Preparations were at once set on foot for breaking camp. Twelve bridges were built over the little stream [under pretence that they were for the conveniency of the foragers] and orders were sent to the troops at Corbeil [to make some redouts upon a higth before that Town] so that the enemy might be still better persuaded that the only object was to assure the foragers on every side. [When both these commandes were executed on the 4th of October, an hour before Sun sett], all the troops were ordered to prepare to march. As soon as it was night the baggage was passed over towards Corbeil in great silence by the lowest path along the Seine. Cavalry and dragoons were placed at the head of the column with orders that on arriving near the town they were to draw up in battle order on the hill behind the redoubts.

[So soon as the baggage had past the bridges] [the troopes in their order began to march; but neither the Guards or Centrys were drawn from the Line, till the whole Army was past over] the little stream. Then the bridges were broken to prevent the enemy from using them and following the King's army, if they should discover it was retreating. [But they were so far from suspecting] this, [that they had designed that very night to have storm'd] the next day [the Regiment of Nettencour] which was with a guard of forty horse in the defence work that covered the two bridgeheads on the other side of the Seine.

In order better to succeed in this, the enemy had prepared great floats of wood which they allowed to drift down the middle of the river from a league further up so that the shock of the timber against the bridges might carry them away. The plan succeeded; and when the regiment of Nettencour wanted to pass over, as it had been ordered, it found the bridges broken. Monsieur de Turenne, being advised of this, ordered the regiment to proceed to Corbeil along the river bank, as he did not judge fit to delay the march of his troops on account of this mishap. The regiment succeeded in passing over at Corbeil and joining the army. On the next day somewhat before dawn, the enemy who had gone to attack the defence work were much surprised at finding it abandoned, but they were still more so at no longer see-ing the King's army; and they were the first to advise their Gener-als of the circumstance. But it was now too late, and even had they known earlier, they could not have done much harm, because after the army had marched a little more than a league, the ground became so favourable that it had nothing more to fear. It was covered on one side by the Seine and on the other by the Forêt de Sennart; the space between was not so wide that the army could not fill it, so that the enemy could neither overtake nor attack it in flank; and the nearer one approached Corbeil the narrower the ground became. The whole army reached Corbeil before sunrise. Although the troops were to remain only one night in order to rest, trenches were dug and palisades set up to prevent their being taken by surprise should the enemy feel any wish to fight. The next morning, being the 6th, the army marched to Chaulmes and arrived in the evening [with intention to pass the Marne at Meaux] and then to join the Court either at Pontoise or at Saint-Germain. That day was difficult and dangerous. The enemy might have attacked the army if they had wished. [The Army march'd so orderly, that in a quarter of an hour they might all haue been drawn up in] battle order. The van advanced in two columns, the first squadron at the head of the left-hand column being the first of the first line, and the squadron at the head of the right-hand column being the first of the second line, following the regular order. They observed the regular distances as if they had been ready to fight. The infantry followed the cavalry in the same order; [the first line of foot marching after the first of horse, and the second after the same manner; the Gens d'armes marching in their usuall place] [betwixt the two lines of foot, and the other wing of horse follow'd the foot in the same method: so that], should the enemy appear, the whole army was ready to receive him by turning to the left.

[The Train of Artillery, with the quessons,[73] march'd on the right hand of the foot, and the baggage on the right hand of them]. As the enemy had undertaken nothing that day, the King's

[73] That is, *caissons*—usually ammunition waggons.

army marched with less constraint to Preslé, to Tournan and Quincé, and [on the 11th they pass'd the Marne neer Meaux, and incamped the same night at] Retz [from whence they marched to Mont l'Eueque,[74] then to Courteuil, where they had the River which runs by that place to cover them]. This retreat, which greatly surprised the enemy, completely ruined their credit with the Parisians who were tired of enduring the burden of a war that overwhelmed them. They more and more wished to see it ended by the return of the King, whose friends now took advantage of this favourable conjuncture. [The Prince of Condé, and Duke of Lorraine, found it was not their intrest to stay any longer] in the neighbourhood of Paris, because a longer stay would finally lose them the few friends they still had there and whom they could only keep by going away. Winter, besides, was coming on and the country was so ruined that it would have been nearly impossible to find subsistance for their troops. [For these and perhaps some other unknown reasons,] the Princes [were forced to a resolution of leaving Paris, and found there was no other expedient but to winter their Armys in Champagne and Lorraine; the Spanish Army being to joine them at Rhetel, and to assist them in taking such places in those Countries, as wou'd secure them in their quarters. As for the Duke of Orleans and his daughter Madmoiselle, it was] decided [that they shou'd remain still at Paris, to use their intrest and endeavours to hinder that Town from receiving the King]. All these resolutions were immediately put into execution, for the King's army being, towards the 14th of October, still only at Courteuil near Senlis, the enemy's army passed near by them on the road to Champagne.

The Court then believed it was to its interest to return to Paris, and Monsieur de Turenne went to Saint-Germain expressly to decide it on this course. He pointed out the necessity of it and said that, the opportunity being favourable, they should take advantage of it and not give the Parisians time to recover from the disgust which they had conceived for the Princes and which their absence and the removal of their troops might dissipate. [To strengthen this advice, he made it manifest, That if the King possessed not himself of Paris, there was no possibility of procuring winter-quarters for their troopes]; that, without that, they

[74] Mont l'Evêque.

would not be in a position, in the following year's campaign, to make head against the enemy's forces which would be very numerous; [for shou'd Paris refuse to admitt the King, the rest of the great places wou'd] [follow their example]; finally, [To conclude, he affirm'd that all depended on the good or ill Success of that affaire. These reasons, which are but lightly touched here], appeared so strong to the Council that they were approved. The Court left Saint-Germain, but on its reaching the Bois de Boulogne by the bridge at Saint-Cloud, the others being broken, there came persons from Paris who addressed certain members of the Council and argued that the enterprise was dangerous and that there was temerity in thus risking the King's person. These gentlemen took alarm and went to the Queen's coach, in which the King was riding, in order to dissuade their Majesties from going further. The coach stopped and Monsieur de Turenne and the rest of the Council were called to deliberate on what was to be done. They [were all of opinion, That their Maties shou'd return to St. Germains]. Only Monsieur de Turenne [persisted in the former resolution, urging all the arguments which had perswaded that opinion], [Adding], that after the step which had just been taken, to go back [would now be both prejudiciall to the King's affaires] and to his honour, [as shewing a manifest want of resolution] which would expose the Court to scorn, [dishearten their Freinds, and encourage their Enemies]. He said that everything was to be feared from a change which would display so much timidity and [That he look'd on those persons who brought this advice, either as covert Enemies to the King by endeavouring to hinder his coming into Paris, or at least as men of weak judgments] whose sentiments ought not to be followed.

The Queen, who was difficult to frighten and whose courage was dauntless, followed Monsieur de Turenne's opinion against the views of the rest of the Council. She said that on so important an occasion it was better to expose herself and her son to the dangers they might incur than to lose their reputation by an action as shameful as their return would be; for this would entirely ruin their affairs and they could never hope to re-enter Paris if they lost this opportunity. It was decided to go forward. The King advanced at the head of his Guard and entered the city by the Porte Saint-Honoré; and instead of the opposition with the fear of which they had tried to frighten him, he was greeted everywhere with acclamations of popular joy and was accompanied to the Louvre by a crowd of people who kept crying out: 'Vive le Roi'. [The Duke of Orleans, as the King enter'd at one end of the City, went out at the other] and Mademoiselle, who had remained in her apartment in the Tuileries, was ordered to leave Paris, and obeyed. [Monsr. de Turenne return'd] immediately [to the Army, and about the end of the month began his march after the Enemy, who] [had possest themselves of Château-Porcien, and Rhetel upon the Aysne], where they found little resistance. [From thence they went to St Menehou] which defended itself well [thō forced at last to surrender on composition].[75] [Besides the ordinary garrison that was in it, there were but four Companies of the Duke's Regiment, which got into it before it was invested].

When the Princes' army left the neighbourhood of Paris, [the two foot Regiments of la Ferté and York, with some horse of la Ferté's troopes, were sent away in all hast, with orders to put themselves into St Menehou, and the places of Barois]. The Marshal[76] [himself went also to Nancy, to secure his government of Lorraine in the best manner he was able, suspecting that the Enemy's design would be to take up their winter-quarter in those parts, as accordingly it came to pass].

The King's army now marching into Champagne, camped on the 2nd of November at Balieux [where they were oblig'd to stop a whole day; because the Soldiers in coming thether found so great a quantity of new wine] and got so generally drunk that there [came not enough up to the quarter, to make the ordinary guard] for the General and the Duke of York. After they were got together they marched on the 4th to [Dizi neer Epernay, where they passed the Marne on the 5th of November, to keep that River betwixt them and the Enemy, who were then about Rhetel], where [the Count de Fuenseldagne[77] had joyn'd them with a con-

75 'fut. enfin forcé de se rendre à composition' (MS., p. 65). St. Menehou is, of course, Sainte-Ménéhould.

76 That is, La Ferté.

77 Luis-Perez de Vivero, conde de Fuensaldaña, soldier and diplomat. He had been the Archduke Leopold's general from as early as 1648, and had led the Spanish cavalry at the battle of Lens. The Baron de Woerden describes him as 'un homme d'une extrême probité, froid, pas communicatif, mais dont l'amitié, une fois donnée, ne se démentait pas' (cited by Miss Godley, p. 415). He was to be a thorn in Condé's

siderable part of the Spanish Army]. This obliged Monsieur de Turenne to keep always at a reasonable distance and behind some river or some defile so as not to run the risk of being surprised. On the 6th the army marched to Chaype [and after they had stayd there three or four days, they] repassed the Marne [and quarter'd at Vitry-le-Bruslé]. On the 16th they marched to Vitry-le-François, [still governing their motion according to that of the Enemy].

While the King's army was camping in these different places, Sainte-Ménéhould was taken about the 13th of November. The enemy there disbanded the troops of the Duc d'Orléans who were in their army and allowed them [to return into France, on condition they shou'd not serve] the King [during the rest of the Campagne] or in any other on that side of the country. [Wherupon they went immediatly to quarters appointed for them in Picardy, and were the next year sent to serve in the Armys on the other fronteers of France]. The enemy then went to besiege Bar-le-Duc. Monsieur de la Ferté had sent to command one named Roussillon [with such a garrison as was sufficient to haue defended it a longer time then he did]. He was nevertheless vain enough to refuse a reinforcement of 500 men which Monsieur de Turenne had sent to Saint-Dizier during the siege of Sainte-Ménéhould [with orders to march for Barleduc, in case the Governour should haue occasion for them]. He thanked [Monsr. de Turenne for his care of him, assur'd him with all, that he was well prepar'd to receive the Enemy whensoever they shou'd dare to approach him]. He repeated this when he was invested and promised [that he wou'd give a good account of the place]. [It was on the 18th, when this news came to Mr. de Turenne, when he was at Vitry le François]. He at once broke camp to go and help him with all possible diligence, [and that the Enemy might have no intelligence of his approache, he repassed the Marne at Vitry], and skirting the river which was on his left, [by break of day came to St. Dizier]. He halted there for six hours to rest his troops, [but just as he was preparing to march again, he received intelligence

side. He and Condé in fact disliked each other from the outset. Condé later complained so bitterly of him in correspondence with Madrid that in 1656 Fuensaldagna was sent as viceroy to Milan, while Caracena, the governor of Milan, was appointed commander in the Netherlands.

that both the Town and Castle were surrender'd to the Enemy];
and this stopped the army's advancing.

This news was the more disagreeable as it spoiled the design
[not only of succuring the place, but also of defeating the Enemy]
or [of puting them to so hasty a retreat, that] at least [they must]
[haue lost their baggage and their cañon]. Never had enterprise
been more judiciously concerted, [for thō the Royall Army was
much inferiour to the Enemys in number, yet the ground was] so
advantageous on the side from which the army was marching on
them, that it ran no risk, the country being covered with woods.

Monsieur de Turenne had 6000 well disciplined infantry, [his
Army having been reinforced both with horse and infantry] which
had been taken [from the garrisons of Artois and Picardy and other
places, which could well spare them when the Enemy was departed out of France]. [By the favour of these] [woods and sud-
dainess of the march] the Army had fallen on the enemy when they
least expected it; [they cou'd haue received no considerable benefit by their intelligence: for such is the Situation of the place, and
such the disadvantage of the post for those who attack the Town,
against] an Army [who comes to releive it], that their entrenchments are useless and cannot be defended. [The woods extend in
length within a league of the Town, and from the woods to the
Castle lyes a spacious plaine]. The castle stands on the level of the
plain, and the upper town is [upon the brink of a descent which
leads to the lower Town]. In the bottom, which is narrow and between two hills, flows a little brook, [and the ascent on each side is
steep and troublesome], so that the King's troops would only
have had to fight against the enemy who were on their side of the
brook and who would have passed their time very ill between the
army which would have attacked them and the castle, and between
the wood and the castle, and they could only have retreated in so
much confusion that they would have fallen over one another.
When Monsieur de Turenne had formed this design, he thought
he would find the whole of the enemy's army together; he was not
aware, as he learned afterwards, that Fuensaldagna had retired
with the greater part of his troops; for the Spanish general did not
know that the King's army was as strong as it was, and he thought
that the Prince de Condé and the Duc de Lorraine [were sufficient to take in all the Barois, and there to make good their winter

quarters]. Thus a great success was missed by the indiscretion of
Monsieur de Roussillon who had so little brains that he allowed
[the four best Companies of his garrison] to be taken [in the lower
Town], although it was defended by a fairly good wall and surrounded by a ditch full of water. He could at least have held out
until a breach had been made; but the enemy, having taken possession of it on the day they arrived before the place and not thinking fit to attack on that side, [the next day raised a battery upon
the Plaine against the Castle; and their guns no sooner playd]
than the Governor, without even waiting for them to make a
breach, agreed to leave the place the next day.

At this siege [the Duke of Lorraine lost Mr. Fouge a Lieutenant Generall, and the best Officer in his Army; he was kill'd the
neight after they had taken the lower Town]. [Being at supper
with the Prince of Condé], [in one of the next houses to the upper
Town, and making a debauch, he grew so drunk, that he ran out]
in a fit of bravado [at a back door with a napekin on his head, to be
discern'd the better], [and to provoke the Enemy to shoot at him.
The Cheualier de Guise and the Prince of Condé himself ran out
after him to bring him back; but before they could hale him in, he
receiv'd a shott which kill'd him]. The prompt taking of Bar-le-
Duc [gave time to the Enemy to make themselves master of
Ligny, Voy, and Commercy, because Mr. de Turenne being ignorant of Mr. de Fuensaldagne's departure durst not come too
near them, for which reason he stayd two or three days at St
Dizier], during which time they made new progress, and these
three places, having only weak garrisons offered little or no resistance.

[From St Dizier the Royall Army advanced] [to Stinville,
where there came up to them a considerable recruit] [composed of
the Duke of Longueville's Regiment of horse,[78] which consisted
of three hundred, and that of his foot which were about twelve
hundred, with them came also the Earle of Bristol's[79] Regiment of

[78] Not presumably commanded by the Duke, who had been one of the Frondeurs.
Henri d'Orléans, duc de Longueville, was the husband of the famous Anne-Geneviève
de Bourbon, Condé's sister.
[79] George Digby. He apparently disliked the Duke of York and in 1657, when
Charles II forced his brother to take service with the Spaniards, Bristol intrigued
against the Duke. He subsequently turned Catholic, and it was he who, in 1662,
moved to impeach Clarendon, a move which fortunately came to nothing.

horse and Company of ordinance; and thō they were all but new rais'd souldiers, excepting the company of ordinance, so that no great service cou'd be expected from them, yet their number did good, because they gave reputation. At this Town of Stinville, Monsr. de Turenne had the first intelligence that the Count of Fuensaldagne was gone] [and upon this notice which was given on the 25th,] he resolved to give battle to the enemy, [or in case they avoided it,] to oblige them to leave the winter-quarters in which they thought themselves so well established that they had already shared them out. The event will show how greatly they had been deceived, [for upon M. de Turenne's advancing to them the next day, they were so far from being able to compass their designs, that they durst not] make head against Monsieur de Turenne. They suddenly broke camp, passing the Meuse at Voy, where Monsieur le Prince was advised that the King's army was marching upon him, and [leaving the River on their left hand, they made what hast they could towards Luxembourg, and Mr. de Turenne follow'd them so close, that for the most part he came about noon to the place where they had quarter'd the night before]. He kept their spurs busy[80] [till he came to St Michel on the 30th on the forenoon]. He did not think fit [to follow them any further, they being so near the shelter of their own Country that they were out of danger].

Monsieur de Turenne now only thought of [finding out means to refresh his Army, especially the foot, which were exceedingly harass'd with the great and painfull marches they had taken, and] were lacking bread. The enemy who had been constantly followed, had eaten up the country everywhere. The waggons were empty, [it being actually impossible for the Commissary of the Victualls to provide bread for them.] Monsieur de Turenne sent to ask the inhabitants of Saint-Mihiel for bread, [but they making a difficulty of obeying him, and pretending they could not furnish] a great enough [quantity in one day], he found himself obliged, in order not to let his army die of hunger, to send all his foot, gendarmes, and cannon into the town, [quartering the horse in the neighbouring Villages. The Army's stay in this was very short, however it serv'd to refresh the soldiers]. But Monsieur de la

[80] 'On leur chaussa ainsy les eperons jusqu au 30ᵉ qu'on arriva le matin a St Mihel' (MS., p. 70).

Ferté being informed of it, himself came from Nancy which was only ten or twelve leagues distant, [to desire Monsr. de Turenne to leave the Town, being] so much [offended at his quartering there] that he did not pardon him for a long time, and this discord was afterwards very prejudicial to the King's affairs. Monsieur de Turenne's army had to leave the day after the arrival of Marshal de la Ferté, whose anger increasing when the inhabitants complained to him about some of the soldiers, he followed the troops' march with his Guards, at the head of whom he charged the loiterers as if they had been enemies. He continued this behaviour as far as [the quarters of the Gendarmes who were not yet march'd out, nor wholly drawn together]. [One of the Earle of Bristol's troope whose name was Manwaring] and who did not know him, seeing the violence with which he was laying about him, thought that these were the enemy, [and sett his pistoll to his brest which fortunatly for both miss'd firing]. One poor Gendarme was wounded with five or six sabre cuts and thrown down, but he recovered. Barkley, a cornet in the same company, got off more lightly; [for hearing the noise which was made by the Mareschall], he as well as Manwaring thought that the enemy had entered the town and advanced to the corner of the street, pistol in hand, but recognising the Marshal he at once lowered it and saluted him, and as the Marshal knew him he got off more lightly than the Gendarme.

[The Army quarter'd that night at a Village call'd Villotte, and the next day march'd to Trouville which lyes betwixt Barr and Ligny: And that evening M. de Turenne sent a party of horse and foot with cañon and all things necessary to attack] this latter place. They first set up the battery at less than a half musket shot from the walls and dug trenches to right and left to put the infantry under cover and made [an epaulement or blind for the horse]. [All this was perfected before Sun-rise the next morning, and then the battery began to play]. A fair breach was opened before nightfall; but the difficulty was to pass the ditch which was full of water, deep [and withall so brode that the ruines of the wall had not fill'd it up]. They none the less assaulted the place and [by the help of plancks and ladders and long] beams, [they passed the ditch] [and came up to the breach] which the enemy at once abandoned, and retired into the castle which was stronger. The

117

next day Monsieur de Turenne marched with his troops to Bar-le-Duc, leaving Monsieur de la Ferté with his troops to besiege the castle of Ligny.

On the night they arrived at Bar they set up [a battery against the lower Town,] [under the shelter of some houses which were almost upon the edge of the ditch, there being but a narrow way betwixt them and it. By morning their guns began to play, and though they were but few, and very small], [two of them being twelve pounders, one eight, and the other two but Six],[81] as these cannon were reinforced and could be given a double charge, [Monsr. de Champfort lieutenant of the ordnance, playd them so warmly, that by Sun-set they had open'd a faire breach].

[The Regiment of Picardy] [was to storme it] under the orders of Monsieur du Tot,[82] the oldest Lieutenant-General in France and the only one in this army. The breach was against the gate on the right as you enter, the gate being flanked only by two small round towers. It was preferred to attack this place rather than another, to avoid the trouble of filling in the ditch and because it would have been necessary to make a bigger breach elsewhere, [which would haue taken up more time then they were willing to spare]; whereas at this point it was easy to pass the ditch by the regular bridge and to jump down by the drawbridge of the wicket gate, [from whence they went under covert of the wall to mount the breach, which was not far distant].

[All things being thus prepar'd], [Mr. de Turenne caus'd the battery to give two or three rounds upon the] Gate-Tower, which alone defended the breach, [that by shattering it, the men might haue the easier work]. Monsieur du Tot, who had orders to open the attack, [in stead of ordering the Commanded men to fall on first, and staying himself with the body], had, as his custom was, drunk a little too much for a commander. He followed the sergeant who was leading the attack and when jumping down from the little wicket gate, he was killed by a musket ball. This place was fatal to drunkards; but the Duke of York renders this justice to the nation that he affirms poor Monsieur du Tot was the only

[81] These figures refer of course to the weight of the cannon balls.

[82] Charles-Henri du Tot had served under Turenne in Germany as maréchal-de-camp. Turenne, who speaks of him both in his *Mémoires* and his *Correspondance* (Vol. I, ed. Marichal) seems to have reposed great confidence in him.

French officer whom he ever saw drunk in the armies. This accident caused no delay. The attackers passed through the wicket in single file and coming to the breach, in spite of the fire of the enemy whom the cannon could not dislodge from the Gate-Tower, they not only carried the breach, [but drove the Enemy from the Barricades which they had made behind it, and the streets, forcing them backward into the upper Town].

[There happen'd an accident to the Governour whose name was Despiller, which very much facilitated the taking of the lower Town]. Not believing that the assault would be delivered that evening, he had remained in the upper town, but the noise of the attack had obliged him to come down and to bring two hundred men to reinforce those who were defending the post. [In riding down, his horse fell with him, and so bruis'd his leg that he was forced to be carryd back into the upper Town]. Not many men were lost in this assault. [Besides Mr. du Tott no man of quality was kill'd, excepting only the Marquis d'Angeau a Volonteer]. [Monsr. Poliac the first Captain of Picardy, who commanded that Regiment, the Major Officers being absent,] had a musket ball in the shoulder, and Godonviller, Captain in the same regiment, received one in the belly. [Both recover'd].

Cardinal Mazarin reached the camp that day, bringing with him a reinforcement of troops which [had been drawn together from divers places, and were commanded by the Duke d'Elbeuf,[83] and the Mareschall d'Aumont[84]]. The Cardinal saw the lower town taken. This success was of little help for the taking of the upper town and the castle. These were attacked only in order to provide lodging for the infantry, the season being too severe for camping. The army found there an abundance of wine and bread which it greatly needed. [As for the horse they were conveniently quarter'd at the] surrounding villages fairly near the town.

Although the frost was hard, the Prince de Condé resolved to try to succour the place. The army was warned of his march in good time and [it was resolved by the Cardinal and the Generalls, that Monsr. de Turenne and the Mareschall de la Ferté should

---

[83] Charles de Lorraine, duc d'Elbeuf.

[84] Antoine d'Aumont. He played a more important part in the war from about 1654 onwards, during the operations in Flanders. He was then a Marshal of France and governor of the Boulonnais.

take the greatest part of the horse,] about three thousand foot and six fieldpieces [and march towards the Enemy]; and that the Cardinal should follow at some distance, while Messieurs d'Elbeuf and d'Aumont with the rest of the troops should continue the siege.

It was learned [that the Enemy was coming by the way of Vaubecourt a bourg, about five leagues from Barleduc]. The King's army [marched towards them, Monsieur de Turenne having the van, and advanced as far as Condit] [which is but a league and a half short of Vaubecourt· where just as the foremost troopes were come into their quarter, they had notice by a party of theirs] which [brought prisoners along with them, that the Prince of Conde was newly march'd into Vaubecourt, intending to quarter there that night, and having no intelligence of the Royalists being so near him]. [Monsieur Turenne sent immediatly to the Mareschall de la Ferté to give him notice of this, and withall to signify his opinion; which was, That they ought presently to march and fall upon] the enemy, [whom they should certainly find in great disorder, the quarter being plentifully stor'd with wine and all manner of provision, which would render it more difficult for their Commander to draw his men together, and cause them] to [get to horse; for their surprise would be so great] on finding themselves attacked, at a time when they thought the King's army was so far off, that one would win an easy victory. [But the Mareschall de la Ferté instead of consenting to this proposition, came himself to Monsieur de Turenne, and told him, He thought it no ways proper for them to attempt any thing of so great concernment, without the participation of the Cardinal who was] not far away; [and therfore advis'd that he shou'd first be made acquainted with it, and his directions receiv'd, before they undertook the Enterprize. Monsr. de Turenne, thō very unwillingly, was constrain'd to yeeld to this opinion; upon which they dispatch'd a Messenger to inform the Cardinal by word of mouth,] of the great opportunity which was offered. [He return'd the bearer in all hast to give his approbation: But thō the Cardinal was only distant about a league or two at most], [the opportunity was overslip'd; for just as the Army was setting forward, another party of the Royalists brought word, that the Prince of Condé already was dislodg'd, as they beleev'd, because the Bourg was all on

Nous, Soussignez, Prêtres Administrateurs du Collège des Ecossois dans l'Université de Paris a Servir Louis Inesse ci devant Premier Aumonier de la feüe Reine de la Grande Bretagne et Ancien Principal en Collège, Charles Wigtford Principal, Thomas Inesse Sous-Principal, George Inesse Procureur et Alexandre Smith Prêtre des Etudes en dit Collège Certiffions a tous ceux a qui il appartiendra, que les Memoires cy joints de feu Roy Jacques II de la Grande Bretagne sont Conformes aux Memoires Originaux Anglois Ecrits de la propre main de Sa Majesté et Conservez, en vertu d'un Brevet Signé de Sa main, dans les Archives ... notre dit Collège Et nous susdits Certiffions en outre que le manuscrit cy joint, revu et corrigé par le susdit Roy Jacques, traduit par son Ordre ... enne de la main de feu S.A.E.me Le Cardinal de Bouillon le vingt sept ou onze de Janvier 1696 et Ecrit de la main de Sieur Dempster, l'un des Secretaires de Sadite Majesté, est Conforme pour les faits, details, Circonstances Reflexions et Generallement tout (le tour du ... seul et l'ordre de la relation exceptés) a une seconde traduction des mêmes Memoires Anglois Originaux faite par l'Ordre de la feüe Reine de la Grande Bretagne, signée de sa main, cachetée du Sceau de Ses Armes, Contresignée par Mylord Caryll Secretaire d'Etat le quatorze de Novembre 1704 et donnée le quinzieme Janvier 1705 par le susdit Louis Inesse a S.A.E.me Le Cardinal de Bouillon pour Servir a l'histoire du Vicomte de Turenne. En foy de quoy Nous avons Signé les presentes et y avons opposé le Sceau du dit Collège. Fait a Paris ce vingt quatre Decembre Mil Sept Cent trente quatre. —

L. Inese
Ch. Wigtford
Tho: Inesse
Geo: Inesse
Al: Smith

3. CERTIFICATE FROM THE ADMINISTRATORS
OF THE SCOTTISH COLLEGE

4. Vicomte de Turenne

fire], and that their vanguard was no longer in sight. On advancing, the army recognised that Vaubecourt was indeed in flames, and another party confirmed the report that the enemy were retiring in extreme haste. Whereupon Monsieur de Turenne retraced his steps to bring the troops back to their quarters, [not thinking it expedient to go further]. [The next day they were inform'd by some inhabitants of Vaubecourt that] the Prince de Condé, having been informed of Monsieur de Turenne's approach, had his men sound the call to arms and to horse, and that, [seeing his men not over hasty to leave] such good shelter, he had caused a fire to be started at each corner of the bourg in order to make them move out more promptly. His so fortunately escaping this danger made him more circumspect afterwards. [He thought it not convenient for him to stay any longer in those parts], seeing that the King's army was numerous enough to continue two sieges at once, and at the same time to come with half their troops to meet him.

He was indebted to Monsieur de la Ferté for having escaped from so awkward a position, [for had not he oppos'd the Counsell of the Mareschall de Turenne, the Prince had certainly been surprised] and beaten. [Neither did Monsr. de la Ferté want either judgment or] experience to recognise that the opportunity was excellent; but since the affair at Saint-Mihiel, [his spleen was such] [that he regarded not what prejudice he did to his Masters seruice], if only he could deprive Monsieur de Turenne of the honour of having executed so important an enterprise. [Vndoubtedly it was] to frustrate this [that he propos'd the sending to the Cardinal, that at least], if the affair succeeded, it might be said that the enemy had been attacked by his orders, and one ventures to say that any other than Monsieur de la Ferté who had [committed such a fault] [had payd deerly]. [But he was so considerable] by his troops, his Government, and his credit that the Cardinal thought it necessary to dissimulate.

When it was known that the enemy had quite departed from the Country, [M. de la Ferté with the greatest part of the foot and some of the horse return'd to Bar] and Monsieur de Turenne put the rest in quarters at Contrisson, Ruvigny-aux-Vaches, and other villages which were only four leagues from Bar. [As for the Cardinal, he was quarter'd at a Village call'd Faine] a league from the town, [where he continued during all the Seige, which lasted not long after the Prince of Condé was retreated]. Yet the besiegers[85] (sic) [suffered two breaches to be made before they] spoke [of surrender]. At the first which was thought vulnerable,[86] the soldiers on mounting to the assault found that there was on the other side a drop of a pike's depth which could not be jumped but [which was not discernable from without]. The army was obliged to set up a new battery against the castle where, [when they had made a considerable breach], the besieged capitulated, surrendered [both the upper Town and the Castle] and remained prisoners of war. This happened towards the 15th of December. From the fact that the first breach we have spoken of was useless, one may draw a lesson which governors of towns may turn to advantage in defending them. Art may do what the nature of the ground did here. [For if a wall be reasonably strong and has a sound foundation], one may dig behind the place where a breach has been made a very deep and steep ditch [so as to render the breach as fruitless to the Assailants].

[In this Town of Barleduc amongst the other troopes which were left in it by M. de Lorraine, there was an Irish Regiment of foot, who seeing themselves prisoners of warr, and like to continue long in that condition, their Collonel dying the same day on which the Town was deliver'd up, and the Lieutenant Collonel having made his escape, sent to offer their seruice to the Duke, in case] the Duke of York [could obtain their liberty from the Cardinal; which being] [granted by him, that Regiment consisting in ten Companies with all their Officers were incorporated in the Duke's]. The Duke was at Ligny and they were sent there.

[And now that Bar was taken, the Mareschall de la Ferté's men] marched to Ligny to [hasten the taking of the Castle, where no considerable attempt had yet been made while the other Seige continued]. They began to batter the wall, but before the breach was large enough, as there was shortage of cannon balls, the besieged fortified the upper part with a strong palisade; whereupon Monsieur de la Ferté [fasten'd a Miner on to the same place], where the ruins of the wall favoured a lodgement. In a short time

---

[85] 'les assiegeans,' which is an obvious slip. The translator should have written 'les assiégés'.
[86] 'insultable.'

the mine was ready to be fired. The regiments of York and Douglas were commanded to attack as soon as it should have produced
its effect, and the regiment of La Ferté had orders to support
them. The Comte d'Etrés,[87] who was commanding the attack,
sent the men forward without waiting for the smoke to clear,
when they could see the effect of the mine.[88] They passed the
ditch on the ice, the ditch being very wide, [but when they came
to the breach they perceived], although too late, that the mine
[had only carryd away the outward part of the Wall as far as
where the Enemy had plac'd their pallisade]. As there was no
means of advancing, the troops were ordered back, but to make
matters worse, the [yce broke under them, and most of them fell
into the] water of the ditch, which gave leisure to the besieged to
open a heavy fire upon them. [Thus for want of a litle patience to
see what effect the Mine had wrought, the Regiment of York lost
four Captains, some Lieutenants and Enseigns, and about a
hundred men], [and the Regimt of Douglas two Captains and
neer fifty private Soldiers], not counting the wounded.

That night the miner was fixed for a second time and the next
day being the 22nd, the castle capitulated, surrendering on the
same conditions as Bar-le-Duc.

The Cardinal, whose appetite had grown with these successes,[89]
desired to push them further and to conclude the campaign with
the taking of Sainte-Ménéhould. After leaving good garrisons in
Ligny and Bar-le-Duc and repairing the breaches as much as the
season would allow, the army left Contrisson on the 27th and
arrived next day at Sommieure where it remained until the 30th.
During this march the troops had to be quartered in the villages
as the rigours of winter made it impossible to camp. [The day
they came to Sommyeur] [the frost was so very sharp, that all the
horsemen were forced] to [march on foot] to keep warm; [thirty or
forty soldiers] perished the same day [throw the extreamity of
cold; for so soon as any of them who were not warmly cloth'd]
[sat down for ease, the frost pierced them, and they were never
able to raise (sic) again]. The Duke of York saw several frozen to

[87] Possibly François-Annibal d'Estrées, marquis de Cœuvres, a son of the Maréchal
d'Estrées.

[88] This may have been due to La Ferté's impatience.

[89] 'que ces succès avoient mis en goût.'

death and a much greater number would have perished but for the care taken by the officers to put on horseback those whom they saw ready to succumb and to carry them to the first villages where they saved several of them by giving them brandy and other kinds of liquor. What made this frost keener and more penetrating was that [they were then marching over the] vast plains of Champagne, where there was no shelter against the [peircing north East wind] which was [blowing directly in their faces]. It was this also which prevented the siege of Sainte-Ménéhould. Monsieur de Turenne represented to the Cardinal the difficulties of undertaking this in such cruel weather; he said that one could not, as at Bar or Ligny, find shelter for the infantry or forage in the neighborhood for the cavalry, since there were no suburbs and the country had been eaten up by the enemy. He added that as the place was strong and defended by a large garrison, it would be necessary to lay formal siege to it and that instead of ending the campaign gloriously [they should hazard the] complete [ruine of the Army and be forced to raise the Seige dishonourably].

The Cardinal yielded at last to such good reasons. The army then marched towards Rethel by way of Menaucour and Grivy, [and on the first of January, 1653, quarter'd at Attigny, which is scituated on the River Aisne]. They passed the river next day and came to Saux-aux-Bois. The siege of Rethel was found almost as difficult an undertaking as that of Sainte-Ménéhould, and this decided them to attack Château-Porcien two leagues further down, because they found there the same facilities as at the siege of Bar-le-Duc; only the castle was defensible, and the town, which they counted on seizing at once, could contain and shelter enough troops to lay siege to the castle.

Monsieur de Turenne arrived on the 6th of January at Soin, where he quartered the greater part of his horse and a part of his foot in the town and the surrounding villages. It is only a league and a half from there to Château-Porcien and it was [the more proper place for hindering any succours from being put into that Town: The Care of advancing the Seige was repos'd on Monsieur d'Elbeuf and M. d'Aumont]. Marshal de la Ferté established quarters for his horse at * * * 90 in order also to prevent any succour being given; and the Cardinal lodged at Balhan.

90 There is also a blank in the *Life* (I, 154).

[Wee shall not relate the particulars of this Seige where the Duke was not constantly present, only what pass'd in the out quarters], where the duty was hard because of the approach of the Prince de Condé, who came to try to raise the siege.

To prevent his doing this [all the horse that were quarter'd in the Villages about Soin] were ordered [to march thither every evening, and continue there all night, returning after Sun rise to their own quarters: The same method was duly observ'd by all the Mareschall de la Ferté's horse]; and these fatiguing manoeuvres lasted as long as the siege, which was fortunately not very long. The town having been taken first, they did not delay in fixing the miner to the castle. When the miner was ready, [the Governour who was call'd Dubuisson capitulated to yield in four days, if during that time he was not releeved]. [The Enemy having notice of this Treaty came as far as Chaumont to try] [to succour it]. It was thought on the last day that they [would have come to an engagement]. Parties brought word that the enemy were marching to attack the King's troops. [They were drawn up in battell in the plain above the Castle], [in the passage of the Enemy]. They remained there until noon when it was learned that the enemy had retired. [An hour afterwards the Castle was deliver'd up according to the agreement], the terms of which, owing to the rigours of the season, were more honourable for the garrison than they would have been at another time of the year. The garrison marched out with arms and baggage. It was this weather that made the Generals desire to take the place on any terms, the whole army being extraordinarily fatigued and the surrounding country ruined. The foot suffered more than the rest and could not be supplied regularly with bread. The Commissary of Victuals had not been able to establish stores in [any of the neighbouring Towns] and [the Soldiers were forced to eat horse flesh] and other wretched food, and especially [the Stalks of Cabbages, which they call'd the Cardinal's bread].

However, when they thought they were going into winterquarters, after passing the Aisne on the 13th and having been quartered at Poilcour and in the neighbouring villages, and then at Pouilly between Rheims and Fismes where they stayed two or three days, the Cardinal ordered the army [to march back over the Aisne, which they pass'd on the 20th at Pont-à-Vere, to retake

Vervins] which [had been Master'd and garrison'd by the Spaniards in the foregoing summer. Thō this place was incapable of maintaining a Seige], [yet it was a good quarter, and would haue given much trouble to the neighbouring Countries; for which reason the Cardinal was desirous that the King's troopes should not end the Campagne before they had master'd it].

Never did soldiers or even officers march on an enterprise with more repugnance and murmuring. After enduring all the rigours of the frost, it was only with great impatience that they could endure the fatigue caused by the thaw in a hilly country where the clay made the roads impracticable, particularly between Pont-à-Vere and Laon, where the baggage nearly remained in the mud. And although after surmounting these difficulties they came into a more open country, the continuation of the thaw made the roads equally bad everywhere. This march ruined the greater part of the equipment and caused the loss of much baggage and many horses.

On the 25th they arrived at Vaupe or Voirpaix,[91] a league from Vervins. The Duke of York who followed Monsieur de Turenne everywhere had gone with him to reconnoitre the place, and having advanced very near with another gentleman, [the better to make their observations], he mistook a small party of horse from Vervins for men of the King's army, and only recognised his error when the enemy had come within pistol shot. They fired at the moment when he was going to ride in among them. But their haste gave him and the gentleman with him time to escape.

[The next day about a thousand foot, and two hundred horse, were commanded] [to begin the attack of the Town, the garrison of which consisted] of nine hundred men, six hundred being foot and three hundred horse; Monsieur de Bassecourt, a Colonel and a brave man, was Governour. [The first night the Souldiers lodg'd themselves under the Shelter of some outhouses and gardens close by the Town wall, and the next night made a battery], which obliged the enemy to capitulate on condition of marching out of the place with arms and baggage.

[The Army receiv'd litle or no loss at this] small [Seige, yet thō it cost so litle time], there was continual murmuring because, after the taking of Château-Porcien, the troops had not been sent straight into winter-quarters; and as the enemy following his

[91] This alternative is not in the *Life*.

custom proffered insults against the Cardinal from the walls of Vervins, [the Souldiers in stead of replying in his defence, only Said, *Amen*, to all their curses].

[The 28th] [in the morning Mr. de Turenne went and saw Bassecourt march out with his Souldiers, and having taken possession of the place, he march'd back with his Army to] Cressy-sur-Saare, [and from thence to Laon,] whence [all the troopes were sent into their severall winter-quarters]; [the Cardinal, and all the Generalls and persons of quality went for Paris, where they arrived on the 3d of February].

[In this manner ended that long Campagne], during which Monsieur de Turenne acquired immortal fame through saving the monarchy several times by his counsel, his conduct, and his valour.

1653

THE DUKE OF YORK'S
SECOND CAMPAIGN
UNDER M. DE TURENNE

IN this year, 1653, his Royall Highness made his Second Campagne, in the company and under the conduct of Monsieur de Turenne, the greatest Captain of this and perhaps of any age, who was not a little delighted in having so illustrious a person for his Schollar in the discipline of warr. Of this Campagne his R. Highness gives the following Account in his Memoires written in his own hand.*

The Campagne of this year began but late on either side, which could not be otherwise considering how long it was before the last ended. Yet thō wee went last out of the feild and many of our troopes had taken up their winter-quarters in Poitou, Anjou, la Marche, and other remote Provinces, Our Army was notwithstanding in Champagne by the latter end of June; with so much

* This paragraph (*Life*, ed. Clarke, I, 159) appears at the head of the entry for the Campaign of 1653. It is obviously a prefatory statement by the person, presumably William Dicconson, who edited or copied James's original memoirs, an edition or copy which was afterwards printed by J. S. Clarke. The statement strongly suggests, though it does not absolutely prove, that what follows is an authentic copy of the original Memoirs. The same applies to the entries, in the Clarke edition, for 1654, 1655; the narrative of the Campaigns of 1657 and 1658; but not to 1656, the prefatory portion of 1657, or the entry for 1659–1660.

The entry for 1653 in the Clarke edition, immediately following the prefatory statement, corresponds so closely with the text of the French MS. (pp. 87–115) that a translation of the latter into English would appear to be no more than a retranslation. I therefore reprint the text of the *Life* (Vol. I, 159–191). One difference must of course be noticed. In the text here reprinted the narrative is in the first person, a fact which has convinced me that the whole of James's original Memoirs was so written. The French MS. on the other hand is in the third person throughout.

The words in italics and brackets were inserted by Clarke to correct what he presumed to be errors, and, occasionally, to fill a gap in the MS. I have left them as they are. The footnotes are mine (Editor).

diligence, that wee beseiged Rethel before the Spanish Army was gott together out of their winter-quarters. This place was of great consequence, being situated upon the River Aisne, and being an inlet into Champagne, of which it is a member; so that partys from thence might make incursions almost to the gates of Paris, and raise contributions even in its neighbourhood. It was taken about nine months before by the Prince of Condé, and put into the hands of the Spaniards upon his conjunction with them.

It seems a little strange that a place of this consequence, and which in all probability would be the first attempt of the French to retake, should be no better provided with sufficient numbers of men for its defence; for thō the Marquis of Persan a very good officer was Governour of it, yet Monsr. de Turenne without staying to make a Line of Circumvalation, storm'd the outworks the first night, and carryd them without any extraordinary loss of men. One cheif reason why the outworks were so easily gain'd was, that thō they had a good ditch and were high enough, yet being only of earth, and having no palissades, but upon the parapett, the French were the more encouraged to venture on them; for when the Soldiers had once got up to them, their advantage was equall to that of the Enemys within, so that the greatest number must consequently carry it.

This success did so hearten our men, and discourage theirs, that the Town itself whose best strength consisted in the outworks, was quickly forced to capitulate; for wee brought our battery so near by the advantage of the outworks, that wee made in a short time two sufficient breaches, at each attack one, in the wall which was none of the strongest. This oblig'd the beseiged to parly on the 8th of July, and the next day to surrender the Town upon termes of marching away with their armes and baggage to their nearest garrison. The Articles being perform'd, our Army stayd a day or two to repair the breaches; and having provided the place with all things necessary, and left in it a sufficient garrison, wee march'd away towards Guise, having been inform'd that the Enemy had appointed their generall Rendezvous near that place.

But in our march thither, when wee lay incamped by a Village call'd Noircour, Intelligence came from the Governour of Rocroy, that part of their Army, which was marching to the Rendezvous, was quarter'd in severall Villages about Chimay, Trelon, and Glajon, on the other side of the great woods of the forest of Ardennes, which were extended down that way; upon which information, our Generalls resolv'd to march with all their troopes and some few feild pieces, leaving only five or six hundred men to guard the baggage, and to pass these large woods in hopes of surprising the Enemy in their quarters before they could haue notice of our march. It happen'd to be Monsr. de Turenne's turn to lead the Van, who us'd all possible expedition, but after having pass'd by a certain Abbey call'd Bussilly, and got with the Van as far as Anort,[1] (*Nost*) which is almost on the farthest side of the woods, wee had intelligence by a small party which brought in some prisoners, that they had been advertis'd of our coming; so that seeing our design to be discover'd, wee march'd back by the same way wee came, and joyn'd our baggage on the 14th where wee had left it at Noircour, after wee had been three days abroad in this expedition; and from thence wee march'd to Haris on the 17th, and so to S. Algis, where the King of France, and Cardinal Mazarin came to us.

On the 25th wee went and camp'd at Ribemont, and in the mean time the Spanish Army consisting at least of thirty thousand men, assembled on the fronteers near l'arbre de Guise, and with proportionable train of Artillery and provisions of Victualls, began their march to enter France; of which the King being informed, it was debated in Councill before him and the Cardinal what was fittest for him to do, having so strong an Enemy to encounter, and our Army in the whole not amounting to above six thousand foot, and being scarce ten thousand horse. Some were of opinion that all our foot, excepting only a thousand commanded musketteers, should be cast into the fronteer Towns, with some few horse to accompany them; and that with this small proportion of Infantry and the body of our horse, wee should keep near the Enemy's Army to incommode and harass them, as much as wee were able, by falling on their foragers and cutting off their Convoy's, in order to hinder them from attacking any of our Towns.

Others were of opinion that wee should not separate our Army, but endeavour with the whole body of it to defend the passage of the Rivers in case the Enemy should advance into the Country,

---

[1] 'Anort' in the MS. (p. 89).

thinking it to be of dangerous consequence (since Bordeaux still held out) if wee should permitt them a free inrode towards Paris, which was lately reduced to the King's obedience.

But Monsieur de Turenne was of a quite different opinion from the two former; For, said he, should wee divide our Army, and put most of our foot and some horse into the Garrisons, wee should leave ourselves so inconsiderable, that the Enemy would easily drive the remaining small body of our forces into what part of the Country they should please; after which they would haue their choice of beseiging any of our Towns, by falling back upon them, and haue leisure enough to entrench themselves before wee could joyn together our Separated forces: besides which they would then be so far advanced in their work, that it would not be adviseable for us to sitt down before any of their places, for before wee could haue made any considerable progress in a Seige, they would haue taken a Town, and bee upon us; So that wee should be sure, according to that method, to haue lost one of our places, without Mastering one of theirs, thō of less importance. On the other side, thō wee kept our whole Army in a body, and lay behind our Rivers, with an intention of hindering the Enemys from passing over and advancing into our Country, wee should faile of what wee proposed to ourselves by that undertaking; for knowing them to outnumber us very much in foot, it would be very difficult for us to maintain any pass against them; and besides it would not only be a very great discouragement to our Soldiers to be forced from their posts, but the consequence would also be very dangerous from the effects it might haue at Paris and in the Countries: So that considering the whole matter, he was of opinion, That wee should keep our Army intire and with it observe the motion of the Enemys, keeping as closs to them as conveniently wee could, either behind or on one side of them, without exposing ourselves so far as to be forced to an Ingagement when wee found it not for our advantage; by observing which method he hoped to (be) able to hinder them from beseiging any place of consequence, in doing of which they must be obliged to separate their Army, which they would hardly adventure to do, whilst wee were attending them so near, that before they could haue intrenched themselves and made their bridges of communication, wee should haue the opportunity of falling on which part of them wee pleas'd; And besides he beleev'd not, that they would advance farr into the Country, seeing that if they did, wee should be able to hinder any Convoys from coming to them, without which they could not possibly subsist, or continue long in the heart of the French Dominions.

These and other reasons offered by Monsr. de Turenne prevail'd upon the Cardinal, and consequently upon the King and Councill; so that orders being given, and measures accordingly taken for carrying on the Campagne, the Court retired from the Army.

In the mean time the Enemy having drawn all their forces into a body, began their march into the French Dominions betwixt the Rivers of Somme and Oyse; and incamped at Fonsomme and Fervaques, from whence they marched onwards on the first of August, and pass'd within sight of us the same day, continuing their march towards Ham, having the Somme on their right hand, and camp'd about St Simon and Clastres, where they imployd a whole day in passing the défilés: In the mean time upon their approche, wee put ourselves on battell, and seeing they came not to us, but continued their march, wee march'd the same day down along the River by which wee lay to a Village call'd Chery-Maiot, not farr from la Fere; where wee imployd all the next day in making bridges for our foot, and passages for our horse, intending to pass that River in case the Enemy pursued their march any further into the Country, of which wee had notice the next morning by our partys: But yet Monsieur de Turenne, unwilling to expose himself by marching over till he were more certain of the way they took, went over himself at break of day with about a thousand horse, and finding that the intelligence which his partys had brought him was altogether true, he sent back his orders for the Army to come over to him, which being performed wee march'd down the River, and camp'd on the third of August at Fargnier, having the woods to cover us from the Enemy, which were of as great security to us as a River; and receiving intelligence that they were advanced as far as Roye, which they took and plunder'd (it being only defended by the Townsmen, who thō they had no troopes amonst them yet suffer'd batteries to be rais'd which playd upon them before they would surrender) wee came on the 5th to Noyon, and hearing there that Roye was taken, wee advanced on the 9th to Magny; which thō on the other side of the woods was yet so fast a Country, that wee were in no manner of danger, and besides it was not our design to keep too far distance from the Enemy.

From thence Monsr. de Schomberg was sent with the Gendarmes, which consisted of about two hundred and fifty horse and a hundred foot, to cast himself into Corbie; and at the same time about three hundred foot were sent into Peroñe, which were the only troopes wee ever put into any place from the Army, and having notice that they were drawing down towards the Somme, not far from Corbie, wee posted ourselves at Epperville closs by Ham on the 10th of August.

Wee were no sooner arriv'd there, but wee received intelligence that the Count of Megen, with about three thousand men, was to march out of Cambray the next day, to convoy great store of provisions and all things necessary for a Seige, with great numbers of Pioneers, and all sorts of ammunition, and that he was to march with them to the River of Somme betwixt Peronne and Corbie, where, after they had mett him, new measures were to be taken: On this advertissement wee took our march passing over the Somme at Ham, and setting out a little before Sun sett, with an intention to fall on that Convoy, which wee hop'd to find on the plaine about Bapaume; And to make the greater Expedition, wee march'd away with all our horse, leaving only some few behind, to come along with the foot, artillery and baggage, which had order to follow with all imaginable diligence. Being come to Peronne by break of day, with our horse, wee took out from thence all the foot which had been sent thither from the Army, and all the garrison could spare beside, and continued our march towards Bapaume: Being come within two or three leagues of that place, wee halted to refresh our horses, and sent our partys towards Cambray, to give us notice of the motion of the Convoy: By noon they brought us intelligence, that the Enemy had begun their march out of Cambray, but being advertiz'd of our coming were return'd into the Town: having received this information, and withall, that the Enemy's Army was come to the Somme near Bray, wee march'd back and met our foot, Artillery and baggage on the 11th that night at Manancourt, a Village which ly's at the head of a litle brook, that runs from thence by Mont St Quentin and so into the Somme, not far from Peronne.

There wee camp'd that night, and having notice the next morning, that the Enemy was making bridges over the River where they lay, it was thought expedient for us to retire, the same day, a litle back to Allayne another Village on the same brook, near Mont St Quentin; having notwithstanding resolved in case they should pass the Somme, that wee should post ourselves some what above Manancourt, in a place which both our Mareshalls had view'd and determin'd there to draw up our Army in battell, upon the first notice wee should haue of their approche to us. But thō this was resolved by both our Generalls together, it was alter'd by one, without staying to hear from the other, on the next morning being the 13th: For Mr. de Turenne according to his usuall custome going out of his quarters by Sun rise, with some few in his Company, first went to visite our horse guard, which was on the other side of the brook; And from thence seeing nothing, nor hearing any news of any of our partys, which he had sent out the night before to bring him notice of the Enemys motion, he went to Peronne to send partys along the Somme, on the other side, to try if they cou'd discover any thing of the Spaniards' march; Not beleeving it possible that they cou'd be coming to us, but that either from Bapaume or by some of our own partys wee should haue been advertized: Yet it happen'd otherwise, for the Enemy march'd with so much diligence, that their Van was past Bapaume before break of day; so that neither our partys which were driven in there, nor any from the Town cou'd give us notice, the Spaniards being gotten betwixt us and them; and the first intelligence wee had of them was by Mr. de la Ferté's horse guards, which were at the head of the litle brook: And he took the allarm so hott, that in stead of marching up to possess the ground, which was resolved on the day before, he having the left wing and being nearest it, march'd back towards Peronne, passing through our right wing; which following the orders they had received the day before, was beginning to march towards the fore appointed place where they were to be drawn up in battell.

In this disorder wee were when Mareshall de Turenne came back from Peronne, and finding that already M. de la Ferté with the left wing was beginning to draw up on Mont St Quentin, he went to his own troopes, which were to compose the right wing and joyn'd them with the left; it being then too late to possess our-

Selves of the former ground, because the Enemys Van was already very near it.

There he resolv'd to expect the Enemy, who came on with great joy, as knowing the advantage they had over us, both in numbers and by getting us into a plaine feild, where wee could neither retreat from them, nor avoid fighting, if they pleas'd to ingage us; And indeed I beleeve that if wee had not chang'd our ground wee should certainly haue been beaten: for, besides that they were much Superiour to us in number, as wee were then drawn up, the ground was such, that wee shou'd not haue been able to haue done any thing; because thō our order of battell was very good according to the new method, and that our second Line was placed at a convenient distance behind the first, and a reserve of twelve Squadrons of horse, with two battailons of foot behind that again, and our left wing placed upon Mont St Quentin, yet our right was in evident danger of being routed, for our utmost Squadron on that hand reached within pistoll shott to the bottome of a litle hill, to which the Enemy were marching, and from thence they could haue gall'd us in the flanck, and playd upon us both with their cannon and Musketteers, before they came down to charg us: so that, as I sayd, wee had manifestly been beaten, without being able to haue fought, it being then too late to haue chang'd our posture: And indeed not only M. de Turenne, but all of us who were on the right wing plainely saw it; neither could I say that ever in my life I perceiv'd so much confusion, and such signs of being beaten, as were visible in the face of the Soldiers. Monsieur de Turenne no sooner had observ'd it, but he gallop'd away to Mr. de la Ferté on the left wing to give him notice; and withall to assure him, That if wee continued in that posture wee should infallibly be routed; that therfore he was resolved to march up the hill, towards the Enemy, seeing wee could not be in a more disadvantageous position than now wee were; neither was there any other way remaining to encourage our Soldiers: Having told him this, and desired him to follow us, he return'd speedily to our wing, and march'd up the hill immediatly at our head.

He was no sooner arriv'd there with the first Squadrons, but he sent Monsr. de Varennes (an old experienced Officer) who had been Captain of his guards in all his German warrs, and in whom he had great confidence, to go before and view the ground over which wee were to pass: Wee had not march'd above a mile, when he came back to his Generall, and let him know, that if he would come along with him, he would shew him such a post as he was sure would be of great advantage, and that it was not farr distant. Mr. de Turenne accordingly went before to observe it, and found it to his great satisfaction such a one as would wholy secure us from the Enemy: for in our right hand wee had the brook, which comes from Roiset, and afterwards falls into the Somme a litle above Peronne; and on our left a hill so inaccessible and steep, that neither horse nor man cou'd climb it; and the distance betwixt both was no more, then that twenty or thirty Squadrons cou'd possibly be drawn up in it. Before us there was a litle Valley, and on that part of it which lay nearest to the brook was a Ravine or small Gully, which wou'd haue been very difficult for any to haue pass'd, and horse especially.

This was the post where wee drew up and where wee were no sooner posted, but the whole countenance of the Army was changed, and our men had their accustom'd cheerfulness in their faces, so that I am confident, had the Enemy attack'd us in that place, wee shou'd haue beaten them: For thō their numbers almost doubled ours, yet our troopes being very good, and well posted, wee had a great advantage; And that wee might make it yet more secure for us and more difficult for them, when they shou'd endeavour to approche us, wee immediatly fell on making five Redans, open behind, and each of them capable of containing an hundred musketteers; between which wee placed our cañon which were about thirty, so that the Enemy must haue endured the fire of all these, before he cou'd so much as see our troopes which stood behind, and then received a charge either of horse or foot, which was in our choice: After all this, the ground was so very narrow, that the Army under Monsr. de Turenne's command (being the right wing and half the foot) was constraint to be drawn up in four or five lines, behind each other. As for Mr. de la Ferté, he drew up with his troopes, which consisted of the left wing and the óther half of the foot, all along the top of the Steep hill I have already mention'd, which cover'd our left hand and fronted that way. So that in case wee had been attacked by the front, he cou'd easily haue drawn his men to haue seconded us of the right wing.

It was, as I remember, betwixt two and three of the clock in the afternoon when wee drew up with our first Squadron in this post, when wee saw the whole Spanish Army march in battell to us, and coming about the end of the wood directly in our faces. This wood ran from within muskett shott of our Redans, all along upon the very height and browes of the steep hill which wee had on our left hand, which also happen'd to straighten the ground by which they were to approche us: In this manner they came on, thinking to haue fallen on us immediatly; but being come within a mile and a half of us, or near that distance, they made a halt, wherupon most of their foot went down to the River to quench their thirst, being sufficiently tir'd with their long march, and almost chok'd for want of water, having met with none since they parted from the Somme, till they arrived at this place; So that it was absolutely necessary for their Officers to give way, that they should drink and refresh themselves.

The Prince of Condé, as I have been since inform'd, would haue fallen upon us that evening, the 13th of August, but the Count de Fuenseldagne oppos'd it, representing to him the weariness of their men, especially their foot, who after so tedious a march through a dry Country, and in so hott a Season, were not reasonably to be put on further duty till the next morning; besides which, it would be very difficult and almost impracticable to draw them from the River-side that evening; that so small a delay could not prejudice the Enterprise because they had us in their power, so that wee could not possibly get from them; but in the mean time their Soldiers would recover their Spirits and Strength by a good night's rest, and then they had the day before them: As for us at so short a warning wee could not do much for the further securing of ourselves; but that they might haue the remainder of the evening to view the posture in which wee lay, and to observe the ground over which they were to pass to us.

These arguments so prevail'd with the Prince, that the thought of doing any thing farther that day was layd aside; and they camped in battaill where they lay. Next morning when he and the rest of their Generall Officers had view'd and consider'd the ground, finding the great advantages wee had by reason of our post, they gave over the intention of attacking us in that place; and so the two Armys continued in presence of each other, during three or four days: in all which time there happen'd no considerable action, but almost perpetuall skirmishes. Yet there fell out one thing, which thō of no great concernment might deserve to be mention'd.

There was a Lieutenant of horse in the Regiment Royall whose name was Bellechassaigne, a great goer out on partys, who was desirous to try if he could take some considerable Officer from the very Camp of the Enemy; having this in his head, he askt leave of Monsr. de Turenne to go out with a small party, which being granted him, he chose about fifteen good men to follow him, and with them put himself into the wood which I have mention'd, which reach'd from our Redans to the Enemy's Camp. Being there he order'd his Soldiers to disperse themselves, and under covert of the wood and favour of the night, one by one to get into the Camp, where they were to rejoyne again about midnight, at such a place as was a very remarkable (*one*) in their Camp, and was seen from ours; where being met, they should receiue Instructions what to do: having given them this order, they all separated from each other, got safely amongst the Enemies, and assembled at the time and place appointed; from thence they went in a body to the Tent of one of the Prince of Condé's Major Generalls, or Mareshalls de Camp. This Officer's name was Monsr. de Ravenel, whom they intended to take out of his bed, and carry away with them; his Tent standing most conveniently for their business, and having no guard before it, which was the reason why they chose him out; all those of a Superiour quality having foot guards at the entrance of their Tents. Some of them therfore alighting from their horses went directly in, and had already seiz'd on two or three of his Servants without noise; when just as they were going to haue taken him, one of the prisoners slipp'd out of their hands, and gave the alarm, which forced Bellechassaigne to leave Ravenel and make what hast he could possibly to Save himself, which he did and brought along with him a horse or two, and as many of those whom he had first secur'd. He might haue kill'd Ravenel himself, but in those Countries they make not Warr so brutally, for I never knew any unhuman act committed either by French or Spaniards all the time I serv'd amongst them.

But to proceed: After the Enemy had stayd three or four days facing us, on the 16th of August about break of day wee heard them sound to horse and beat the march for the foot; and by that time it was break of day, wee saw them begin to march: Vpon which wee stood immediatly to our armes, and Monsr. de Turenne himself with two Squadrons of our horse guards went up towards their Camp, the better to observe which way they bent their march, that therby he might make some kind of conjecture what place they intended to beseige. When he was come about half way distance betwixt our Camp and theirs, he left behind him one of the Squadrons and advanced with the other, yet somewhat farther and then stayd with it; sending me, with Monsr. de Castelnau[2] and about twelve more, all Officers or Volonteers who were excellently hors'd, to go on as far as conveniently wee cou'd, with order not to engage, but to come off in case wee should be push'd. Accordingly wee went up into the very Camp of the Enemys, and as far as the hutts of the foot, when the Reer of their Cavalry were not yet gotten out of the Camp. There wee made a stand and had a perfect view of their whole Army, after which wee went within pistoll shott of their last Squadrons, not offering to disturb them, nor they us: Thus when wee had satisfyd ourselves with looking, and saw plainly they bent towards St Quentin, wee return'd to Mr. de Turenne, who straight going back to his own Camp, dispatch'd away Mr. de Beaujeu one of our Lieutenant Generalls, with twelve hundred horse and six hundred foot, to cast himself either into Guise, which place he beleeved the Enemy intended to beseige, or into any other place before which they should offer to ly down. And Beaujeu made such expedition, that he got into Guise just as their first horse appear'd to invest that Town: which when the Enemy perceived, and withall the great diligence which our whole Army had us'd for the same intent, they layd aside the

[2] Jacques de Mauvissière, marquis de Castelnau, was a grandson of the famous Mauvissière who had served for some ten years as ambassador in London during the reign of Elizabeth I. His *Mémoires* are a valuable source for the history of the later Valois. Jacques, marquis de Castelnau (1620–1658) had entered the army at the age of fifteen and taken part in many battles. Captured and imprisoned at Cambrai in 1637, he had escaped and later distinguished himself at Nordlingen (1645). He was at this time a Lieutenant-General. James criticises his behaviour on two occasions, particularly when Condé was covering the retreat of the Spanish army across the Scheldt in August 1655, and Castelnau failed to interfere seriously with him. On the other hand he was a model of loyalty and chivalry, and very popular in the army. In 1658 he inspired enthusiasm and confidence in the English troops, and his great cavalry operation at the battle of the Dunes played a decisive part in Turenne's victory. He was killed shortly afterwards and was posthumously promoted a Marshal of France.

thoughts of that Enterprise; and after having stayd some few days in that neighbourhood, march'd back, and incamped at Caulaincourt, within a league of the Abbey of Vermand, upon the same brook, about two leagues from St Quentin, it being so far on the way from thence to Peronne.

As for our Army, so soon as Mr. de Beaujeu was detach'd, wee march'd also, causing our baggage to pass the River before us through Peronne, which was the only Pass therabouts. When they were gott over, wee began to march through the Town with the whole Army; when wee saw the Enemy at such a distance from us, that there was no farther danger of their marching back to fall upon our Reer, before wee cou'd get on the other side of the River. And thō that Town be very long, and that there is one bridge only over the Somme; yet by that time it grew dark, Mr. de Turenne with the Van got as far as Golancourt, which is within a league wide of Ham. 'Tis true the Reer cam not up till the next morning, but however it had the same effect with the Enemy as if they had been there in a body, for their partys who saw us cross the River gave them an account of our being there; So that as I observ'd, not only the march of Beaujeu, but also our diligence, hinder'd the Enemy from beseiging Guise: And, as I remember, Mr. de Turenne answer'd some about him, who were representing to him that it was impossible for half our Army to come up that night, considering the length of his intended march and the expedition he used in marching, That what they objected was very true; notwithstanding which if he could but reach his quarter with the Van that night it would produce the Same effect, as if the whole Army were in presence; because that wee being cover'd by the Somme, their partys could give no other account of us, but by the fires which they observed; and seeing them in great numbers they would return with a false intelligence, that wee were advanced so far. And certainly not only in this particular, but generally in all others, never did any Generall take better measures in his marches, or guess'd more probably at the designs of the Enemy then he.

The next morning when the troopes were all come up, and that he was advertis'd from Guise that the Spaniards were at a loss, having miss'd their purpose, wee thought it expedient to continue where wee were without advancing any farther, as being well warn'd by our late Escape; So that the Enemy coming to Caulin-court, wee remained at Golancourt to observe their motions.

While wee lay in that quarter Mr. de Turenne having notice from his partys, the Enemys foragers were accustom'd to pass the brook behind which they lay and come up towards Ham, having with them only a small Convoy, orderd Mr. de Castelnau to take a thousand horse, and to try his fortune on them, in case they came abroad to forage next day: In the evening the ten Squadrons were commanded out, and as soon as it was dark Mr. de Castelnau march'd with them to Ham; where having drawn them up, in stead of passing through the Town, as he ought to have done while the darknes continu'd, he stayd on the outside till break of day; then going through the Town himself, he sent out two partys, to see if those foragers were abroad, leaving still his body on the other side of Ham; and when at last his partys had brought him intelligence that the Enemys were at forage, he sent for all his horse to come over to him, which indeed they did, but by that time wee had travers'd the length of the Town, and were begin-ning to march towards the Enemy, wee saw they were almost all gone back into their Camp, having taken the alarm at the partys which were sent out to discover them, So that wee tooke not above twenty or thirty at most of all their men, thō wee detach'd some after them, who glean'd up to the number I haue mention'd.

Thus what Mr. de Turenne had so well design'd, was wholy frustrated by the unskillfulness of him who commanded us: for thō he was perfectly stout, and was besides a good foot Officer, who understood very well how to carry on a breach, yet he was very ignorant in commanding horse, which he not only shew'd on this occasion, but by what he did afterwards; so that many men were of opinion, that what he knew was rather gain'd from the ex-perience of a long practice amongst the foot, then by any naturall talents beyond other men: But the whole management of this Action was only a chaine of the greatest faults in conduct; for after that which he had already committed, in stead of returning back immediatly into our Camp (which was his duty (*when*) he had fayl'd of his Enterprise) he march'd on directly towards that of the Enemy, over a bare plaine, till wee came within half a league of it, and there halted, staying there I am certain above an hour, which was the greatest madness imaginable; for by it wee were expos'd, and that unavoidably, to be routed in case they had come upon us, as in reason they ought to haue done, and there was scarcely an Officer, or even privat Soldier there, who did not plainly see it and apprehend the consequence; for the Enemy could see at least a league and a half behind us, the Country being very bare and open, and that wee had none to second us, and cou'd count our numbers to a man; and alltho they were to pass the brook, behind which they lay, yet that was so just under the command of their whole Camp, that wee cou'd not haue hinder'd their coming to us. Having stood thus, as long a time as I have mention'd, looking on the Enemy to no manner of purpose, he drew us off, and then left an ambuscade for the Enemy of about a hundred horse in a small Village, as wee march'd away, which was as foolish as all the rest; for the Enemy were too cautious to permitt any of their men to pass the brook afterwards.

In the mean time Monsr. de Turenne being concern'd for us, because wee had Stayd out so long, and fearing wee might be prest in coming off, came himself from the Camp with four or five Squadrons of horse, and three or four hundred foot, passing over the River through the Town and advancing a litle way from thence; placing his men So, that they might make a retreat for us, in case wee had been pushed or forced to a hasty retreat. He had not long been there when to his great comfort he saw us coming back, and not in that manner which he apprehended.

After this wee continu'd in the same quarters till the first of September, and then the Enemie first decamping from Caulincourt, began their march towards Rocroy in order to beseige it. Into which place it was impossible for us to cast any man, tho wee knew the garrison was weak, and that wee had notice of the Enemies march that way. For the Enemy when they went from Caulincourt, immediatly sent off a considerable body of horse to invest it, and to hinder any succours from being put into it; and the Situation of the Town is such, that standing in a litle plain environ'd with woods, whoever is first posted there can easily forbid any passage to it. Therfore tho wee endeavour'd to reinforce that place, wee were never able to effect it.

So soon as wee had information of their march that way, wee began ours, and passing the Oyse by la Fere continued in our march straight to Mousson, Leaving Laon on our right hand, and

142

quarter'd at Espe; from thence to Condé sur Aysne, which is not far from Château-Porcien, and so to la Chesne, and to Remilly which is within a league or two of Mousson: And the next day being the 10th of September wee passed the River below that place, and took up our severall quarters, Mr. de Turenne below the Town and Mr. de la Ferté above it. Mr. de Turenne's horse were upon one Line stretching from the neighbourhood of the River to the top of the hill, somewhat more then cañon shott from the Town; As for himself, he with his foot and Gendarmes, camp'd in a litle Valley about half cañon shott from the place; and finding yet another valley, which was narrower, and somewhat nearer the Town, he there quarter'd the Regiment of York, and that of Guyenne: and the same night, without farther delay, fell to opening the Trenches from the place where these two Regiments were quarter'd. At this time also Monsieur de la Ferté began his approches, but quarter'd not so near, himself or his Soldiers, as wee had done. But before I proceed further, it will be necessary for me to give a short description of the place.

Mousson stands upon the Meuse, about midway betwixt Stenay and Sedan; over the River it has a bridge which was cover'd by a hornwork: The Town is fortifyd with a good old wall, well flanck'd with round towers, some of which especially one towards the hill was very large; it had also a very good dry ditch with a strong pallisade in the midst of it and in most parts of it. The out parts of the ditch are faced with stone, which is no small strengthning to a place; and because that side of the Town which is farthest from the River is somewhat commanded by a hill at the foot of which it stands, they had made an Envelope of an half bastion, and three or four whole bastions to cover it: And on both sides down to the River, severall half moons with other outworks. As for the garrison of Mousson, it consisted as near as I can guess in fifteen hundred foot and betwixt two and three hundred horse; the Governour was call'd Wolfe, an old German Collonell. That which occasion'd this garrison to be made So strong, was, that the Enemy when they design'd to beseige Rocroy, had sent away the Count de Briol with a body of men, with which he was order'd to secure this place, Stenay, Clermont, and St Menehou; not doubting but wee should sit down before one of them, so soon as they began with Rocroy. Briol upon our marching that way, Satisfied himself with putting into Mousson so many men as made up the number I have mention'd, keeping the rest in reserve, to provide for the other places, which belong'd to the Prince of Condé whose officer he was.

Having given this account of the place and the strength within it, I proceed to the Relation of the Seige. The first night of our being before the Town, as I sayd, wee began our approches, and carryd them on a considerable way: Wee also rais'd a battery of five or six guns, which was perform'd with litle loss by the Regiment of Picardy the first of the old Regiments, it being the custome of the French Army that the first Regiment has allways the honour to break ground first in all Seiges, how many soever are made in the Campagne. The next night the Regiments of La Feuillade and Guyenne had the guard of the Trenches, and made a very good advance without any considerable loss. At the same time a Regiment of foot, which was quarter'd in some houses near the bridge, had orders to storme the horn-work before it, which they perform'd and carryd it with litle or no loss, the Enemy not thinking convenient to dispute it, but drawing off into the Town as our men advanced. The third night the Regiment of Turenne took their turn, and carryd on the Trench so near, that the next night the Regiments of York and Palleau brought it to the very edge of the ditch belonging to the outworks; and the same night fasten'd a Miner in the face of the half bastion of the Envelope I have already mention'd, having broken the pallisades which were in the ditch, to make his passage thither. He continued working till the afternoon; about the beginning of which he call'd out to our Soldiers which were in the head of the Trench, That he wanted drink and candles, and till he were supplyd with them he must cease from working: Upon which a Sergeant of York was order'd to carry him what he wanted, and that his passage might be more secure, all the men in the Trench were commanded to stand to their Armes, and those who were at the head of it, to give a Voly, when the Sergeant was ready to take his run to the Miner; and they and the rest to continue firing till they were sure he was in safety: This was accordingly perform'd, and he pass'd through the ditch to the Miner without having one shott made at him.

That night the Regiment of Picardy had again the guard of the Trenches; and the next day as I was going to the head of the approches, accompanyd by Monsr. d'Humieres, Monsr. de Crequi[3] and somme others, while wee stayd a little time in the first battery a great shott came from the Town, which pass'd through three barrells of powder, without firing them, which had it done, all who were in the battery had inevitably been blown up: But the danger came so suddainly and was so soon over, that none of us had time to be concern'd for it.

The next day came up a battallion of the Regiment of Guardes, consisting of above six hundred men in ten Companies, and commanded by Monsr. de Vautourneu; and according to their privilege had the guard of the Trenches the same night, relieving the Regiment of Picardy: And when Monsr. de Castelnau, the only Lieut Generall then in the Army, came according to his usuall custom into the Trenches, to command there, they absolutely refus'd obedience to him, pretending they were not to obey any man but the Generall himself: of which Monsr. de Turenne being inform'd, he went thether to accommodate the business, but finding Vautourneu very obstinat and positiue in that point, he desir'd Mr. de Castelnau to retire into his tent, and repose himself that night, because he had taken so much paines and so litle rest the night before; adding, That he himself would do his office for him, and watch in the Trenches: Castelnau obeyd and went away, and Monsr. de Turenne did, as he had Sayd, there being indeed a necessity incumbent on him So to do, for any farther dispute in that matter which he was also unwilling to decide: But he immediatly dispatched a Messenger to Court, to informe them of it, who sent a positiue order to the Guardes, That they should obey the Lieut Generall. This command came back before it was their turn to mount the Trenches the second time, after which the dispute was no more revived. But yet it prov'd of advantage to the seruice, for the Guardes thought themselves obliged in honour to

[3] François, chevalier de Créquy (1625–1687) was a younger brother of Charles, duc de Créquy. He had already fought in the Thirty Years War. He appears to have been conceited and perhaps rather selfish. Bussy-Rabutin, who was jealous of him —and not without reason—criticises his behaviour at the battle of the Dunes. His promotion as a Marshal of France in 1668 is said to have turned his head, so much so that he refused to serve under Turenne. This led to a temporary disgrace. He had however become an excellent strategist and the only French general whose abilities could compare with Schomberg's. In 1679 he marched into Germany, defeated the Elector of Brandenburg at Minden and compelled him to sign a peace treaty.

make a very great advance that night; which they perform'd, being both encouraged by the presence of the Generall and by the prudence of his directions; for they did not only make a blind all along the bottom of the ditch of the Envelope, by the help of the pallisado's which were in it, which went directly upon the great Tower, but also made a lodgement along from the place where the ditch of the Envelope joyn'd with that of the Town to a half moon, which was on their right hand and which also was abandon'd by the Enemy, from whence wee design'd to get down into the Town ditch and there to lodge our Miner.

Thus far wee had advanced very speedily, but when wee came to make our descent into the ditch of the Town, wee found more difficulty then wee expected; for the next night endeavouring to continue at the same rate wee had begun, by making a lodgement against the pallisado's which were in the midst of the ditch, thō wee carryd on that work with great vigour, yet when it was almost perfected, the Enemy beat our men out of it, by throwing down great store of hand granades, fireworkes, and fire it self, so that it was impossible to continue longer there, and make good our undertaking: yet (*we*) were not discouraged by the unsuccessfulness of this first attempt, but for two nights following very obstinatly pursued the design of lodging ourselves, but all to no purpose: for thō wee finish'd our work, yet the Enemy burnt us out, by throwing down upon us such vast quantities of fireworks, and combustible matter, that they ruin'd our work.

This made us cast about to go on some other way with more security; and therefore the next day, wee endeavour'd to make our descent into the ditch, by cutting a trench from the top of it, where wee lodged, and so sloping along the side: but wee also fail'd of effecting this; for, besides that the Enemy had a low flanck, in which was only one small piece of ordnance, which lay so much under our battery that wee could not bear upon it, or dismount it, and that when wee descended into the ditch, it playd levell on us, wee also found (when wee had got down half way) the wall I formerly mention'd, which of itself would haue stopt us; thō the great gun had not gaull'd us from the flancker. So soon as it was day that single peice destroyd all the blinds wee had been making; After which wee were constrain'd to haue recours to the old method of sinking a well, out of the lodgement wee had in the ditch of the half moon, and so that way to go in to the bottom of the ditch: Wee fell in hand with it as fast as possibly wee cou'd, and also endeavour'd to fasten our Miner to the Town-wall by the means of Madriers, which are planckes nine inches thick at least, cover'd with tinn or raw hides, or both, the better to resiste the force of fire; Those they carryd, and set up against the wall under which the Miner fell to work; having barrells fill'd with earth on each side of him for his security from the small shott of the flancker, as the Madriers were to preserve him from the hand granado's, stones, and fire, which they threw incessantly upon him with great violence, thō without effect: So that they were convinced that unless they cou'd invent some other means of dislodging him, he would soon haue gott so far into the Wall, that there would be no farther hope for them; finding also that thō it was a dry ditch, wee had made so great lodgements all along the edge of it, that they could do nothing by a sally, they invented another way that was more secure, which was by hanging a bomb or great granado down by a chaine and closs to the side of the Madriers, which firing blew them all away, and then they threw over so much combustible matter, as burnt the Miner in his hole. The Miner at the other attacke had no better success, for Monsr. de la Ferté having the same desire to make a quick dispatch fasten'd a Miner to the body of the place before he had made a lodgment under the Wall, so that the Enemy having found him, immediatly smother'd him with smoke, he being already so far enter'd that the fire cou'd not reach him, but as I sayd, the smoke stiffled him.

During the time of this whole Seige, wee were much troubled and hindered by perpetuall raines and stormes so violent, that they very often blew away our blinds, and wash'd down some part of our Trenches which for the most part were fill'd with water, the Sky being seldom clear for above three hours togather: and that which makes me remember this the more particularly, was, that one morning very early, going down with some others to the approches, when wee came into the ditch of the Envelope, which went straight upon the great Tower, and was our only way to the lodgement, where wee were working att the well I have already mention'd, wee kept closs to the pallissado, where the blind should have been, and thō nothing but the very beginning of it was left standing, all the rest being blown down, yet all of us were so busily imploy'd in piking out our way (the ditch being full of dirt and water) that not one single man tooke notice that the blind was ruin'd, and consequently wee (*were*) in open view, till wee were gotten half our way, and then, one of the company who observ'd it first, propos'd that wee shou'd return; to which I well remember I would not consent, urging, That since wee were now so far onward, the danger was equall in going forward or in returning: so wee continu'd going on to the head of the attacke as wee first intended; but in all the way while wee were thus exposed, there was not one shott made at us, at which wee wonder'd; but afterwards when the Town was surrender'd, the Governour inform'd us of the reason, That he himself happening to be upon the wall at that very time, and knowing me by my Starr, had forbid his men to fire upon the Company, which is a respect very usuall beyond Sea. But he had not the same consideration for those afterwards, who were commanded to repair the blind; for I hauing given notice to the Officer who was in the Trenches, of its condition, he gave order to haue it mended, and severall of those who were employ'd in that work were slayn, and others hurt.

About the same time, when wee began to sink our Well in the ditch of the half moon, wee also lodged a Miner at the foot of the great Tower, under shelter of the Madriers, who had better fortune then the former, and work'd into the wall; when he was gott within as far as he design'd, but not yet begun to make his chambers, he sent out word to Mr. de Turenne, that he heard the Enemy at work in a Countermine, and that as near as he could guess, they would be upon him in some few hours, long before he could finish his undertaking; Upon which, he gave immediat orders to put some barrells of powder in the hole he had already made, and then to stop it as firmly as they could, intending by this only to ruine the Enemies Countermine and Miners, well knowing it could not bring down the Tower: his orders were speedily put in execution, and because the powder must needs blow backwards, he withdrew his men from such parts of the approches as were neighbouring to it, or in danger of any hurt from it, and himself and severall others went and stood in the first battery, which was distant from the Tower about half muskett Shott; under this shelter he expected the effect: when fire was given, it produced all that wee design'd, for it only enlarged the hole which our Miner had made, and as wee learn'd afterwards kill'd those of the Enemy, throwing to a far distance severall great stones with as much violence as if they had been shott out of a cañon, some of which hitt the battery behind which wee stood, and others wee saw fly much farther. So soon as the blow was over, Monsr. de Turenne, having seen what it perform'd, sent back the Miner into the hole, which was now widen'd, and sent along with him a Sergeant, and six men to guard him who might easily be lodged in it, with all Security from the Shott of the Enemy.

This which concern'd the firing of the Mine pass'd all in the day time; when it was night wee thought it convenient to open the Well which wee had sunk, and which was now as low as the bottom of the Town ditch, for it would haue taken a longer time, then wee cou'd spare, to go all the way under ground as far as to the wall, and being already sunck so low were secur'd both from great and small shott, and had nothing farther to apprehende in our opinions but hand granado's, fire works, and fire it self: But wee had no sooner open'd it, then the Enemy discovering it, by the light of the fires which they had made, roull'd from off the walls a Bomb, or Mortar-Granado, by the means of two strong pieces of timber fasten'd together; the Bomb lighted full into the mouth of the Well, and kill'd four or five of our men who were working within it, and withall, so terribly shook the lodgment just above it, where Mr. de Turenne, myself, some Officers, and many volonteers were then standing, that wee all beleev'd at that moment it would haue been shatter'd to peices: yet it stood; but it was above a quarter of an hour before any could go down to work again by reason of the smoke and dust; And then, thō the Enemy continually plyd that place with hand-granado's, fire, and fire works, and now and then a Bomb (none of which last happen'd to be So justly directed as the first) yet wee carryd on our Trench as far as the palisado's which were in the midst of the ditch; but by reason of that storme of fire works which the Enemy without ceasing powr'd upon us, wee were obliged to cover it again with planks, fascines and earth upon them, for the security of our men. When wee were advanced as far as the palisado's, wee were forced again to drive under ground, the Enemy still heaving over vast quantities of wood and combustible matter, and wee being then so very near the wall, that it was impossible to go forward any other way.

Advancing in this manner wee fasten'd our Miner at length to the body of the place; wee lost that night a considerable number of our men. La Feuillade had his head broken with a hand-granado, Mr. d'Humieres had likewise a blow on the side of his, with a small shott, which first came through the lodgment, and then after glancing from his head, pass'd through the leg of a pioneer, and lastly strook the toe of my boot, without doing me any harm. Mr. de Turenne continu'd on the place all night, with out whose presence I am confident the work had not been done.

At the same time Mr. de la Ferté was so far advanced in his attacke, that his Mine was ready to spring next day, it was accordingly sprung after dinner: M. de Turenne with severall of his Officers and Volonteers went to see what effect it would produce, but went not down into those Trenches, his coming being only out of curiosity. The Mine was made in the angle of a Tower and the wall, and was so order'd as to blow up not only the Angle, but also that part of the Tower and Wall which was nearest to it: when it was fired and the smoke gone off, wee saw it had only done its intended work upon the Wall, and very angle, but that the Tower was yet standing; only there was a great crack quite through it: but immediatly after the firing of the six guns upon the edge of the ditch, all togather, that part of the Tower came also down to our great satisfaction.

I have been told by some who were then in the battery with Monsr. de la Ferté, when this happen'd, that when he perceiv'd that part of the Tower next the Angle came not down with the other, he was in great rage against the Cheualier de Clerville, an Engeneer, who had the care of carryng on the Mine, threatning him furiously for his negligence and ignorance: At which the poor man much frighten'd, and fearing som severe usage from the Mareshall, but withall observing that the part which was yet standing shook, desir'd that the six guns which were in the battery might all be levell'd at that part of the Tower and fir'd at it all togather, which he said would probably bring it down: This being immediatly done had its desired effect, and he escap'd a cudgelling.[4]

[4] This paragraph is paraphrased in the French MS. (p. 111), and the order of the sentences somewhat altered, and not improved.

The breach that was made by it was very faire, so that our men the same night made a lodgment on it, which being perform'd and our two Mines on the other side of the Town in readiness to spring, the Governour thought it now high time to begin a Treaty for the surrendring up of the place; and the next morning beat a parlee, at the same time sending out Officers to treat. The articles were soon adjusted, which were that he should march out next day with armes and baggage, and be conveyd as far as Montmedy a neighbouring garrison of the Spaniards.

Thus, wee master'd the Town of Mousson in the space of seventeen days from the opening of the Trenches, without the loss of many men, or of any considerable Officer, or Volonteer of quality, excepting the Vidame de Laon, a nephew of Monsr. de Turenne, and second Son to the Count de Roussy, who was shott dead in the Trenches, as one evening he was going down to the head of them betwixt Mr. d'Humieres, and Mr. de Schomberg. The greatest loss wee had was in our horses, of which very many dyd by reason of the ill weather and clay ground on which they were camp'd.

But here I think it will not be amiss if I make a short digression to give account of some of their methods in France for the carrying on a Seige,[5] and of the extraordinary care and pains which the Generall Officers usually take on such occasions, to which I cheifly attribute their speedy taking in of Townes: They trust to no body but themselves to view, and make their observations; Mr. de Turenne went in person to view all the ground about Mousson, taking with him Mr. de Castelnau, when, as in another Army, I have seen the Generalls trust a Sergent de bataille or some inferior Officer to do it, so that they were wholy guided, and in a manner govern'd by their (the) eyes and advice of other men: but Monsr. de Turenne made use of his own judgment, where he thought it most proper to break ground, and which way to run the Trenches; when night came, he himself was present at the opening of them, and continued there allmost till break of day: Besides it was his constant method, during this whole Seige to go into the Trenches both morning and evening, In the morning to see if the work was well perform'd, at evening to resolve what would be the

---

[5] The observations that follow are made more rapidly, and with less of preamble, in the French MS. (p. 112).

work that night, having in his company the Lieut Genl: and some of the cheif Officers who that night were to command in the Trenches, to instruct them himself what he expected to be done. Again after supper he went to see them begin their work, and would continue with them more or less, as he found it necessary for the carrying on of the present design.

While he was once in the Trenches, during this Seige, I remember an odd accident, which happen'd when I was present and which I will relate, thō besides my present purpose: A Captain of the Regiment of Guyenne, being newly come to the Army, and that Regiment being then on duty on the Trenches, he approch'd Monsr. de Turenne to salute him; It happen'd, that, at the same time he was bowing down his head, a small shott from the Town struck him in the skull, and layd him dead at the Generall's feet: at which unhappy chance, some who were present made this unseasonable raillery, That if the Captain had been better bred, he had escap'd the bullett, which only hitt him there, for not bowing low enough to his Generall.

But to proceed: the Commander in cheif, is not only thus diligent, but all the inferiour Officers are obliged to be as carefull in their severall stations: particularly in all the time of this present Seige, in our side of the attack wee had not so much as one single Ingeneer, nor did I ever observe them to be made use of at any other place, but only as overseers of the work, most of the Officers understanding very well how to carry on a Trench, and to make a lodgement. As for the Mines, they haue a Captain of Miners who has a care of carrying them on, when the Generall has resolved where they shall be.

And not only from my own observations, but by what I have learn'd from others who haue had more experience and seen more seruice then myself, I find and am settled in my opinion, That no Generall ought wholly to confide in any Ingeneer for the carrying on of a Trench, it being not reasonable to beleeve, that one who is to be allways there, will hazard or expose himself as far as Officers, who are to take their turns, and who are push'd on by emulation of each other to make dispatch, and carry on the seruice with all diligence: And besides it gives more opportunity to Officers to understand that work, then otherwise they would haue; which appears most plainly by the Army of the Hollanders, for there, where all was resolv'd on by their Generall[6] upon consultation with the Ingeneers and the overseers, few Officers ever arrived at any knowledge in carrying on the Trenches, their imployment being only to guard them, and the workmen, and command their Soldiers to fire, they not being answerable for the advancing of the work: so that unless an Officer were naturaly industrious to learn and applyd himself to it, he receiv'd but small improvement. But what I have said concerning the carrying on of their approches in Holland, I confess I have not spoken of my own knowledge, but only from hear-say of persons, whose judgment and integrity I suppose I may reasonably trust: yet this I can affirm, that I have known very few of whatsoever Nation who were much the better for what they had learn'd in that Country; thō I haue known many good Officers who haue serv'd there, yet they gain'd their experience els where.

At this Seige was made no line of Circumvallation; for besides that wee were affraid in case wee had gone about it, so much time would haue been taken up, that the Enemy would haue compass'd their business, and gain'd Rocroy, before wee could haue taken Mousson (and then our Lines would haue signified litle to us) the Situation of the place was such by reason of the River Chiers, which cover'd us on the Luxembourg side, and then runs into the Meuse betwixt us and Sedan, that it was in stead of a line to us to hinder smaller succours from being put into the Town; wee having small advanced guards upon all the passes of that River, so that nothing could come that way without being discover'd, and that time enough to be prevented. On the other side the Enemy was so thorowly imployd at their Seige of Rocroy, that they could not think of endeavouring to releeve Mousson.

On the same day when the Town was surrender'd, which was the 27th of September, wee march'd to Amblemont in our way towards Rocroy with intention to try what could be done in order to the releif of it; but when wee were come as far as Varnicour, wee heard of its being deliver'd up.

After these two Seiges, there happen'd litle of Action betwixt either Armys during the remainder of the Campagne; for besides

[6] In the French MS. (p. 113) James ascribes this habit to 'le feu Prince d'Orange', and what follows (eight or nine lines) is a very brief summary of what he says in the *Life*.

that the Season of the year was too far spent to undertake any considerable Seige, the Spanish Army had suffer'd much more at
Rocroy, then wee at Mousson, and their numbers were so dimi-
nish'd, that out of that consideration, and our keeping so close to
them, therby to prevent our frustating any new undertaking, they
durst attempt no more that year; but imployd their time in
marches and countermarches, on the other side of the Somme,
eating up all the forage of the fronteers, as wee did on this side of
the same River in observing all their motions.

But while wee thus continued to hold them in play on that Side
of the Country, the Court having got together some troopes, besides the guards of horse and foot, which are constantly attending
on it, and some which were detach'd to them from the Army, undertook the Seige of St Menehou, which at first was carryd on by
three Lieutt Genlls; Monsr. de Navaille commanding the troopes
belonging to the Court, Mr. de Castelnau those which were sent
from Monsr. de Turenne, and Monsr. d'Vxelles such as had been
spar'd out of Monsr. de la Ferté's troopes. And thō two of these
three above nam'd were as able Officers for all Sorts of Duty as
any others in the Kingdom of France, and thō Mr. de Castelnau
thō not so proper for feil Seruice understood the business of a
Seige as well as any man, yet these three being all in equall command, manag'd the main affaire so ill, and went so slowly on with
it, that the Cardinal was forced to send the Mareshall de Plessis-
Praslin to take the supreme command upon him, after which the
Seige advanced with more Success.

Some days after the begining of this Seige, M. de la Ferté with
the greatest part of his horse came and quarter'd about * * *[7] to
hinder any releif from coming into the place, because the Duke of
Lorraine was marching down that way with his Army. In the
mean time M. de Turenne was quarter'd with his forces behind
the Somme betwixt Roye and Corbie; from which place seeing
litle probability of action there, I ask'd leave of Mr. de Turenne
to go to the Seige of St Menehou; and being obliged to take
Châlons sur Marne in my way thither, at which place the Court
then resided, I was stayd so long on one pretence or other in that

---

[7] There is a blank here in the *Life* (I, 190). The MS. *Campagnes* avoids the difficulty by merely saying that La Ferté marched to prevent the Duc de Lorraine from
bringing help to Sainte-Ménéhould (p. 115).

Town, some times for want of Convoy, another while, upon the
news of the King's removal within a day or two, so that they could
not spare any; that notwithstanding my continuall pressing to be
gone, the Town of St Menehou sent out to treat of a surrender the
same day I waited on the King of France to the Castle of Ham,
which is within two leagues of St Menehou: so that I miss'd the
seeing of that Seige, and went the next day with his Maty to view
the approches, and the breach which had been made in the body
of the place, before they came to Articles of Capitulation.[8]

8 . . . 'avant qu'elle [la place] battit la Chamade' (MS. *Campagnes*, p. 115) –a
more picturesque expression for 'to sound a parley'. The *Life* (I, 191) has an additional paragraph as follows:
'Thus ends the Relation given of this Campagne by his Royall Highness, who upon
the removall of the French Court, return'd likewise to Paris where he arrived the
beginning of Xber, and there spent the ensuing winter: towards the end of which, the
King his Brother took his resolution of leaving France by reason of the Treaty of
Amity then of foot between that Crown and Oliver Cromwell newly made Protector; For Cardinal Mazarin thought it at that time necessary for the preservation of
the French Monarchy, to keep fair with that Vsurper. The Duke attended his
Brother on his way towards Germany as far as Chantilly, where they took leave of
each other, in hopes of a more happy meeting thereafter.'

BOOK II

Of The Wars In Flanders
1654[*]

THE DUKE OF YORK'S
THIRD CAMPAIGN IN FRANCE

THIS Year the French Army under the Command of Monsr. de Turenne, and the Mareshall de la Ferté, was not assembled soon enough to prevent the Spaniards from beseiging Arras. On the third of July they satt down before it, with an Army consisting of thirty thousand men well furnish'd with all things necessary for so great an Enterprise. One thing which induced them to undertake that Seige, was their being advertis'd of the weaknes of the Garrison, which was not So strong as it ought to haue been, thō not so weak as to oblige the Governour to quit any of his outworkes which were very great. Our Generalls being sensible of this defect, sent away about a thousand horse in three bodies, one commanded by the Chevalier of Crequi, another by Monsr. de St Lieu, and the third by the Baron of Equancourt. St Lieu got into the Town with about two hundred horse, the first or second night after the Town was invested, through the Prince Condé's quarter; The Baron d'Equancourt two nights after him with three hundred horse through the Lorraine's quarter, and the Chevalier de Crequi forced his passage into the Town some days

---

[*] 'Of the Campagne here ensuing his Royall Highness gives the following account in his Memoires' (*Life*, ed. Clarke, I, 192). I here reprint the text of the Clarke edition (pp. 192–243) for the same reason as applied to the entry for 1653. See above, p. 128.

The entry in the French MS. (p. 116) is headed:
      Memoires du duc d'York
          Liv. II
               des Guerres en Flandres
   An 1654.

156

after both, through the Spanish quarter before the Line was finish'd. This was all the succour could be spar'd from the French Army. As for foot, wee durst not venture to send any, it being so plaine a Country about the Town, that they might haue been easily discover'd and defeated when once the Enemy had taken up their quarters before the Place.

Another reason why they lay down before Arras was, that wee had beseiged Stenay; which place they hop'd would haue endur'd so long, and taken up so many Troopes, that they might have compass'd their design before wee could haue ended our Seige, or at least as soon; and that, during this, our Army would not be of strength enough to undertake any thing upon them which indeed was not ill conjectur'd: for wee were (*so*) very weak that wee stirr'd not from about Peronne to approche their Lines till about the 16th of July, when wee heard they were near finish'd, for fear of ingaging ourselves so near a great Army, in a Country so bare and open.

I joyn'd the Army by Peronne before they march'd, being to Serve that year in quality of one of the Lieutenant Generalls, under Monsr. de Turenne, and tooke my day according to the date of my Commission as the youngest who serv'd in that Army. About the 16th, as I have sayd, wee began our march towards Arras, and camp'd at a Village call'd Sains, near Sauchy-Cauchy which lys betwixt Cambray and Arras about five leagues distant from the last of these places; The next day wee continued our march to Mouchy-le-Preux,[1] Mr. de Turenne taking that compass about the Country to cover himself by some brookes, that in case the Enemy should draw out upon him, he might be able to avoide fighting, And he was so cautious the day before he came to Mouchy-le-Preux, that when he arrived at a brooke which was half a league short of the foremention'd place, he there drew up his Army in battell, and afterwards pass'd over himself with some horse and dragoons to view the ground where he intended to incampe, and gave not orders for the Army to come over to him till the evening, but stayd upon the place to see if the Enemy had any intentions of drawing out against him; resolving that in case they should that day haue attempted any thing, our Army should not

---

[1] 'Mouchy-le-Preux' is the spelling in the Clarke edition, here reproduced. It should be Monchy-le-Preux.

haue gone over: When evening came, and the Enemy appear'd not, wee pass'd the brooke, but it was then so late that nothing could be attempted by them in all lykelyhood for that night.

Our Troopes no sooner were camp'd, but they fell to work about our Line, every Regiment both of horse and foot labouring at it on that part which lay before them; and this they perform'd with So much diligence, that next day they were in some tollerable posture of defence; but when once it was finish'd wee thought ourselves absolutely secure, it being a very advantageous post, and not of too great a front, for the Army wee had then; The brooke which I have already mention'd covering our left wing, as the Scarpe did our right: so that if the Enemy had drawn out to engage us there, when we first put ourselves in battell in that post of Mouchy-le-Preux, or before our Lines were finish'd, wee should haue had faire play for it, notwithstanding they were so much stronger, because they could not outfront us nor fall into our flankes; And wee had so good an opinion of our own courage, as never to be unwilling to venture an Engagement with them where they could not outwing us.

I have heard since when I was in Flanders and elswhere, many taxing the Spaniards for not coming out against us the first day of our being in that post, or as wee came to possess ourselves thereof; and some report that the Prince of Condé propos'd it to the Spaniards: But I can not affirme this, neither will I take it upon myself to censure them for not doing it, because I have not heard their reasons for this omission, though they may be easily conjectur'd. But whither they had it under their consideration or not, wee took our precautions in coming thither, as if wee believ'd they would make some attempt on us; and, being once posted, wee lost no time to intrench ourselves: for certainly that post of Mouchy was very strong, because that not only both our flancks were cover'd, as I have alread said, but also our Line ran along upon a heigth from Mouchy which was in the midst, and both overlook'd and commanded on either side down to the brooke and River of Scarpe; So that had the Enemy advanced upon us in the day time, our cañon, which for the most part were planted on that height of Mouchy, would haue gall'd them terribly, after which wee had still the advantage of the ground.

Monsieur de Turenne's own quarter was at this place of

Mouchy, having with him the greatest number of his foot, his horse were incamp'd on two Lines, which reached to the brooke, together with the rest of his foot; Monsr. de la Ferté had his quarter at the right hand of all our Line down by the side of the River Scarpe, at a Village called Peule. One part of his foot were incamped by him, the other part at Mouchy, and his horse also upon two Lines betwixt Mouchy and his quarter: Our reserue was in its proper place just behind Mr. de Turenne's quarter, which was in the midst. Thus our Incampment was in order of battell, only wee had some foot at each extremity of our Lines, and in the midst of our wings of horse, that our Line might be the better defended.

When wee were thus posted, and our Line finish'd, wee sent out considerable partys of horse, almost every night, to hinder any Convoys from coming into the Enemie's Camp; and notwithstanding that they sate down before Arras as well appointed with all things necessary, as was usuall for Armys at that time, yet so great a body of men as they were within their Lines was of necessity to haue some communication with their own Country; and whether it was, that they were really in want of powder, or that it was only out of precaution, from almost the first days of our being in their neighbourhood, they sent out partys of horse to supply them with it, which went to Douay, Cambray, and other places of theirs, and some of their Garrisons sent to them, each trooper carrying a bag of fifty pound weight of powder behind his horse: These partys they kept continually going, scarsely intermitting any night, and thō wee had partys very often abroad to intercept them, it was never our fortune to surprise any of them, the Country being so very open, that unless by accident they should fall into the midst of our partys, they could not be intercepted: Yet wee seldom sent out less then a thousand or twelve hundred horse under the command of some Lieutenant Generall, who march'd out of the Camp in the evening. They who were sent abroad out (*of*) Monsr. de Turenne's Army, posting themselves betwixt the Camp and Bapaume in some Valley or other place where they could not be easily discover'd, till they came out against the Enemy, having small outguards round about them to give notice of any thing that pass'd and, besides them, Centry's every way that they might not be surpriz'd; and Mr. de la Ferté did the like on his Side, his party's advancing betwixt the Camp and Lens.

But though neither ours, nor his could meet with any of these powder-carriers, yet by an accident hapening amongst themselves, one of their Convoyes chanced to miscarry; For one night as wee were with Mr. de Turenne, visiting the guards, wee perceived a great blaze of fire, quick and violent like that of the blowing up of gunpowder; and it seem'd to us, as if it had been at the quarter of Monsr. de la Ferté: But as (we) went down that way to inquire of it, our Sentinels who were upon the heigth of Mouchy, inform'd us, that they had likewise seen it, and that it was not where wee had imagined, but on the plaine farr beyond those quarters towards Lens, which caus'd us to wonder the more what it might be. The next morning wee were fully Satisfied concerning it, that an entire Regiment of horse, consisting of Six score, going from Douay to the Enemie's Camp, all of them Officers as well as Souldiers having behind them a bagg of powder, besides about fourscore horses laden with hand grenades, which were led by Countrymen on foot, had been all blown up, but by what accident, none of those who were brought prisoners into the Camp could tell. Indeed it was a very dismall object, to behold a great number of poor men, who were brought into our Camp with their faces disfigur'd and their bodies burnt by powder, so that few of them recover'd, their Companions having been all kill'd outright. These prisoners were brought in by some of our partys who were out on that side of the Country, who seeing the flash at a great distance, rode up to the place to gaine a more clear knowledge of the matter; they also brought along with them some few scorch'd horses, and a paire of kittle drums which belong'd to that Regiment, and all the men who had any life remaining in them. I happen'd since, when I was in Flanders, to talke with a Lieutenant of horse who was the only man that could give an account, how that accident befell them; for seeing his face had been burnt, I casually ask'd him how he came by that misfortune? He answer'd me, that it was by the blowing up of powder at such a time near Arras; and upon my examining him concerning the particulars of it, he told me, That happening to be in the Rear of the whole Regiment, he saw one of the Troopers with a pipe of tobacco lighted in his mouth; wherupon he rode up to him, and taking it gently from him, threw it away after which he beat him with his sword: The Soldier being drunke, pull'd out his pistol, and presented it to his breast; upon which the Lieutenant threw himself from his horse apprehending what might happen, and the Trooper at the same instant firing at him, it lighted on the bag behind the sd Lieutenant's horse, which taking fire, blew it up, and so, from one successiuely to the other who was next, it spred through the whole Regiment: he being on the ground escap'd best cheape, having only his face, his hands, and some parts of his bod scorched.

This accident was So very remarkable, that I could not but mention it, especially because it was the only party of the Enemy which miscarryd, or which indeed wee mett with excepting twice; one which was rencountred by the Marquess de Richelieu commanded by the Comte de Lorge, but there the advantage was not on our side, for the Comte resolutely forc'd his way through the Marquess's men, beat them, and took three or four of his Captains, loosing only twelve horses laden with powder, and getting safe with the rest into the Lines of their own Camp. The other was yet of worse consequence to us, by the considerable loss wee Sustain'd in the person of Monsr. de Beaujeu, the Lieut Genll who commanded our party: he being sent out by Mr. de Turenne with a body of eight hunderd horse, and having notice of a Convoy which was to come into the Enemy's Lines by the way of * * *[2] immediatly taking that way about break of day he mett a party of the Enemy commanded by Mr. Druot (*Droot*) a Colonell coming from the Enemies Camp; the numbers of both sides were in a manner equall, but the Enemy had no advertisement of our being there; yet it so happen'd that most of our men were at that time dismounted from their horses, expecting intelligence of the Supposed party which came the other way, which made it easy for Droots men to overrun as they did the two first Squadrons, before they could mount; And as for Beaujeu, his misfortune was such, that as he was going to put the next Squadron in order, he was slayn, and that body also beaten: So that if the Regiment of Beauuau (*Beauveau*) had not made a stand, and put a stop to the Violence of the Enemy, by beating their first Squadron which had done all this execution, Our whole party had been absolutly defeated. But this advantage gave leasure to the rest of our men to put themselves in order, and to receive a charge from the Enemy,

[2] There is also a blank in the MS. (p. 122).

which was not very vigorous, Droot having been hurt in the former by the Regiment de Beauveau; so that there was no great mischeif done at that bout on either side, they only disordering each other: wherupon the Enemy, not knowing the certain number of our men, and fearing they might be stronger then indeed they were, judg'd it convenient for them to march away, and our Soldiers having lost their Commander were enough content to escape as they did, and thought not of following them; so that in this action, it might be said that both were beaten: As for the number of the Slayn and prisoners on either side, it was very inconsiderable excepting the loss of our Lieut. Generall.

For my own particular I was once a broad in my turn, with about a thousand horse, and being posted in a litle Valley with my party, my Centryes being out every side, a party of the Enemy consisting of an hundrd horse coming from their Camp to go for Cambray, surprised a Corporall and two Centryes, just as he was about to releive them; who being ask'd by those who had made them prisoners, what our numbers were? The Corporall answer'd, About a hunderd, and that most of us were dismounted, feeding our horses: which they beleeving came furiously down upon us at a great gallop their trumpett sounding the charge before them; but when they were with in pistoll-shott of us, perceiving their mistake, and that in stead of a small party, and those off their horses, they were to deal with severall Squadrons all on horseback, they retired faster then they had come on: Which I observing, was a moment in doubt what I should do, imagining at first they would never haue advanced with so much fury, if they had not been well seconded; but immediatly weighing with how much precipitation they ran off, I concluded their number to be no more then what I saw, wherupon I order'd the Squadron upon the head of which I was, to disband after them, myself with the rest riding softly after: but they made such hast, that our Soldiers could not overtake them; yet they escap'd not, for they fell into the hands of another party of ours, which took them every man. The same morning also, another party of theirs was taken by me; for as I was marching back towards the Camp, a small detachment of mine brought me word, that they had discover'd about a hundred horse of the Enemy, putting themselves in ambuscade a litle before day in a neighbouring Village: upon which intelligence I march'd with my whole party as near the Village as I could, without being seen by them, sending a small number of my men to draw them out of their ambuscade; with order, that when the Enemy came out to charge them, they shou'd retire to the main body. This they perform'd so dexterously, that the Enemy were closse upon us before they perceived us, So that none of them escap'd from being taken.

While these things pass'd without the Camps, the Enemy before Arras having finished their Line on the 14th August open'd their Trenches the same night, following the Seige with all manner of diligence, and pressing the Town so very hard, that thō Monsr. de Mondejeu who was Governour, perform'd all the parts of an expert Commander, and was assisted by Monsr. de St Lieu, the Cheualier de Crequi and the Baron d'Equancourt, with all imaginable gallantry; yet the Spaniard gain'd ground upon him every day, and by the * * *[3] of August had made themselves masters of the corne de Guiche, and not only of the outward but of the inward also, as may be seen by the plan of it; continuing to push on their work with vigour, notwithstanding the resistance which they found. This obliged the Governour to send out severall Messengers to our Generalls, some of which came safely into our Camp to inform us of the condition of the place.

One of these Messengers having swallow'd the Note he brought, wrapt up in lead (that in case he had been taken and searched it might not haue been found about him) and coming at a time when the Generalls were very impatient to hear from the Town, the Messenger was not able to voyd the paper in above 24 houres, though severall purges were given him to bring it out of his body: This gave them great anxiety, and particularly Monsr. de la Ferté cryd out with a great passion, *Il faut éventrer le coquin!* 'the rascall must haue his belly ript up', since he will not voyd it: This put the fellow into such a fright, that being then just at the door of the Tente, the peice of lead came immediatly from him; and by the account it brought, made us defer attacking the Lines of the Enemy before the Stenay troopes were come up to us, the Town not being so prest as wee had reason to beleeve it was by some letters wee had intercepted from the Enemy's Camp to some in Flanders, wherin they confidently affirm'd they should be masters

[3] There is a similar blank in the MS. (p. 124).

of the Town by St Laurence's day at furthest; which with the news wee had from the Army before Stenay, that the Seige there did not advance so fast as wee expected, and so no liklyhood of having those troopes before that day, had made our Generalls resolve not to stay for them, and forthwith to attacke the Lines, ordering every Squadron of horse and battalion of foot to provide themselves with such a number of fascines and hurdles within two days. The reason of this provision was, because the Enemy had made without the utmost ditch of their Line, about six rowes of holes, of a foot and a half or two foot diameter, and three foot in depth, that our horse might not be able to pass to the edge of the out ditch, and with the help of these hurdles wee hop'd to get over them: But as I have already Said, those apprehensions were all blown over by the Note which the Messenger had brought them, and by the good news which arriv'd the next day from before Stenay, which imported that it would soon be taken; They thought it reasonable therfore to attend the coming of those troopes, and in the mean time wee continued our preparations for attacking the Lines when it should be judg'd fitt.

About the * * *[4] of August wee had notice from Mr. d'Hocquincourt, to whom the Court had newly given the Command of the troopes that had been before Stenay (for it was not he but Mr. Faber Governour of Sedan who had commanded them before when they took Stenay) that he was within * * *[5] days march of the French Army, and desir'd to know whither he should come up and joine us, or incampe at some other place; to which they return'd this answer, That Monsr. de Turenne wou'd meet him with fifteen squadrons of horse at * * *[6] and that if Mr. d'Hocquincourt would come thither before and bring with him all his horse, they too would go together, and view a post upon the brook (*de Crinchon*)[7] near Riuiere; where they beleeved would be found a convenient place for him to campe, and where by intrenching himself a litle, he might be secure from any attempt which the Enemy could make on him.

Accordingly Monsr. de Turenne and the other, mett at the

---

[4] There is also a blank in the MS. (p. 126).
[5] This part of the sentence is omitted in the MS.
[6] 'a un certain endroit' in the MS.
[7] Not in the MS.

place appointed on the 17th of August: But instead of going as they had resolved, to view that post, having immediatly received notice of a great Convoy coming to the Enemy from St Omer and Aire, by the way of St Paul, under the command of Mr. de Boutteville, they march'd away on the instant with their horse, and left word for Mr. d'Hocquincourt's foot, cañon, and baggage which was then about Bapaume, to make what expedition they could after them to St Paul; taking their way by Buquoy, and so along by the woods, to cover them as much as they could possibly, because they had no horse to guard them. In the mean time, wee with the Cavalry were come as far as St Paul, where wee had intelligence that the Convoy having had notice of our coming that way, was return'd to Ayre, for which reason wee went no farther after them: But finding the enemy had possessed themselves of that Town, and had left four or five hundred dismounted troopes in it for its defence, it was thought fitt by our two Generalls to stay where wee were till our foot came up, and then to attack it, it being a very considerable post which had been of great seruice to the Enemy; for most of their Convoys had come Safely to them by that way, and it was their usuall resting place betwixt their garrisons on that side of the Country and their Camp, so that it was necessary for us to take it from them. It cost us litle time and labour, for as soon as our foot and cannon were come up which was on the 18th when our Batterys were made, they capitulated, and, as I remember, were made prisoners of warr.

This being perform'd, the next day wee marched back towards the Lines and quarter'd at Aubigny, where, coming early to our quarters, Monsr. de Turenne according to his custome took with him a Squadron or two of horse and went on towards the Enemies Lines; and when he was come near an old Roman Camp, which was call'd by the Country-men Coesar's Camp,[8] where the Scarpe and a litle brook joyne together, he found the Enemy had there an advanced guard of horse, which upon our coming towards them retir'd to the other side of the brook; by which means Monsr. de Turenne had the leisure to view that post which was not distant from the Line of the Enemy above twice cannon shott.

And he found it so proper for his turn, that he propos'd it to Monsr. d'Hocquincourt, as a much securer and better post to all

[8] 'Camp de César.'

intents, then that of Riuiere: Wherupon the next day being the
20th wee march'd thether, and to render it yet more secure,
Monsr. d'Hocquincourt ordered his men to make a Line from the
River to the brook; and finding that the Enemy had put five hunderd men into the Abbey of Mount St Eloy, which was but just
on the other side of the River, he resolved to attack it the next day
notwithstanding its neighbourhood to the Enemies Lines; that by
possessing it he might the better keep them in.

Being thus resolved, the next morning early he pass'd the River,
which is there but very small, and drew up all those troopes in
battell betwixt the Abbey and the Line, excepting such of the foot
as were commanded to attack the place: At first the Enemy made
shew as if they intended to mentain the Outwall, but upon the advancing of our foot they quitted it, and retir'd into the Abbey it
self which had a good old wall about it, flancked with round
Towers. So soon as wee were masters of the Outwall, wee made
Embraseurs through it for our cañon, and began to batter the
wall of the Abbey; But finding that our cañon could not do much
at so great a distance, wee rais'd a slight battery, which was indeed no more then a blind within the Outwall, and brought thether our great guns, where in four hours they began to make a
breach, and while the cañon perform'd their part, the foot did
theirs also: for having got by the shelter of some walks, and litle
garden-walls within pistoll-shott of the foot of the main-wall, they
fasten'd a Miner to it by the help of Madriers, and just as the
Miner was ready to go on with those who were to carry the plancks
to secure him, our foot which were cover'd by the garden-walls
drew out from behind them, and stood firing as fast as they were
able, for half a quarter of an hour together, at the Enemys loop-
holes, that the Miner might lodge himself with more safety;
which being done they drew back behind the walls again. They
were the French and Suisse Guards who perform'd this, and notwithstanding they approched so very near, and were seen from
head to foot when they drew out, yet they lost very few men in the
Action. At the same time the Regiment de la Marine found the
means of lodging themselves, by the favour of a litle banck close
to the Tower which wee were battering: so that those within the
Abbey thought it was now high time for them to capitulate, which
they did, yeelding up the Abbey and themselves prisoners of warr.

This being done, Monsieur d'Hocquincourt drew back over
the brook to Coesar's Camp, and Monsr. de Turenne march'd
away from thence, with his fifteen Squadrons of horse and two
Troopes of Dragoons, to his own Camp. In his way thether he resolved to take a view of the Enemies Line on that Side, and in
order to it, march'd down from Mont St Eloy, straight upon them,
till he came within half cañon shott of them, and so keeping still
the same distance from their Line, continued his march round that
part of it which was on that side of the River Scarpe, till he had
fully view'd it. During all this time the cannon shott from the
Line playd hard upon us, and not without doing execution, there
being not any of the Squadrons that escap'd without the loss of
two or three men at least, and many of them lost more, besides
horses, which caus'd some of the old horse Officers to murmure
that they should be expos'd in that manner, as they then thought,
to no purpose. And this was the only time while I serv'd in the
French Army, that I ever knew Monsr. de Turenne blam'd for
hazarding his men unnecessarily. But the same Officers acknowledge they were in the wrong for taxing their Generall, after wee
had forced those Lines which they came then to obserue; for then
the reason was evident why he expos'd not only his men, but his
own person to that danger, it being at that very time, that he chose
the place where he resolved to attack the Line. And indeed had he
not gone so near with his whole body, the Enemys horse guards
would not haue retired as they did within their Line; and then he
could not haue view'd it so exactly, for wee approched so near with
some few loose horse, that Mr. Jermyn's (*Lord Germain*)[9] horse
was kill'd under him with a small shott from the Line, which
peirced him through and gave his master a terrible blow on the
leg afterwards.

Thus Monsr. de Turenne by passing so near them, had the opportunity of viewing most exactly the strength of each quarter of
the Enemy, all their troopes standing to their armes as wee
marched along by them. He observed the quarter of Don Fernando de Solis to be the weakest, not only in men, but in the forti-
fication of it; for which reason he resolv'd to make his strongest
impression there. Some of our Officers as wee were marching

[9] The MS. *Campagnes* (p. 130) has 'Mr. Germain', but the reference is probably
to Jermyn.

down towards the Lines from Mont St Eloy, were bold enough to represent to Monsr. de Turenne, the extreme hazard which he ran by going so near the Enemy in so open a Country, who (*where*) they could tell every man wee had, and therby knowing our force, might draw out and defeat us without any danger to themselves; which he freely acknowledg'd they might do, and that were it on the Prince Condé's side as it was on the Spaniards, he would not haue made the Venture: but having serv'd amongst the Spaniards, he well knew their methods of proceeding, And he was certain, that upon our first approche towards their Lines, Don Fernando de Solis would not dare to do any thing of himself, without sending first to the Count of Fuensaldagne who was Governador de las Armas; and the Count would either go himself or send to advertise the Archduke of it: after which they would send to the Prince of Condé, whose quarter was quite on the other side, and give him notice, at the same time desiring him to come to the Archduke's quarter where they were, to haue a Junto to consider what must be done on that occasion; And while this consultation which must pass through so many formes was making, wee should haue leisure to view their Lines, and afterwards to pass by them without running any other hazard then that of their cañon from their Lines. It happen'd just as he had foretold it would, and all those very Formalities were actually observ'd by the Spaniards, as the Prince of Condé himself told me afterwards in Flanders; but by that time they had resolved at their Junto to fall upon us, wee were wholly out of their danger and gotten in to our Camp.

Monsieur de Turenne having taken this view, it was now time for us to put some thing in execution in order to releeve the Town; for by a letter from the Governour, our Generalls had notice that he had very litle pouder left, so that unless he were speedily succour'd he must be forced to capitulate. This hasten'd our resolution of attacking their Lines; which had never been attempted but by the means of Monsr. de Turenne, who consider'd nothing but the public good, and the carrying of the King's Seruice; most of the other Generall Officers having by-ends and interests of their own, which made them declare openly against the taking of such a resolution, and oppose it with all the arguments they could invent. For Mr. de la Ferté, he was unwilling to run the hazard of losing so many of his Soldiers, as in all probability must be kill'd in the attempt; for being of so much consideration at Court by reason of his troopes, he was unwilling they should be lessen'd. Monsr. d'Hocquincourt was Governour of Peroñe, which if Arras was once taken, would then more fronteer then it was before, and a considerable part of the contributions belonging to that place, would fall to him: The same reason prevail'd with Mr. de Navailles Governour of Bapaume, and with Monsr. de Bar Governour of Dourlans, both of the Lieutenant Generalls; and most of the rest, excepting only myself and the Count de Broglio looking on it as a desperate peice of seruice, gave their opinions against the attack; for by weaving the attempt they secur'd their persons, and if the attempt were made and succeeded not, they might be able to say, it was undertaken contrary to their judgment: And this is not sayd as my bare conjecture, but was very apparent; for Monsr. d'Hocquincourt and his Officers propos'd to make a tentative, as they call'd it, or an offer, without pushing for the Saving of our honours, judging it impossible to effect the Enterprise. M. de la Ferté even after it was resolved on, a day or two before the attack, sent his Trumpett to Monsr. de Turenne, hoping by the Relation he should give, to fright him from attempting it, which appear'd by the manner of his coming; for he came in to Monsr. de Turenne's Tent as he sat at Supper with severall Officers, and told him, he was sent by his Master to give him an account of what he had seen in the Enemies Lines, he being newly come from thence, and adding, that he was bound in conscience to give him a true relation of it. He then told him, That they had made their Lines extraordinarly strong, having inlarged their ditch and rais'd their Line; that their out ditch was very difficult to pass, and that without it there were severall ranks of holes, with stakes betwixt every hole, and that their Lines were well furnish'd with Souldiers to defend them. Upon this Monsr. de Turenne grew angry, and commanded him to be gone, telling him withall, That were it not for the respect he bore his Master, he would haue layd him by the heels for talking in that manner: For indeed this discourse being made in a publick place, might haue been of ill consequence to discourage all who heard it, had they not guessed he had been order'd by Monsr. de la Ferté to give this tragicall account.

But Monsr. de Turenne's judgment was too well settled, to give way of his artifices, So that in stead of suffering his own reason to be shaken by them, he made the falsness of their arguments appear. As for the tentative, he convinced those who upheld it, that they (*were*) under a manifest mistake, for in stead of saving their reputation it would haue a quite contrary effect; because by making a faint (*feint*) attempt, without pursuing it, everyone would see they intended nothing more, so that they should haue the disrepute of Sacrifising two or three hundred men to no purpose: And then as to the probability of our succez in attacking the Line, he said, Wee should fall on with no less then fifteen battallions upon one front, that some of these would find none to oppose them or at worst only some scatter'd men; That those who found no form'd body to make resistance, would doubtless fix themselves on the Line where they fell on, and that consequently all the rest of our foot coming to that place, if they could not force their way where they attack'd, must by being masters of the fire, beat off the Enemy and make an entrance for the horse; That by attacking them in the night, one quarter durst not come to the assistance of the other, for that by reason of the false attacks, each fearing for himself, would not dare to forsake his Station, and help his Neighbour till break of day, and before that time wee should haue forced our passage through their Lines; That what he most apprehended was some disorder or accident in our march thether, for he was very confident, that were wee once ready drawn up, where wee intended our attack, wee should be able to force our way: And to strengthen these his reasons, the Court was absolutely for the attempt, so that infine it was resolv'd on, notwithstanding all the trickes and reluctance of those who oppos'd it.

The time appointed was the Eve of St Lewis his day, being the night of the 24th of August; and thō none in the Army besides the three Generalls knew the certain time, yet the whole Army had orders to prepare for it, and to provide themselves of fascines and hurdles and all other necessaries for such an undertaking; neither were they obliged only to make these preparations, but those which were full as necessary, which were publick prayers at the head of each Battalion and Squadron for severall days before, and as many as could, confessed, and received the blessed Sacrament: So that I am confident no Army ever show'd more markes of true deuotion then ours at that time. And now that the night for the attack drew near, Monsr. de Turenne did on all occasions discourse with the Officers concerning the mañere of it, and what resistance wee were like to find, instructing them how to behave themselves according to the Severall occasions which might arise, and accidents which might happen: But above all things he recommended to them the care of keeping their Men in perfect order when they were once with in the Lines, and to be very cautious that they advanced not too fast, after they were gotten in; for then was the criticall time of care and discipline, there being more danger of being beaten out, then there was hazard in entring, for it was to be expected that all the forces of the other quarters would come powring in upon us: and that wee shou'd not think of going straight forward to the Town, but shou'd march along the Line and clear that before us, and beat the Enemy before wee thought of marching to our freinds. These kind of discourses he had every day with his Officers, as occasion was presented, in common talk, and more especially with the Generall Officers. And I am apt to beleeve that from this manner of conversation, historians haue made speeches for many Generalls who never made any to their Armys when they were upon the point of giving battell; for such ordinary discourses as I have mentioned, appear to me to be much more usefull then set formall speeches, which can not be heard but by very few, in an open field, where they are commonly feign'd by writers to haue been spoken: whereas by familiar conversation with Several Officers, the Generall do's not only instruct them much better, and at more leisure, but is ready at the same time to answer any of their objections, and to clear any doubt which may arase. I know not whither any of the two other Generalls did the same; but I am a witness that it was done by Monsieur de Turenne.

And now all things being fully prepar'd for the attack, all the men of quality at Court, who were of age to draw a sword, came from thence into our Army to haue their share both of the honour and the danger of so great an undertaking. And some of them happening to dine with Monsr. de Turenne, and myself, at the Marquess d'Humieres his tent, about two days before the attack, after diner had a desire to see the Enemie's Lines. Monsr. de Turenne therfore gott on horseback with all those who had din'd together, and went out of our Line towards one of our out horse-guards. Just as wee came out wee saw a small party of ours pursuing a party of the Enemies, which had fallen on our foragers, who were then returning to our Camp. Monsr. de Turenne observing this, commanded us who were with him, to try if wee could get betwixt them and their Line, and cutt off their way, at the same time ordering the horse guards to second us. But thō wee were well hors'd, the Enemy got to their guard before wee could joine them, and upon our advancing up towards the Enemy, they drew into their Line, and left some few foot, which were making fascines in a litle wood which was about half cannon shott from their Line, to our mercy; and these wee made prisoners: and here Monsr. de Turenne took this opportunity of Viewing that part of their Lines, which he had not seen before.

But he continu'd not long there, for they plyd us very hard with their cañon, and wee saw them getting in horse back as fast as they could, So that it was evident they would come out upon us, it being the Pce of Condé's quarter: Therfore wee drew off and went towards a Castle call'd Neufville S. Vât which was not above a league distant, in which wee had foot, and as we were descending from the high ground on which wee were, wee saw about a league from us the Convoy of our foragers, consisting of twelve Squadrons of horse commanded by Monsr. de l'Islebonne, a Lieut Genl, marching home to our Camp.

At the same time Seeing the Enemys horse beginning to draw our of their Lines, Monsr. de Turenne alter'd his course a litle, and march'd towards Monsr. de l'Islebonne, sending before and ordering him to come up to us with all speed: Having hopes that in case the Enemy should follow us, wee should be able to do somewhat on them. By this time our number was increased, so that besides the Squadron of guards, which was with us, wee were about sixty or seventy officers and volonteers: But the Enemy follow'd us no further then the top of the hill which was within cañon shott of their Lines, and thether came the Pce of Condé himself with about fourteen Squadrons of horse. When Monsr. de Turenne saw they follow'd us no farther, he sent word again to Monsr. l'Islebonne that he should continue on his march to our Camp; and sent back the Squadron of the guards to their post, himself going with the Officers towards the Castle I have already mention'd.

But he had not gone farr, when some few scatter'd men came from the heigth, where the Pce of Condé was in person, and endeavour'd to gain the top of another rising ground up which wee were marching, to discover what strength there was behind us; which being observ'd by Monsr. de Turenne, he was not willing they should get above us, and by that means discern that wee had none to second us, and for that reason commanded out half a score volonteers to hinder their design; of which number were Mr. Jermyn, Mr. Charles Berkley, Briscara, Trigomar, and others, whose names I do not remember. At the same time wee drew up in a body upon the top of the hill, and faced towards the Enemy: But our young Volonteers were not Satisfied with performing only what was order'd them, but followed these loose men farther then in reason they ought to haue done, that is, even to (*the*) bottome, which was betwixt us and the Enemys bodys of horse; which the Pce of Condé seeing, commanded one of his Squadrons of horse, namely the Regiment d'Estrées with the Duke of Wirtemberg at their head, to come down at full speed upon our young men, and endeavour to cutt off the way of their return. This obliged Monsr. de Turenne to order us with our small body to meet and charge them, thereby, to disingage our friends; And then again he sent for Monsr. de l'Islebonne and the Squadron of guards to Second us.

It was all wee could do to save our Volonteers, but in preserving them wee ingaged ourselves by charging the Duke of Wirtemberg, and thoug our body was not neer so strong as his, wee routed him, and pursued him down into a litle meadow, which lay in the bottom; from thence wee follow'd him up a litle balk, where his men turn'd upon us, and gave us a volley of their Carabins, which gave a litle Stop to us by their knocking down severall of our men and horses. This being observed by the Enemy renew'd their courage, and they charg'd down upon us the Second time with so much vigour, that they forced us back, press'd upon us, and made us begin to turn our backs. But at the same time the Squadron of guards, who as they were going to their post had seen the beginning of the skirmish, came into our releif, and just as they came up to us, myself and Monsr. de Joyeuse turn'd and put ourselves at their head, leading them up to charge the Enemy in the flanck: but at the instant when wee were puting this in execution, the whole Squadron ran and left us two ingaged, non staying with us but two or three of our Servants.

Almost at the same point of time Monsr. d'Arcy a gentleman of quality had his horse kill'd under him, and wee endeavour'd to get him off; I call'd to him to get off, but he seeing a loose horse which had lost his rider, would needs catch him, and stayd so long in endeavouring it, that though I and Monsr. de Joyeuse did all wee could to lay hold of him and gett him off, wee were not able to performe it: and indeed wee endeavour'd it So long, and ingaged ourselves so far, that wee were both in danger of being taken, and had much ado to escape ourselves. As for Monsr. de Joyeuse he had the misfortune to receive a shott through the Arme, of which afterwards he dy'd, but I got off without any harme. Mr. Jermyn was like to haue been taken in endeavouring to save one Beauregard, whose horse being also kill'd, he help'd him up behind him, but the horse would not carry double, and bounding threw him off; Therupon Jermyn advis'd him to lay hold on his stirrup, by which means he brought him a litle way from the Enemy, till at length being press'd by them, he was forced to quit him, and then Beauregard was made prisoner. Mr. Berkley help'd to get off Monsr. de Castelneau, whose horse was shott in five places, so that he was hardly able to bear him from the Enemy; which Berkley seeing, dismounted, and lent the other his own horse, after which he gott upon another on which (*one of*) Monsr. de Castelneau's pages was mounted, and with much difficulty escaped.

The Enemy had the chase of us for almost a mile, and had pursued us farther, had not Monsr. de l'Islebonne with his twelve Squadrons come to our relief; but seeing him they retir'd time enough for their own safety, without being oblidg'd to run for it. Besides d'Arcy and Beauregard, there were some others taken, and almost all the pages who were there with their Master's cloakes. Very few were kill'd and not many hurt; yet it vex'd Monsr. de Turenne to haue received that litle affront in person, and made him desirous to haue some kind of revenge, and he hop'd to haue had it that very night; for having receiv'd intelligence that the Enemy were accustom'd to come out of their Lines and forage in the night, he resolved to fall upon them.

And to that purpose so soon as it was dark, he march'd out of his Camp in person with all his horse then in his Camp with him, which were about fourty Squadrons, and took along with him three or four Lieut Generalls, amongst whom he divided them, himself marching at the head of all: But whither the intelligence were false, or that they, having notice of our design, were gone off before wee could reach the place where wee were inform'd they us'd to forage when wee came thether wee found no body; so that having miss'd of our expectations, Monsr. de Turenne made the Van of that which was the Rear, and march'd back, as he thought, towards his Camp. The night happen'd to be exceeding dark, and our guides mistaking their way, in stead of leading us to their Camp brought us to the Lines of the Enemy.

It was the Prince of Condé's quarter which they mistook for ours; and upon the Centry's asking who went there? they were answer'd Turenne; he repeated the question, and demanded farther if it was not Lorraine they meant? but they answer'd again that it was Turenne, upon which he fir'd at them; Then some of our men who continued still in their errour, cryd out to him not to fire, for Mr. de Turenne was there in person: This obliged the Enemy to fire some few small shott at us, and one great gun, which absolutely undeceived us, but withall put us into the greatest disorder imaginable, causing such a panique fear in our common men, that I was confident, if that moment fourty horse had come out upon us, wee had been defeated. The cheif, or rather the only cause of the first disorder was the darkness of the night, our Squadrons being therby obliged to march so close to one another, for fear of loosing the File, that upon the sudden stop which was made by the first Squadron when the Centry fir'd, those behind came shouldring one upon another and broke their order; But upon their firing afterwards from the Line, the formost giving a litle back and altering their course immediatly to wheel about towards their own Camp, the confusion was so great, that of ten Squadrons which ought to haue been behind mine, there was not one at our marching back, So that I happen'd to haue the Reer in coming off; but the hurry was soon over, for wee all gott safe into our Lines, as also those Squadrons which had lost their way.

This happen'd, as I said, about a day or two before wee attack'd the Lines, And now our fascines and hurdles and other necessarys for such an attempt, being fully provided, our Generalls resolv'd to attack the quarter of Don Fernando Solis with their whole

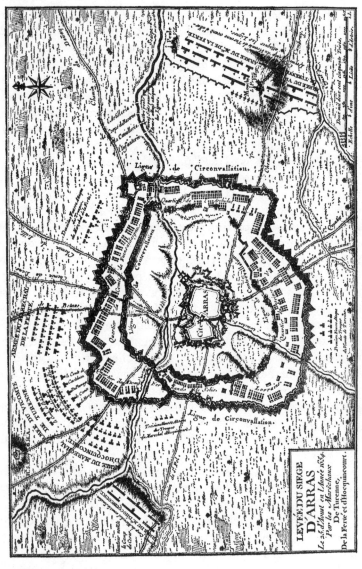

Raising of the Siege of Arras, August 25, 1654

forces, as being the weakest in all respects, and farthest distant from the Prince of Condé: This quarter began on the north side of the River above the Town, and joyn'd to that of the Count of Fuensaldagne. To favour this undertaking, three false attacks were order'd to be made on the other parts of the Line; the time appointed, an houre before day on the 25th of August.

In performance of this resolution, Monsr. de Turenne and Monsr. de la Ferté with their two Armys began with the Van of their troopes to pass over the Scarpe out of Monsr. de la Ferté's quarters, about Sun sett. It was Monsr. de Turenne's turn that day to lead, and they had a great march to come to the place appointed for the attack; but it was so well order'd that there happen'd no confusion in the way, there being very many bridges over the Scarpe made, and such care taken, that no ill accident arrived to them in their march. Every man knew his own business. The first line of the foot pass'd over the bridge, which was on the left hand of all the others, and nearest to the Enemies Line. On the next bridge to that on the right hand of them, the horse pass'd over which were to second them. On the third, the Reserve of horse and foot: On the next to it, the Traine of Artillery, with all that belong to it; so that with only faceing to the left wee were in battalia, and in a readiness to falle on; every battalion having their Pioneers, and commanded men, ready at the head of them, and each Trooper carrying two fascines a horseback before him, to deliver to the Foot when they should haue occasion for them. As for our baggage it was order'd to be in a readiness, but not to stirr out of the Camp till it was broad daylight, because no guard was left with it; but afterwards to come to us as they could.

This was the order of our march, which was perform'd with such conduct and exactness, that wee came just at the houre appointed, to the place where wee were to meet M. d'Hocquincourt with his troopes. In all this way wee halted but once, and that but for a very litle time, without hauing given the least allarme to the Enemy in the march; though for the greatest part of the way, had not our musketeers observ'd their orders very carefully in hiding their metches, the Enemy from their Lines must needs haue discover'd them. I remember that once that night, out of curiosity to see how they observ'd their orders, I went without our Foot at a litle distance from them, and could not so much as perceive one lighted match.

And here it will not be amiss to mention our order of battell, and how our Generall Officers were disposed, but I shall only be very particular in those who belong'd to Monsr. de Turenne: He divided his eight Lieut Generalls equally betwixt the horse and foot, four to each. To the first Line of foot compos'd of five battalions he appointed three, The Count de Broglio commanded Picardy and the Suisse which were the two right hand battalions: Monsr. de Castelneau those of Plessis and Turenne which were on the left hand, and M. du Passage that of la Feuillade which was in the midst. To command the horse which seconded these, consisting of about twenty-four Squadrons, he appointed also three: Mr de Barr had the charge of those on the right hand behind Mr de Broglio, Myself on the left hand behind Monsr. de Castelneau, and Monsr. d'Eclinvillers in the midst. The reserue of foot consisting of three battalions was commanded by Monsr. de Roncherolles, and that of horse by Monsr. de l'Islebonne who had under him eight Squadrons: This was Monsr. de Turenne's order of battell for that occasion.

Monsieur de la Ferté who drew up on his left hand, had one only line of foot consisting of six battalions, two lines of horse behind them, and a reserue of horse; Monsr. d'Hocquincourt who was placed on the right hand, had first four battalions of foot, then a line of horse, and behind them a second line of foot of four battalions more, with some horse on their wings, and a small reserue of horse not exceeding three or four Squadrons. Wee also had three false attacks; the first, of Monsr. de Turenne's troopes compos'd of two battalions of foot, being York and Dillon, and six Squadrons of horse, all commanded by Monsr. de Tracy who had orders to get as neer as he cou'd without being discover'd to the Prince of Condé's quarters; but not to fall on, till he heard the attack begun on the other side by us, and then to march directly to the Barrier of that quarter which he had been shewn some days before, and through it to endeavour to force his passage into the Town. The false attack from Monsr. de la Ferté's troopes was commanded by Mr. de la Guillottiere, who was to fall upon the Count de Fuensaldagne's quarter with two battalions, six Squadrons, two troopes of Dragoons, and two great guns. The false

178

attack of Monsieur d'Hocquincourt was not considerable, being only of four Squadrons, and some ropes with metches ty'd to them, commanded by Mr. de St Jean, who was to make his on Prince Francis of Lorraine's quarter. These were the orders of the Severall Armies for the attack of the whole Line.

And now Monsr de Turenne being come to the place appointed, found Mr d'Hocquincourt already there in person, but without his troopes which were not yet come up, thō they had but a very litle march to make. Hocquincourt said, his men were just coming, and would immediatly be upon the place, till which time he desir'd the attack might be deferred. But Monsr. de Turenne answer'd, That he could not possibly delay it, being now so neer the Line, that the Enemy would soon discover him, that therfore he desir'd him to make what hast he could to fall on after him: And his own troopes being by this time in order, he led them on himself (*on*) horseback to attack the Line.

Wee had in our march thether a very still faire night, besides the benefit of the moon, which sett as favorably for us as wee could desire, that is, just as wee came to the place appointed. As the moon went down, it began to blow very fresh and grew exceeding dark, in so much that the Enemy could neither see nor hear us, as otherwise they might; and they were the more surprised when the first news they had of us, was to find us within half cañon shott of them. I remember not to haue seen a finer sight of the nature, then was that of our foot when they were once in battell, and began to march towards the Lines; for then discovering at once their lighted metches, they made a glorious shew, which appear'd the more by reason of the wind, which kindled them and made them blaze throw the darkness of the night; for the breeze keeping the coal of their metches very clear, whensoever any of the Musketeers (*happened*) to shog against each other,[10] the metches struck fire, so that the sparkles were carryd about by the wind to increase the light.

Wee were no sooner discover'd by the Enemy then they fir'd three cannon at us, and either made fires or sett up lights along the Line: Our foot then lost no time in falling on; but had not the vigour of the Officers who led them, and the horse by keeping so

[10] '. . . et les soldats qui marchoient serrez venans a s'entrechoquer, . . .' (MS. p. 145).

close to their rear, obliged the common men to do their duty, they had not perform'd it as they ought, nor as I allways till that time had observ'd them to do, for I never knew them to go on so unwillingly as then; which notwithstanding, they stopt not till they came to the Line itself, where the resistance they found was not So great as they suspected; for in a very litle time all our five battalions made themselves masters of that part of it which they attacked; and then they who were appointed for that worke, began to make passages for the horse to enter, and every Squadron of horse went up to the very holes which I have mention'd and then threw down their fascines, which the foot immediatly took up and help'd to fill up both the ditches. This being perform'd the horse wheel'd off, and drew up about thiry yards behind, expecting till passage should be made for them.

While this was doing, one came to the left hand of the attack where I was at the head of the horse, and whisper'd to me that M. de Turenne was hurt, and that matters went no well on the right hand: Upon which intelligence to incourage the foot, and to let them understand how near wee were to them, I commanded the kettle drums to beat, and the trumpets of the Squadron of horse at the head of which I was to sound, which being heard by all our other horse, they did the like. This incouraged our foot sufficiently, but was of some prejudice to my own Squadron, and to that which was next it, for from a Redan on my left hand the Enemy by the beat of the kettle drums and sound of the trumpetts found where wee were, and plyd us with their shott. The Kettle drum was soon silenced, he being the first man who was kill'd of that Squadron where I was.

This happen'd just as Monsr. de la Ferté was beginning his attack, he having not put his men so soon in order as Mr. de Turenne had: But he either had not so good fortune, or found more resistance then our foot; for thō his Officers led up their men with good resolution into the very ditch, yet they were not able to master the Line, but were beaten off, and came running away to shelter themselves amongst the horse which I commanded. The disorder was very great, the Officers complaining aloud, that they had been abandon'd by their Soldiers, and the Soldiers crying out, that they had follow'd their Officers, who had not behav'd themselves as became them: which part had justice on their side I know not, but beaten off they were, and the horse far'd the worse for their ill success; for the Enemy seeing their lighted metches, plac'd their small shott amongst them with much more certainty then they could before.

By this time the Foot of our attack had made passages for our horse to enter, and Monsr. de Turenne's Regiment of Foot had found a Barriere which they open'd, and therby sav'd themselves the farther trouble of making a passage: Upon notice of which, Monsr. de Turenne order'd Mr. d'Eclinvillers to enter the first with four Squadrons of horse, and to be seconded by me; accordingly he enter'd the Lines with his three first Squadrons, but as the fourth was going in, they who had beaten off la Fertés Foot came along the Line to this Barriere, and finding only this Squadron of horse entring there, (the foot which had first master'd this Barriere having drawen off from thence, and advanced farther within the Line somewhat more on the right hand, as not thinking it necessary for them to stay and maintain that post when once the horse was enterd) powr'd into them a volly of small-shott, and threw severall hand granados in amongst them; with which the Collonel who commanded that Squadron, one Bodervitz a German, being shott from his horse thō not slaine, and his Major also much wounded, they were beaten off and the Enemy shutt that Barriere upon us.

Seeing therfore I could not enter there, I went along the Line on the right hand till I found another passage, by which I enter'd at the head of Mr. de Turenne's own Regiment of horse, which on that occasion made but two Squadrons; and finding the Enemys hutts on fire, which prov'd of great advantage to us (and As I heard afterwards was first thought upon by one Bout-de-bois Lieut. Colll. to la Feuillade) I advanced farther to see if any of the Enemy were yet drawn up behind them, and notwithstanding that some of their horse were still continuing there, it was so dark, that with the two first Squadrons I pass'd betwixt them without either seeing them, or being discover'd by them; But the third, which was the Regiment d'Espence[11] (*de Beauveau*) lighted on them, beat them, and took the Marquis de Conflans prisoner, who commanded the Regiment wch they defeated. By this time the day began to break, and I still advancing, came to the Countervalla-

[11] d'Espange (MS. p. 148).

tion, where finding no passage in it * * *[12]; [yet I found none, till I came to the River above the Town which divided the Lorraine quarter from that of Don Fernando de Solis]. And seeing that none of ours had yet pass'd over into the Lorraine quarter, I alter'd my resolution and thought it proper for me to go over the bridges into it.

This I undertook with the Regt. of Turenne only, which made but two Squadrons, the rest of the horse which should haue follow'd me having lost their way, and advanced as far as Prince Francis of Lorraine's Tent without finding any opposition. But being there, I saw four or five Squadrons of the Enemy drawn up, about the distance of muskett-shott from me upon another litle heigth. Wherupon I thought it best to halt a litle, till more horse came up to me, and drew up both my Squadrons upon one front, which just fill'd up the distance betwixt the Line and the Tents; after which I sent away three or four persons severally to bring the horse I wanted. While I was there expecting them, the Duke of Buckingham came up to me, and ask'd me, Why I would not pursue the Victory, and charge those which were before me? To which I answer, That I had no mind to receive an affront, and expose my self to a certain defeat, what I saw of the Enemy already being twice our number, besides what part of them might be behind the heigth on which they were; That should wee advance and be beaten, the Enemy might make himself master of the bridges which wee had pass'd, and break them down, by which means they wou'd both save themselves and the baggage of that quarter; That if they came up and charg'd me where I then was, I should at least ingage them on equall termes, because they could not outflanck me, besides which I had here the advantage of the ground; In short, that I expected more horse every moment, which being come I would then go and charge them. Thus resolved I continued there, and would not give way to his importunitys.

The Enemy and wee stood looking on each other for some time,

[12] There is a gap here in the text printed by Clarke (I, 222). The French MS. however (p. 198) supplies the missing words: 'Ou ne trouvant point de passage vers la ville Il [i.e., James] la costoia, l'aiant toujours a sa gauche et n'en rencontra point qu'en arrivant a la riviere au-dessus de la ville qui separoit le quartier de Loraine de celui de Fernando de Solis. . . .' Clarke, who notes this omission quotes the above passage from the text printed by Ramsay. This is the same as in the MS. (p. 198), although Ramsay modernised the spelling.

no horse coming to me; but, in mean time, some scatter'd men of ours fell to plunder Prince Francis his Tent, where besides his plate, there was a month's pay for his Army in ready mony, which had like to haue occasion'd our paying dear for it; for our horsemen hearing the noise which those plunderers made in taking it, in spight of their Officer's commands and threatnings, quitted their ranks one after another, and fell to ransack the Tent for their share of the booty; so that at last there were none left with me but Officers, and the twelve Cornetts; which being in full sight of the Enemy, I expected every moment to be charg'd and beaten: Being in this perplexity and hearing no news of those severall persons whom I had sent for horse, I thought it expedient to go myself and fetch them, and recommending to Monsr. de Montaulieu the Lieut Colll to make good that heigth till my return, I rode back, and found the Second Squadron of Villequier on the other side of the bridge going towards the Town, which I stop'd, and putting myself at their head, march'd over again: But scarce had the rear of the Squadron past the bridge, and the head being gott off from a small causwey begun to draw up into order again, when those horse which I had left to face the Enemy came running down the hill upon me in great disorder; At this the Squadron which I brought with me took such a fright that they also ran and left me, it being impossible to stop them. Wherupon I repassed the bridge, having seen four Squadrons on the other side of it, intending with them to come over again into the Lorraine quarter: But before I could bring them to the bridge, the Mareshall d'Hocquincourt with all his horse, and severall Squadrons of the other two Armies were come thether, and began to pass.

Seeing this, I thought there were horse enough that way, and so in stead of following them, I march'd directly the other way, betwixt the Countervallation and the Town, towards the Count de Fuensaldagne's quarter with my four Squadrons, two of which were Gendarmes commanded by Monsr. de Schomberg, the other two the Regiment de Gesvres, under Monsr. de Querneux. Being come with these upon a heigth from whence I could take a large view of all about me, I saw upon another heigth before me, betwixt the two Lines, severall Squadrons of horse drawn up facing towards the place wee enter'd. At first thought they were the Enemy; but seeing one of the Squadrons in red coats, I alter'd my opinion, and beleeved them to be our horse, taking that particular Squadron to be either the King's Chevaux-Legers, or his Gendarmes, their coats being of that coulour: Upon which conjecture I marched towards them to joyn my Body to theirs, because by observing their posture I knew they were facing an Enemy; but what that Enemy was I could not discern, a higher ground being interpos'd on my left hand which hinder'd my sight.

But by that time I was gott to the bottom of the hill and was beginning to march up, an Officer came to me from Monsr. de Turenne, with orders to come immediatly to him, and told me, that those whom he had taken for friends were enemys, and that Monsr. de Turenne was on the heigth over against them, who was in great want of troopes: Being thus inform'd I march'd back to joyn him, and came very opportunely with my four Squadrons, he having at that time about him only three Squadrons, and one Battalion which was rather for shew then of any use, it being compos'd of men and Officers rallyd together, who had been broken either by the Enemy, or by plundring.

And here it will be proper to give an account how Monsr. de Turenne came thether, and how he happen'd to be in the posture in which I found him. The Reader is then to understand, that Monsr. de la Ferté being repulsed at his own attack, enter'd the Line where wee had gone in before him: Being once there, he was desirous of doing something extraordinary; and putting himself at the head of ten or twelve Squadrons of horse, some of which were his own and some belonging to Mr. de Turenne, it being now brode day light, he advanced along betwixt the two Lines towards the Count de Fuensaldagne's quarter; and at the same time, some of the Foot of both their Armies advanced also, amongst whom was the Battalion of the French Guards belonging to M. de la Ferté's Army, but these last came up in a disorderly manner along the line of Countervallation. Some horse of the Enemy were drawn up, and yet standing on a heigth: These being seen by Monsr. de la Ferté, he march'd down the hill where he then was to charge them. But just before he ingag'd them, Monsieur de Turenne came up to the place from whence la Ferté was newly gone, and was much troubled to see him go on in that manner; he would willingly haue stopt him, but he came too late: so that all he could do was to stay two Squadrons which were follow-

SEDAN.

LE VICOMTE, A L'AGE DE DIX ANS COUCHE SUR L'AFFUST D'UN CANON.

Bonnard del.

J.B. Scotin Sculp.

5. VICOMTE DE TURENNE, AGED TEN, AT SEDAN

LOVIS DE BOVRBON PREMIER PRINCE DVSANG
Prince De Condé Duc Danguien Et Dalbret Pair. Et Grand Maistre
De France Gouuerneur De Bourgongne Et De Berry, De
Champagne & Brie.
B. Moncornet ex cum priuilegio

6. Louis de Bourbon, Prince de Condé

ing him, to draw them up upon the heigth, and to rally the battalion I have already mention'd; telling those that were about him, That he fear'd they should presently see la Ferté rowted; after which he himself should be hard put to it, to maintain that hill on which he was. As he said, so it happen'd, for M. de la Ferté was sufficiently beaten; and at the same time when they charg'd him, they sent some horse to fall upon our foot which were without the Countervallation, and cutt most of them in pieces, taking, as I remember, severall Officers of the Guards, but not offering to follow their advantage, or to advance up the hill where Mr. de Turenne was drawn up; but in stead of doing so, withdrew to the heigth from whence they came when they charg'd Monsr. de la Ferté.

In this posture I found affaires when I joyn'd Mr. de Turenne, who immediatly commanded me to draw within the two Lines, and draw up my Squadrons on the left hand of those who were already there: He then inform'd me of what had happen'd there, and that he apprehended, if the Enemy could gett together any foot, they would advance upon us and give us work enough to defend ourselves, there being no relying on those whom wee had there with us. After this, he enquired of me where I had been, and what was become of his Regiment of horse, and I gave him an account of all that had happen'd to me, and others, where I had been.

By this time some of our cañon, I think seaven, were got into the Line, and came to us, to our great Satisfaction, with some few other Squadrons of horse; and our cañon began to play upon the Enemy's horse, doing great execution amongst them. But notwithstanding this, Monsr. de Turenne was not without some apprehentions of what might happen, as doubting that the Enemy might advance upon us with foot; for seeing how ill our horse maintain'd their order, and that almost all our four (*foot*) were in confusion by their plundring, so that no body of our men was left in order, but that which was about himself, it was with no small reason that he fear'd some ill revolution in our success, in case he should be worsted where he was: But he continued not long in this apprehension, after our great guns began to play; for whether it was that they made the Enemies post too hott for them, or that for other reason they thought it not expedient for them to stay any longer there, about half an hour after the first gun was fir'd against them, they began to draw off. Once wee perceived some of their foot appearing, but immediatly they drew out of sight again; and this happen'd some what before their horse drew off.

I have since been informed by some who were then with the Prince of Condé (for it was he who was there and perform'd all that was considerable on the Enemys side) That he intended, if he could haue got two battalions of foot up to him, to haue come and charg'd as M. de Turenne beleeved he would; and that once he had gather'd that number, which were those whom wee saw appear, yet so soon as they came within rach of our cannon, they wou'd not be perswaded to advance one foot farther, but shog'd off.

And here 'tis admirable to consider, that these two great men, without being any other way advertis'd of each others being there, yet found it out on both sides by their mutuall conduct; Monsr. de Turenne positively affirming that the Pce of Condé was on the other hill, and that otherwise he would haue press'd those troopes more then now he would adventure to do; and the Prince of Condé saying the like of Monsr. de Turenne, adding farther, That if any one besides him had been there, he would certainly haue charg'd him.

This very consideration made Monsr. de Turenne, when the Prince drew off, not to follow him or endeavour to press upon his Rear; being satisfied with what already was perform'd, and unwilling to trust fortune with any thing farther, when the main of his design was already accomplish'd.

But Monsr. de Bellefonds, with some of the horse belonging to the Town, was not so cautious; for endeavouring to do somewhat on the Prince's Rear as he passed the River into the Archduke's quarter, he was received so warmly that he was beaten off with loss: After which the Prince went over at his ease, for the rest of our troopes took warning by the success of their fellows, and ventur'd not again to charge him; and when he had pass'd through our old Camp, he began to rally his scatter'd men beyond the brook, and march'd away for Cambray. As for the Archduke (and) the Count de Fuensaldagne, they went to Douay with not above a Squadron or two in their company, and pass'd through our baggage, where the Archduke was known by some of Monsr.

de Turenne's Servants; and had one Squadron of our horse been there, they might probably haue taken him.

Tis now reasonable I should give some account of what was done by Mr. d'Hocquincourt. I have already mention'd in the beginning of this Relation, that, when Monsr. de Turenne fell on, he was not in a rediness with his troopes, and as I have been since informed by some of his Officers, it was break of day before he began his attack. He storm'd the Line on the right hand of the place where wee enter'd, and found litle or no resistance; So that the greatest Imployment of his foot was to make a passage for his horse, at the head of which enter'd the Mareshall himself, and came directly to the bridge, over which he pass'd into the Lorraine quarter, after I had been there and was gone out of it. And along with him went most of the horse belonging to the other two Armys. He met no opposition till he came to the brook which divided the Lorraine from the Pce of Condés quarter, where he found Mr. de Marsin drawn up on the other side with severall Squadrons of horse, which stopt him there a considerable time; the Army having some few foot, or some Troopers with their Carabins who maintain'd that passage so long, that most of the foot in that quarter had leisure to get off: and when some of our horse coming out of the Town upon him, oblig'd him to draw off, he made his retreat in so orderly a manner, that he march'd out of the Line without being broken, making use of his foot or Troopers who stood in stead of them, as he had done formerly at the brook: For as he drew out of the Line he placed them behind it, from whence they fir'd upon our horse, who not being so well order'd nor led on as they ought to haue been, were kept at a distance by the fire they made; so that under their favour Mr. de Marsin gott out of the Line, and So march'd off in excellent order, till he joyn'd the Prince of Condé at the same time when he was rallying his men as I have related.

Much about this time, when Monsr. de Marsin was making his retreat out of the Line, Mr. de Mondejeu Governour of Arras being come out of the Town, some (of) the old horse Officers seeing him, desir'd he would put them into better order, because neither M. d'Hocquincourt nor any of the Generall Officers there present, had perform'd that part of their duty as they ought: But he absolutely refused it, saying, he came only there as a Volonteer,

187

and thought it very unreasonable for him to pretend to share in any part of the honour of that day with them: that the ordering of their men belong[ed] wholly to them: and as for himself, that he had gain'd sufficient reputation in the defence he had made, and was now come out with no other intention then to serue those who had so bravely releeved him.

It remains now that I relate what happen'd in our false attacks. As for those of M. de la Ferté, and M. d'Hocquincourt, they follow'd their orders punctually, and no considerable accident befell them, but that the first had the best part of the plunder belonging to the Count of Fuensaldagnes quarter, which was the place appointed them for their false attack: But Monsr. de Turenne's had not so good fortune, M. de Tracy who commanded them, and who follow'd also very punctually his orders, having had a much different adventure: For being commanded to march without the least noise into a bottom which was within canon-shott of the Enemies line, and there to ly closs, without falling on, till some time after wee had begun our attack, which wee supposd that of necessity he must haue heard, it happend quite otherwise; because the wind proving contrary, and with all blowing fresh when wee began to storme the Line, he heard nothing of it. At last the day breaking, and no noise coming to him, he and all his men were verily perswaded that some accident had hinder'd our attack: however he resolved to stay in his post somewhat longer, and there he continued till he saw some horse coming out of the Line which he conjectur'd to be such as were sent abroad to make discoverys; and presently after them a Squadron or two which he took to be the horse-guard coming to their accustom'd post, but seeing more still coming out, he concluded it was to fall on him as having discover'd where he lay. Vpon which he orderd his two Battalions of foot, to Save themselves by marching to the Castle of Neufville vitas, which was close by them; and himself with the horse took their way towards Bapaume. He had march'd a good part of his way thether, before he was sensible of his mistake, but the foot whom he left at the Castle were sooner undeceived, for most of the Lorraine horse and many out of the Pce of Conde's quarter drew off that way, it being their nearest passage to Cambray; which our foot seeing, they commanded out the Aide-Majors of each Regimt with fifty men apeece, to skirmish with them as they past by. This

188

they perform'd, but at length they advanc'd so far, that some of the Enemies horse gott in amongst them, and kill'd every man of that party.

I will not take upon me to give an exact account of what numbers were slain on either side in this memorable action; But by what I saw myself of the bodies lying on the place, as well freinds as foes, I could not guesse them to be above four hundred. Wee had never a Generall Officer amongst that number, and I remember but one Collonell, M. de Puymarais, Colll of horse, a brave young gentleman, Son to Monsr. de Barr, one of our Lieut Genls, but very few Captains. It fell so heavy upon none as upon that Squadron of Eclinvilliers who had behav'd themselves so ill a day or two before, where Monsr. de la Ferté led up to charge when he was beaten: They were it seemes desirous to recover the reputation they had lost, and therfore charg'd so home, that the rest giving ground sooner then they, they were beaten worse, and I was inform'd most of their Officers kill'd upon the place.

The number of our wounded men was not considerable: Monsr. de Turenne had a bruise, besides a shott upon his armes, and his horse shott under him. Monsr. de la Ferté had his horse kill'd. But of all our Genl Officers I remember not any hurt, excepting the Count de Broglio who was shott through the thigh; and of inferiour Officers the number was not great. The Volonteers all escap'd well, excepting those who were with Mr. d'Humieres, who received so home a charge from one of the Enemies Squadrons, that the Marquis de Breuauté et la Clotte, two of them, were so desperatly wounded that they dyd afterwards. Biscara and others of them were much hurt, as also the Cheualier de St Gé and severall Officers of his Regiment.

On the Enemies' side the General Officers escap'd well, for I remember not to haue heard that any of them were hurt or taken, excepting the Baron de Briolle, one of the Pce of Condé's Mareshalls de Camp, who was a very brave old gentleman; and who, thō he had the misfortune to be taken and wounded in fighting against his King, yet some days before he dyd of his hurts which he then received, show'd he was no Rebell in his heart, however accidentally he had been one: for Sending for his Son who had been made prisoner with him, he told him some houres before his death, by what inducements and in what manner he had been drawn into rebellion; after which he commanded him on his blessing, never to be seduced again, on what pretence soever, to take up armes against his Soveraign. Vpon which admonition of a dying Father the young man so heartily repented, that he prov'd himself both a loyall Subject, and a dutifull Son: Vpon which account he was sett free.

I can not be exact in the number of the prisoners: but it was comonly reported that they were about three thousand, And I am apt to beleeve the account was true, for fifteen hundred of the Lorraine foot were all taken together in an envelope which was in their quarter. Wee found about sixty three brass cannon of all sorts within the Line, and all things proportionable for so great a Train. As for their baggage, they lost it all, amongst which our Soldiers found good plunder, the General Officers in those Countrys being all serv'd in plate, and every one obliged to haue a considerable quantity of baggage, because it was impossible to subsist without it in such Armies: And to shew in what Vast proportion they use to be furnished, some few days after this, when our Army passed over the Escaut below Cambray, it was commonly reported by some who pretended to haue reckon'd the number, that wee had above seaven thousand waggons and carts attending us, our Army at that time not consisting of many more then twenty thousand men; thō when wee were all together at forceing of the Lines, wee were about fourteen thousand foot, eleven thousand horse, and four hundred Dragoons.

The day after wee had thus releeved our Town, I was sent with two thousand horse to Peroñe where the Court then was, to convoy it to Arras, where they continued for some few days; During which time our Army camp'd within the Lines of the Enemy, our men making use of their hutts, and finding their quarters so well furnish'd with forage, that wee never sent out for any, while wee stayd upon the place.

On the last of August wee march'd towards Cambray and camp'd at Sauchy-Cauchy, and at the same time the Court return'd to Peronne. On the 3d of September wee march'd to Thun[13] St Martin, which stands on the Escaut, and there pass'd it on bridges which wee made, advancing the next day as far as Saulsoy, which is the midway betwixt Cambray and Valenciennes; And the

[13] Thuyn St. Martin (MS., p. 162).

next day they came to Kircurayn,[14] (*Kievrain*) which is two good leagues short of St Guilain. The 6th wee fell back upon Quesnoy, a Town situate between Valenciennes and Landrecies; in which place thō there was a Governour, yet he had no considerable garrison. The Town of itself was not Strong, the outworks having been demolish'd after the Spanish fashion, which is only enough to hinder them from being defended, but with all so litle slighted, that they may be repair'd with ease, and put into as good condition as before. This place was surrender'd to us, the day after wee came before it. It was no sooner in our hands but wee employd ourselves in repairing the old out-works, and raising new where they were wanting.

Some few days after, leaving a strong garrison in Quesnoy wee march'd to Bavay, and so to Binche on the 11th. The Town last mention'd lyes two or three leagues wide of Mons, and is of equall distance with Mons from Brussels. Binche was deliver'd to us on the same day wee came before it. Here wee stayd till the 22, only to eat up the Enemies' Country, and give leisure to our men in Quesnoy to fortify themselves.

During this march Monsr. de Turenne, who was then our Sole Generall, the other two Mareshalls having left the Army when wee left Arras, gave more employment to the Lieut. Generalls, then they were used to haue: for before this time none but he whose turn it was, had any thing in particular to do, more then to attend the Generall; but he now order'd, that as he whose day it was, march'd at the head of the horse which had the Van, so also he who had been releeved, should march at the head of the Foot, and he who went out before him, at the head of the other wing of horse which had the Reer; so that every day there were three Lieutenant Generalls on duty. And he found so great ease and benefit by this new order, that during all the time I continued afterwards in the French Seruice, he kept it up. And he further directed them, that whensoever they came to any brook or défilé, they should not stay till those before them were passed over, but make a passage for themselves, on the one hand, or on the other, keeping still the Van betwixt them, and that side on which the Enemy might come: by which means he was inabled to make greater marches; for generally after this, observing the method

[14] Keurain (MS., p. 162).

above mention'd, wee pass'd over the défilés at once in three places.

In the time of this march the Enemys Cravats[15] were very busy about us, so that it was not safe for any man to straggle, thō never so litle, from the body of the Army. And sometimes they would get up by two or three in a Company into our Army, and when they found their opportunity, take some or other, and carry him away: One of them was once so bold, as to put himself into the rancks of the first Squadron of the Reer of horse, at the head of which I march'd. I remember that immediatly after I had pass'd a défilé, and through some bushes, which were on the other side of it, hearing a noise in the Squadron behind me, I turn'd about to ask the reason of it; when some of my Soldiers brought before me a Cravat, who had placed himself in the midmost ranck of that Squadron, as if he had been a Trooper belonging to the Regiment, and was so unfortunate to put himself the very next man to one, whom he had taken some few days before, being also at that very time mounted on the horse which he had then taken from him: But he was soon discover'd by the Trooper, who therupon calld out aloud, This is he who tooke me prisoner some days since, and this is my horse on which he rides. He layd hold on him immediatly and brought him to me. The fellow confessed, that himself and some others of his Camarades, the Cravats, had put themselves in ambuscade behind those bushes which I had newly pass'd, and had resolved to disperse and mingle with the Army: That had it not been his misfortune so to haue placed himself as to be discover'd, he was confident that before night he had taken a prisoner, instead of being one himself.

In this our march I know it was wonder'd at by some, that so considerable and victorious an Army as ours then was, should undertake no Seige of consequence that Year; But if they had consider'd, how far the season of a Campagne was then declin'd, and

---

[15] From the French 'cravate', a Croat or Croatian. They were Croatian mercenaries, light-armed cavalry in this instance and probably as a rule. The first example of the use of the word in English, cited in the *Oxford English Dictionary*, is from the *London Gazette*, No. 3903/2 (1703): 'Monsieur de Guiche, Colonel-General of the Regiments of Horse called the Cravates.' Defoe (*Memoirs of a Cavalier*, 1721) spells the word 'Crabats'. The article of neckwear known as a Cravat was first adopted in France 'in imitation of the linen scarf worn round their necks by the Croatian mercenaries', says the *O.E.D*.

that wee were not furnish'd with provisions of any sorte for a great undertaking, they could not haue thought it strange, that wee contented ourselves with taking of Quesnoy; for thō that Town of itself was not very considerable, yet it was of great advantage to us for the carrying on of our designs in the next Campagne: for Monsr. de Turenne, even thus early, had contrived the business of the next year. And thō it was a bold undertaking to make good that place, seated as it was in the very midst of the Spanish garrisons, yet our fortifying it, renderd his designs for the ensuing year more easy to be compass'd, and in particular the taking of Landrecies, of which I shall say more in its proper place: So that in reality the taking and making good this Town, was of more consequence to us, then any other Town which wee could haue master'd at that Season of the year.

While wee stay'd at Binche, the Enemy drew together their baffled Army at Mons, sheltering themselves under favour of the Town, and endeavouring by their partys to molest our foragers. But such was the vigilance and conduct of our Generall, that they did us litle harm; thō their Cravats were still plying about us, and laying many ambuscades with small success: Yet one day I remember, they miss'd but narrowly of taking an advanced guard, with Mr. d'Humieres, and severall Officers of the guard in my company. Being come up to that post, wee saw a party of the Enemys horse about our own number, coming out from a wood, which was on our left hand, towards us; but when they were at the distance of half cañon-shott, they turn'd off again as if they were affraid of being follow'd: wherupon some of the Officers propos'd to me, that I should pursue, and push them; Monsr. d'Humieres and some few with him, who were somewhat advanced before the rest, began immediatly to gallop after them; which been (*being*) seen by those about me, they spurr'd on eagerly, and left me, without receiving my answer whether or not I would approve it. At this I put on my horse to his full speed, and got to the head of the formost: It was all I could do to stop their rashness, and they grumbled sufficiently, that I had hinder'd them from taking the whole party, But I told them, I was as morally certain as I could be of any thing, that by stopping them I had preserv'd them from some ambuscade, and that I could not beleeve the Enemy would haue come so near us, but out of design to decoy us into some inconveniency. My opinion prov'd true, for no sooner had I stop'd my men, but the Enemy turn'd about and fac'd us, offering to draw us on by skirmishing; But when they saw that they could inveigle us no farther, they march'd away towards Mons: Immediatly after which I saw two hundred horse go off, which had hidd themselves in a litle bottom behind a wood not far distant, and thether it was that the first party had design'd to haue drawn us. Upon which discovery both Monsr. d'Humieres, and the rest of the Officers thank'd me for preventing their pursuite: for had they gone forward, in all probability most of them must haue been taken, because our main-guard, which was posted on the other side of the brook, could not haue releeved them time enough; the défilé over the brook and afterwards through the Village, on the other side of which the advanced guard was placed, being so great, that the Action had been past, before their friends could haue come up to their assistance.

After wee had stayd at Binche about ten days, and eaten up all the forage of the neighbouring Country, Monsr. de Turenne thought it was now high time for him, to draw back towards Quesnoy, before the falling of the rains which would haue made the ways troublesome for our cañon, and so vast a quantity of baggage as wee had then in our Army.

Having taken this resolution he chose to return by the way of Maubeuge, because the Country betwixt that place and Binche was more open and had fewer défilés then the direct way to Bavay. And besides this consideration he had another full as prevalent, which was, that the Spanish Army lay then at Mons; so that in case he should haue taken his march by them, he must haue had no less an Enemy then the Prince of Condé in his way, before whom there was no making a false step; and wee could not but expect to haue him on our wings, in our drawing off, and watching all opportunitys of the least advantage which should be offer'd to him.

Monsr. de Turenne therfore to avoid an affront on his first days march, which was the 22d of September, sent off all the baggage at break of day, with about six or eight Squadrons of horse, and M. de la Ferté's Dragoons, which march'd at their head, or on their flancks, as occasion offer'd. They were no sooner in their way, but he follow'd the Reer of them with his Van, and that he might be the less expos'd to any attempt, he march'd in a closer order then he formerly had used, as by the draught of it may more easily be seen. Here the draught * * *16

Yet he so managed it, that he could suddainly put himself into his ordinary forme of battell, and that without the least confusion; for upon the right hand of all march'd the first Line of that wing which had the Van that day, upon their left hand half of the first Line of foot; Again on their left hand the second Line of horse of that wing which had the Van; and on their left hand, the other half of the first Line of foot: And so after the same manner on their left hand, the other wing of horse, and the second Line of foot; and on the left hand of all, the reserue of horse; so that wee march'd with four Battalions and five Squadrons of horse afront, Each file consisting of * * * Battalions and * * *17 Squadrons. In this order wee march'd with our greatest cannon in the Van, and some few small pieces in the Reer, and as wee came to any pass or défilé, the Reer faced about with their feild pieces, while the Van past over; which when they had done, then they drew up on the other side, and faced about also, leaving sufficient space for the rest of those who were to follow them, to draw up after they had pass'd: In this maner they continued, till all were come over to them, and then the whole body began to march again.

By that time wee had march'd above a league, wee discover'd about fourty Squadrons of the Enemies horse coming towards us on our right hand: The main-body of them came not within cannon-shott of us, keeping still a narow brook betwixt us and them, and only sending over it their Cravats, with a Squadron or two of horse to second them. The Cravats came so very near us, that severall of our Foot just stepping out of their rancks, fir'd on them betwixt the Intervals of the horse, which having done, they re-turn'd into their order. Thus they march'd along by us, skirmish-ing, and wee never making any stop for them. They follow'd us till they came to a pass not far distant from Maubeuge, expecting still to find an opportunity of doing some execution on us. But

16 James had probably intended here to insert a sketch, showing how the troops marched. The translator began by writing 'comme on peut le voir par le plan', then deleted these words in the MS. (p. 167) and went ahead as below.

17 There are similar blanks in the MS. (pp. 167, 168).

our Generall was so carefull, and order'd his march with so much caution, that thō the Prince of Condé himself was at the head of those Squadrons, he was never able to fasten one charge upon us, or to put any of our horse into the least disorder; neither indeed were they in any liklyhood of doing it, unless it were once, and that was at the pass I mention'd near Maubeuge. Att that place they press'd a litle on our last troopes in their going over; but seeing our men turn'd so readily upon them, and in so good order, they thought it not expedient to charge them, but after having thus tasted them, suffer'd them to draw off quietly: By this time they found it was to no purpose to follow us any farther, for they durst not adventure to pass the défilé after us, for fear of exposing themselves too much, and therfore march'd back towards their own Camp, while wee continued our way to Maubeuge.

It was dark night before wee got thether, and thō our Camp was mark'd out to us betwixt the woods and the Town, yet what through the darknes, and what by confusion in which wee found our baggage, and more them (*than*) both by the straightness of the ground betwixt the Town and woods, none of our troopes could find out their appointed quarters; so that they fell into a very great disorder, and were so intangled amongst the baggage, that Monsr. de Turenne could not possibly disengage them, or bring them into order. At last finding there was no remedy for the confusion, he got together two or three battalions of foot, and plac'd them without all our baggage, in that side on which the Enemy might possibly haue come. He stayd with them all night in person, and so soon as it was broad day light drew up the Army again into good order, and that day being the 23d of September wee march'd to Bavay.

In our going thether, the whole Regiment of the Enemies Cravats pursu'd a small party of ours to the very Van of the Army, and came so near us, before they were aware of it, that all of them were in danger of being taken: for our first two Squadrons disbanded after them, and follow'd them so close, that they had no other way for their Escape then to gain the shelter of the woods; many of them being forced to quitt their horses for their own preseruation: And truly, I beleeve, they lost more men and horses on that occasion, then ever at any time before or since.

At our arrivall at Bavay wee demolisht the walls of that litle

196

Town, the inhabitants wherof had abandon'd it the first time wee camp'd by it. It had four Roman ways mett in it, and being not above three or four leagues from Quesnoy, it might haue been very troublesome to that garrison, and disturb'd them in raising their contributions, if the Enemy had put any troopes in it during the winter.

From Bavay wee march'd the next day to Baudignies, and camp'd close by the Quesnoy. There wee stayd till the 28th, and then march'd to Château Cambresis, after wee had consum'd the forage therabouts. During the time of our abode there, the workes of the Quesnoy were so far advanced, and the place so well furnish'd with all kinds of stores and other necessaries, that the winter now coming on apace, it would haue prov'd too difficult a peice of work for the Enemy to undertake, after wee were drawn off into our winter quarters.

While wee continued at Château en Cambresis, one of our Convoys of forage was like to haue been defeated, and was so near it, that the Count de Renel, a Collonel who commanded it, was made prisoner at the first charge, in leading up the foremost Squadrons which were broken by the Enemy; and had not the remaining horse, which were of the old Regiments, as namely, la Valette, Grammont, and others, after that, done their part with great bravery, they had been cutt off intirely and all our foragers expos'd: But notwithstanding that they saw their Commander taken, and their first Squadrons routed, they advanced upon the Enemy and forced them to draw off, without any further attempt; after which they march'd away with the foragers to our Camp, without having lost any of them. The Party of the Enemy which made this onsett, came from Cambray, and, as I was inform'd, consisted of eight Squadrons of horse, ours were about the same number; and had the Enemy improv'd their first advantage, they must certainly haue beaten the whole party, and taken as many of our foragers as they could haue driven away with them.

This adventure obliged Mr. de Turenne to be more cautious afterwards in his forages, and to send out Stronger Convoys with them. Two or three days after this accident, when they went abroad again, he himself went along with them to the same place where the Count de Renel had been taken, but with a much stronger Convoy; for he took with him above twenty Squadrons of horse, two Battalions of foot, and about four feild peices, supposing the Enemy would now come stronger out upon our foragers then formerly, and he was not deceived in his conjecture: for some time after he had posted his troopes for the best security of his foragers, wee saw about six Squadrons of the Enemy coming out of a wood which was close by us, and where they had been in ambuscade. They cam on at a round gallop, as if they would haue fallen on two or three Squadrons of our Gendarmes, who were drawn up in a litle bottom betwixt the wood, and a Village where many of our foragers were at that time loading their horses: On one side of this Village was Monsr. de Turenne himself with the greatest part of the horse, and one battalion of foot; but, there being a small pass betwixt us and the place where the Gendarmes were posted, which were commanded by Monsr. de Schomberg, had the Enemy push'd on vigourously, they might haue routed him, before wee could haue come to his releif: he therefore, considering the danger in which he was, found there was no way of saving himself, but only by a bold action; and accordingly advanced towards the Enemy, who seeing him come up to charge them, and not being able to discern what was in the bottom from whence he came, in all probability imagin'd he had more behind to second him, for immediatly they withdrew into the wood again: he was very glad of their retreat, as he had reason, and stopt short upon the litle higth where he then was, without offering to follow them, because he was not strong enough, besides he knew not what other troopes they might haue, either within the wood or behind it. There he stayd, more horse being sent from us to strengthen him, till our foragers were all loaded, and that wee began to draw off; which wee did without seeing any other Enemy appear.

Even after this wee sent such strong Convoys with our Foragers, that for the rest of the Campagne the Enemy made not any attempt upon them: And wee were full as carefull of the Convoys which wee sent to the Quesnoy with provisions, for all of them were so well guarded, that the Spaniards thought it not for their advantage to sett upon them.

The last that went thether while wee stayd at Château en Cambresis, was commanded by me, after which wee march'd into forage-quarters, and spent some weeks upon the fronteers. There

wee took two Castles, one call'd d'Anvillers, and the other Giron-
delle not far from Rocroy, which wee demolish'd: And then it was
time for us to march into our winter quarters, the cold season being so far advanced that it was become too late that year for the
Enemy to attempt anything upon the Quesnoy.[18]

---

[18] The entry in *Campagnes* (p. 172) stops at this point. In the *Life* (I, 243–244)
there are two additional paragraphs as follows:

'The Campagne of 1654 being thus ended, His Royall Highness repair'd as
formerly to the French Court at Paris, where he arrived about the middle of December, and there spent the remaining part of the winter; Towards the end of which his
brother the Duke of Gloucester took his leave of him, the King his brother having
sent My Lord of Ormonde on purpose to bring him to him at Colen.

'The summer following his Royal Highness went to make his fourth and last Campagne in France, of which he gives the following account in his Memoires.'

This is followed by the entry for 1655, which I reprint below.

The reader will at once notice the contrast between the regular syntax and correct
orthography of this passage, which comes presumably from the pen of William Dicconson, and the rambling, irregular syntax and fantastic spelling (incorrect even in an
age when orthography was not yet fixed) of the passages in the first person which have
been copied from James's own memoirs—copied with, as I presume, an accuracy as
unsparing as it is no doubt faithful.

1655*

THE DUKE'S FOURTH AND LAST CAMPAIGN IN FRANCE

THIS Campagne of 1655 began with putting in execution what was design'd the year before, when wee took and fortified Quesnoy; for wee open'd it with the Siege of Landrecies, and then our Army found the benefit of having that place to freind.[1] For immediatly after they sat down before Landrecies, the Enemy came and posted themselves betwixt that Town and Guise, thereby to hinder all communication betwixt our Army and our own Country; so that had not this been timely foreseen, and their design frustrated by our laying up a magazine of all necessarys in Quesnoy, sufficient for the carrying on of that Seige, Monsr. de Turenne must haue been put to great extremities; Wheras he was now so much before hand with the Spaniards, that the post which they had taken up, was of small advantage to them, and no manner of hindrance to the French in pursuance of their Seige, convoys passing every day with great ease and security from Quesnoy to the Camp: So that no other inconvenience follow'd from the Enemies being posted near Guise, then that it hindered some Officers and Volunteers from getting into the Army, while the Seige lasted, whose affaires had hinder'd them from marching with it, when it came before the Town.

Of this number I was one; for which reason I shall not give a particular description of that Seige: Most of us who came short, and could not joyn our Army time enough, were either at Guise or la Fere while this Seige continued; I was myself at the last of these places, expecting the opportunity of some Convoy to favour my

---

* Reprinted from the *Life*, ed. Clarke, I, 245–264, for the reason indicated in connection with the entries for 1653 and 1654 above. I have not however reproduced the last three paragraphs (pp. 264–266), because these are summarised in the first paragraph for 1656 in the French MS.

[1] More concise in the MS. *Campagnes* (p. 173).

desire of being present at the Seige; but the Spanish Army was so posted in our neighbourhood, that the passage was render'd too difficult for any of us to attempt. Monsr. de la Feuillade, with two or three officers and a small party of horse, ventur'd to haue pass'd, but they were mett by the Enemy and beaten, la Feuillade himself being taken and desperatly wounded. This ill success of his, so far discourag'd all of us, that wee layd aside the thought of it; so that till the Enemy drew off, which was a day or two before the surrender of the Town, wee came not to our Army.

This Seige was a very favourable one to our Soldiers; those of the Town contenting themselves with a bare defence, according to the ordinary formes, and not making any vigourous Sallys during the whole time it lasted; so that wee lost as few men, as could possibly be expected, in the mastering of such a place, and no officer of note but Monsr. de Tracy, who had the Command of all the German horse, as being the eldest Collonel of them. The Garrison held out only, till a breach was made by a Mine in the face of one of their Bastions, and a lodgment made upon it, after which they capitulated and Surrender'd.

After the Town was deliver'd up to us, our Army stayd by it some days to repair the breaches and outworks, and to slight our Line of Circumvallation; and the Enemy drew back into their own Country betwixt Mons and Valenciennes behind the Rivers, not thinking themselves strong enough, as indeed they were not, to hazard a battell with us on equall termes; So that their business was to attend our motions, and endeavour to hinder our undertaking any other considerable Seige.

And now by that time wee were in a readiness to march, the King and the Cardinal came to the Army, and wee march'd down along by the Sambre, as far as la Bussiere, which is within a league of Thuyn, a small Town belonging to the Pays de Liege. Having spent some time in this march, and stayd a day or two at la Bussiere, wee march'd back, and passing by Avênes invested la Capelle; and thō wee camp'd within a league or two of it with our whole Army, yet on better consideration wee did not beseige it, as not judging it a place of so great importance, that our Army should lose so much time as was necessary to reduce it. And therfore leaving it, wee pass'd the Sambre, advancing into Haynault as far as Bavay on the 11 of August. The Town I last mention'd is betwixt Quesnoy and Mons; and our intentions were to advance yet farther into the Enemie's Country, and to pass the Haisne, a litle River which coming from Mons, takes its course by St Guislain, and falls into the Schald[2] at Condé: But sending to view the passages upon it, wee found that the Enemy had fortifyd the River from St Guislain as far as Condé, with a very strong Brestwork and Redouts, with platformes ready made in them at the distance of every three or four hundred paces; which together with the difficulty of approaching the River itself, by reason of the lowness of the Country, which was full of ditches, and there being no way to come to the River but along narrow dikes, made the passage very hard to be forced. Which notwithstanding, in a consultation that was held in the King's presence, where were assisting the Cardinal and the two Generalls, Mr. de Turenne and Mr. de la Ferté, together with the Mareshalls de Villeroy, de Grammont, du Plessis, and myself, it was once upon the point of being resolved, that wee should attempt to force our passage au Pont de Haisne; And had it not been for Mr. de Turenne, that opinion had taken place: for the Cardinal hauing propos'd it as an undertaking which would be of high reputation in the world, if wee could make a way over a River in the face of a formidable Army, he was seconded and his advice confirm'd by most who were there present, whither out of complaisance, or by the force of his reasons,[3] I shall not pretend to judge; but resolv'd on, it had been, had not Mr. de Turenne oppos'd it, by representing the great difficulties which would be found in that attempt.

For, said he, Besides that the whole River is strongly fortifyed all along, there is no approaching it but by the side of a Dike, by reason that all the ground of our side is full of ditches, so that the Enemy would haue a double advantage over us; and thō at last, I beleeve, wee may force our passage, wee should unavoidably loose many men in compassing our design: he added, That it was not

[2] The Scheldt. James elsewhere calls it by its French name of Escaut. This description of the Haine is omitted in the MS. *Campagnes* (p. 175).

[3] James or his translator ascribes this, not to Mazarin's arguments, but to Turenne's. Thus the text of the MS. *Campagnes* reads (p. 176): 'Mais les sentiments de Mr. de Turenne qui etoit contre cette entreprise, prevalut, soit par la complaisance qu'on eut pour luy, soit par la force de ses raisonnements. Il en fit voir les difficultez. . . . ' It seems more likely that the text of the *Life* (I, 247–248) gives the accurate account, and that in this Council it was Mazarin's opinion which so far impressed the others that it nearly prevailed.

this consideration alone, which mov'd him to disuade that undertaking, but the beleef he had, that the thing wee aim'd at, might be
effected without running So great a hazard, or venturing the lives
of so many Soldiers; That instead of our endeavouring to force a
passage there, wee should rather march, and pass the Escaut
somewhat below Bouchain, and then passing by Valenciennes and
leaving it on our right hand, should march to Condé, and there
pass the Escaut again; That in so doing, wee should take the
Enemy on the flanck, and therby render that great intrenchment
of no effect to them.

With these and other arguments he convinced the Cardinal,
and all those of the Councill who had abetted his opinion: And
in pursuance of M. de Turenne's proposall, wee march'd immediatly from Bavay towards Bouchain, upon notice of which the
Enemy march'd also toward Valenciennes, and posted themselves
very advantageously, having their Right cover'd by the woods of
St Amand, and their left by the Town, and the old Line ready
made to their hands, upon Mont Azin, from the woods to the
Town; and instead of endeavouring to hinder our passing the
River, they fell on repairing the old Line, which by the next
morning was put into very good defence; which whilst they were
a doing, wee past the River on our bridges of boates, and by eight
next morning, being the 14th, pass'd over our whole Army, leaving some few troopes behind to secure our baggage from the
garrison of Bouchain.

I have been since inform'd by some of the Enemys own Officers, who were then upon the place, that they came thither with an
intention of making good that post, for upon the proposall of that
march, the Prince of Condé oppos'd it, unless they would absolutely resolve to maintain it when they were once there; telling
them plainly, That he would not stirr a step, unless the Spaniards
would ingage their promise to do this: They gave him all the
assurances he could desire: Yet he foretold them, that in that post,
wee should certainly come upon them, and then it would be too
late to think of retiring, by which they would expose their whole
Army to be beaten, But whatever arguments he urg'd were not
sufficient to divert them, for march they would; but at the same
time they confirm'd their promise to him, of making good that
Post: So wee found them there.

And now our Partys having brought us word how they were posted, as soon as wee could put our troopes in battell, wee march'd towards them; and being come within a league of them, seeing they were well intrenched on that advantageous post, wee halted till our cañon and ammunition, which were somewhat behind, could come up to us. During this our stay, Monsieur de Turenne went with a Squadron or two, to view their Line, advancing till he came within cannon shott, and then they fir'd at him with their great guns; which confirmed him in the beleef, that they would maintain their post: upon which he commanded Mr. de Castelnau with his Camp-Volant, which consisted (*of*) about twelve Squadrons and two or three Battalions, to march, and post himself on the Enemys right hand on the high way which comes from St Amand; that at the same time wee should attack their front, he might see what could be done upon their flanck.

No sooner was Castlenau gott thether, but he perceived the Enemy was drawing off towards Condé, of which (*he*) immediatly advertis'd M. de Turenne; who order'd him to press upon their Reer, and by that means retard, if possibly he could, their march, till he could come up himself with the body of the Army: and till wee receiv'd that advice which wee had from Mr. de Castelnau, wee perceived nothing of the Enemys retreat; neither indeed could wee by reason of the ground; their Line being, as I have said before, upon a heigth, so that wee could only discover such troopes as they would shew us.

It seems that so soon as the Arch Duke, and the Count de Fuensaldagne were inform'd that our whole Army was past the River, and that they saw us marching up towards them, they repented themselves of being So far ingaged; and, as the Prince of Condé had foretold them, resolv'd to march back to Condé, and there to pass the River. This resolution they took without consulting him, so that the first notice he had of it, was by an Adjutant, who brought him word, that the Arch Duke was marching away, and desir'd him to bring up the Reer, and make good the retreat, thō it was the turn of the Spaniards to haue done it: And that they might haue as litle disorder as they could, they sent their great cañon into Valenciennes, and only carryed off with them their small feild peeces.

Had Monsr. de Castelnau done his part as he ought according

to his orders, and also as he might, the Prince of Condé would haue been reduced to great extremitys: Tis true he fail'd not in point of courage, but meerly in conduct, for he was so hasty that coming to the Pont de Beuerage (where runs a brook which coming from the woods falls into the Escaut on the other side of Valenciennes, where Monsr. de Marsin was posted with severall Squadrons and some Dragoons) he would not stay for his foot, but endeavour'd with his horse alone to haue forced the pass upon him, and charg'd over the bridge twice or thrice, thō he was still beaten with some losse, and at last was forced to Stay till his foot were advanced to him; who were longer in coming up then they needed to haue been, by reason that all his horse were gott before them into the way. But so soon as the Enemy discover'd his foot advancing, they immediatly drew off, and left the bridge free for him to pass over, which he did. And by this time, Monsr. de Turenne was come up with his Van, to the Reer of Mr. de Castelnau's troopes, and sent severall Messengers to him with orders, that he should press the Enemy as much as possibly he could, therby to hinder their march, that he might come up with them in their retreat: But Castelnau perform'd not what was expected of him, suffering himself to be overreach'd by some of the Prince his Officers, who bringing up the Reer of their Army and seeing M. de Castelnau advance before his troopes, ask'd to speak with him upon parole; To which he consenting, because they were of old acquaintance, he order'd his men at the same time to halt a litle, while they were passing their compliments: Mean while the Prince of Condé commanded his men to make what hast they could, to secure themselves by getting off; and so amused[4] our Lieut Genll,[5] till a man whom they had left on the top of a rising ground, which was behind them, made a signe to them, and then they took their leave immediatly of Castelnau, and gallop'd after their troopes: By this means they gain'd so much time, that they pass'd the River, before our men could come up with them again.

Soon after this, Monsr. de Turenne arriv'd at the place where Castelnau had drawn up his men, within cañon-shott of the River, and saw the Enemys Army drawn up on the other Side of the

---

[4] i.e., beguiled.
[5] 'et Castelnau fut pris pour duppe' (MS. *Campagnes*, p. 179). James is rather more severe in the French MS. than in what we presume to be his own *Memoirs*.

River by Condé: And then Monsr. de Castelnau gave Monsr. de Turenne an account of what had past, and added, That the last Squadron of the Enemys horse were forced to swimm the River to Save themselves: This mistake of his caused some Sharpnesse more then ordinary between the Prince and Monsr. de Turenne, by an accident which happen'd some days after as the Reader will find in the following account.

The Enemy had no Sooner past over the River, but they broke the bridges, so that they were in a further danger, and, as I remember, march'd the same afternoon for Tournay. Wee quarter'd that night at Frane, closs by Condé, and the next morning fell to making our bridges over the River, about a league below the Town; intending so soon as they should be finish'd to attack that place. At first it was resolved that only Mr. de Castelnau and Mr. d'Vxelles, with the troopes which they commanded, should be employd to take the Town, while the two Mareshalls, with the rest of the Army, should cover them from any attempt from the Army of the Spaniards. And so they began to make their approaches to the Town; But the very first night they found so vigourous a resistance from the Defendants, whose workes indeed were very slight, but lin'd with great numbers of men within them, that it was found too hard a taske for them alone to undertake.

Of this the two Mareshalls being advertis'd, they came them selves, and carryd on one of the attaques, leaving the other to the conduct of the two foremention'd Lieutenant Generalls. And here wee found a very favourable shelter, from the houses of a small fauxbourg which was before the gate: for thō the Enemy had burnt it, yet not haueing time to pluck down the walls, it prov'd beneficial to us; for from thence wee began our Trenches, which was but litle above half musket shott from the Town. The first night of their being open'd at our attack, they were mounted by a Battalion of the Guards commanded by Vautourneux, the eldest Captain of these ten Companies; and at the Lieutenant Generall's attack was the Regiment of * * *.[6]

That night wee made a very good (*attack*) at both places; yet wee lost betwixt three or four hundred men at those two attacks, of which number were Severall Officers. At our approche wee lost

[6] There is a similar blank in the MS. *Campagnes* (p. 181).

Monsr. de Vautourneux, who seeing one Captain LLloyd (a Welshman and an Engeneer, who had been bred up under the Prince of Orange and was a stout colerick man)[7] coming back from the Trenches after he had perform'd his duty, traced out the work, and sett the workmen upon their imployment, ask'd him, why he returned so soon? Saying withall, That he was certain he could haue not perform'd all he had to do in so short a time; after which he let fall some words, as if he doubted of his courage: At which the Engeneer was so incensed, that it made his Welsh blood boyle with him; So that he told Vautourneux, That if he pleas'd to go and look upon what he had trac'd out, he should find he had not been wanting in any part of his duty. Vpon this they both went together to view it, and the shott from the Enemy flew so fast, that Vautourneux was kill'd before he could get to the head of the workmen, and Captain LLloyd shott through the head.

The next night a Battalion of Suisses had the guard of the Trenches at one attack, and the Regiment de * * * at the other, both which attacks carryd on their Trenches within pistoll shott of the Town: that night wee lost at least as many men as the former. The third night, an other Battalion of the frech Guards releeved the Suisses at our attack, and the regiment de * * *[8] at the Lieut Generall's. That night at our attack, there happen'd a very great mistake, which caus'd the loss of many men: It was the turn of Monsr. de la Ferté to be in the Trenches, who coming in the Evening to take a view of what had been perform'd there, and to resolve what was to be farther done, suppos'd that he was now neer enough to endeavour to make a lodgment against the pallisades, which both he and all the Officers concluded to be without the ditch on the very edge of it; And accordingly, he order'd his men to lodge themselves at the foot of them, which so soon as it was dark, they attempted to haue done: but when they came to the ditch, they found the pallisades were not before it, but upon the barme, which, notwithstanding, they pass'd the ditch which was but shallow, and not broad, in obedience to their orders, and endeavour'd to haue lodged themselves at the foot of the pallisades upon the barme, which they disputed so long, that they lost a considerable number both of Soldiers and Officers; and at last were

[7] 'a stout colerick man'—not translated in the French MS. (p. 181).
[8] There are similar blanks in the MS. *Campagnes* (p. 182).

constrain'd to draw off, and content themselves only with carrying on their Trench to the edge of the ditch. And here it is not to be wonder'd at, that this mistake was made; for the ditch, as I said, being narrow, and it being generally the Custom, that the pallisades were placed without it, they took it for granted, that so they were: to which I might add, that it was exceeding difficult to the eye to distinguish att a distance, where they were sett.

The next day the Count de Henning Governour of the place sent out to treat, and made his conditions to march forth with his armes and baggage on the day following, which was the 19th of August. He accordingly perform'd his Articles, and came out with upwards of two thousand foot, and some few horse.

While wee lay before this place, Monsr. de Bussy-Rabutin,[9] Mestre de Camp de la Caualerie, being sent out with seven or eight Squadrons of horse to convey and guard our foragers, while they were about their work on the other side of the Escaut, betwixt St Crepin and Valenciennes, having plac'd his troopes before the Villages in which our men were foraging, and towards the Evening, when our foragers had almost ended their work, and were most of them gone home loaden, seeing two Squadrons of the Enemies horse appear in the plaine betwixt him and Valenciennes, he was desirous to fall upon them; being also prest to it by Severall Volonteers and persons of quality who happen'd to be with him, amongst which were the Prince de Marsillac and the Count de Guiche: He therfore march'd to them with all his horse; Vpon which they drew off at a round rate, and he follow'd them: But when he was almost got up to them, they faced about on the suddain, and at the same time twelve or fourteen Squadrons came out of a litle bottom, where they had been all that time in Ambuscade, which so much surpris'd both him and all his company, that at first they knew not what resolution they should take; and at length when he was going to haue charg'd them, he hauing then no other choice to make, as he had order'd matters, but either to charge there, or to retire back and make good a défilé that was behind them, he was determin'd by the men themselves; who

---

[9] See the *Mémoires de Bussy-Rabutin*, ed. L. Lalanne, I, 435 et passim. Bussy's memoirs throw valuable light on the campaign of 1657 (see, e.g., II, 28–29, 36, 39, 43, 46, 47) and especially the campaign of 1658 and the battle of the Dunes (II, 53, 58–59, 60–61, 66).

without waiting for his command, chose the latter, which they had reason enough to do, seeing themselves so far outnomber'd by the Enemy, so they faced about, and made the best of their way to the défilé, crying out, as they broke and ran, *Au défilé*! meaning they would rally at the pass, and they were as good as their words; for so soon as they were come thether, they rallyd very well, and the Enemy being Satisfied with what they had taken in the poursuit, press'd them no farther. These Regiments that did this, were of the best of our Army, and most of them old Troopers as well as Officers, and had they not done that they did, the loss had been much more considerable.

In this rencounter wee lost above a hundred horsemen, and a Cornett or two of the Regiment Royall, who happening to be taken by some of the Prince of Condé's troopes, he sent them back to the King by one of his own Trumpeters; but his Maty refused to accept of them, and so those troopes of the Regiment which had lost them, march'd without any during the rest of the Campagne.

There happen'd also about that time an accident, which caus'd a worse understanding betwixt the Prince of Condé and Monsr. de Turenne, then is usuall betwixt persons of their quality commanding against one another:[10] For a letter which the Mareshall had written to the Cardinal being intercepted, wherin he gave his Eminence an account of what had past in the retreat, when the Spaniards quitted their post neer Valenciennes; The Prince, into whose hands it fell, after hauing read it, sent a Trumpeter, with a letter to Monsr. de Turenne, which was full of very Sharp and ressenting expressions, some of which were to this purpose, That had he not known M. de Turenne's own handwriting, he should haue thought, that the account which was given to the Cardinal in that paper, had rather been written by some Gazettier, then a Generall; and clos'd his letter with these words, That had Monsr. de Turenne been at the head of his Army, as himself was at the Reer of his, he would haue seen the contrary of what he writt, none of his horse being forced to swim the River to Save themselves in their Retreat. Monsr. de Turenne grew very angry at the reading of this letter, and told the Trumpeter, That it concern'd him to haue

[10] This little preamble is omitted in the MS. *Campagnes* (p. 184), where we read simply that 'It was about this time that a letter which Mr. de Turenne had written. . . .'

a care, how he brought any papers of that nature; and warn'd him of it, That if he committed the same fault again, neither his character nor his Livery should protect him; but that for this time he was contented to let him go, though he had well deserv'd to be punish'd for bringing so injurious a paper. The Prince was not long ignorant, that Monsr. de Turenne had written nothing but what had been told him by Monsr. de Castelnau, and therfore was sorry that he had written so angry and offensive a letter; yet, till the conclusion of the Warr, they were never heartily reconciled; I mean, they liv'd not with that Civility towards each other, as men of their quality and posts are accustom'd to do in those parts.

And now Condé being taken, and wee hauing left a sufficient garrison within it, our Army march'd on the next day which was the 20th of August to St Guislain, and beseig'd it, Monsr. de Turenne having his quarter at a Village called Hornu, and Mr. de la Ferté his, on the other side of the River. At this place the King of France and the Cardinal came to the Army, and were quarter'd at the Castle of Bossut, a litle below the Town, on the same River. This Town is very strongly situated, standing very low, and the River of Haisne running through it; so that they can drown at their pleasure most of the ground about it, as now they had, for which reason wee found difficulty enough in the carrying on our Trenches: 'Twas also very hard to make a line of Circumvallation, because bridges of communication could not be made without great trouble: So that at the best, notwithstanding all our endeavours, our Trenches were full of water, especially when wee came neer, and our approches might more reasonably be call'd blinds of fascines, then any thing else; because the water being even with the ground, wee could neither sink ourselves, nor make use of that earth to cover us. Yet surmounting all these difficulties, wee carry'd the Town in the space of three days, after wee had broken ground.

When wee came first to our quarters at Hornu, (*Horn*) it was exceeding dark; so that, thō severall of our Generall Officers had houses mark'd out for their reception which were within lesse then cañon-shott of the Town, they knew it not, till next morning, when they were waken'd with the thundering of the great Guns from the Town; and the houses being all paper buildings, they were soon dislodged, as in particular Monsr. de Passage, with others, who were all obliged to seek their quarters out of gune shott. I onely made bold to stay in mine, which indeed being litle more then muskett-shott from the Town, they neglected it so much as not to shoot at it, as supposing that nobody would stay in it; so that I remain'd there in great security during the time the Seige lasted.

At this place the French Guards according to custome, had the guard of the Trenches the first night; it being an indisputed right in those Countrys, that how many Seiges soever, thō of very short continuance shall happen in a Campagne, the eldest Regiment has allways the honour of first breaking ground. There happen'd a dispute that night betwixt Mr. de Montpezat the eldest Lieut Generall, and the Grand Maistre de l'Artillerie, occasion'd by the first mention'd sending his orders to the latter, to furnish him with some necessarys which he wanted for carrying on the Trenches, the first night they were open'd; which the other refused to obey, pretending he ought to receive no orders but from the Generall himself: Of which Mr. de Montpezat complaining the next day, the dispute was decided in favour of the Lieut Generalls, that the Grand Maistre was obliged to receive orders from any of them: Upon which result, for so long time as he continued in the Army, he officiated no more as Grand Maistre, but had a Comission, granted him for Lieut Generall and served only in that capacity.

Wee lost no many Soldiers at this Seige, nor do I remember that any Officer of note was kill'd; only the Cheualier de Crequi and Monsr. de Varennes were wounded, besides some other Officers, as Monsr. de Chavigny Aide Major to the Regiment of Guards, and since Pere de l'Oratoire; The Cheualier de Crequi was wounded at Monsr. de la Fertés attack, and dangerously hurt in the head, of which notwithstanding he afterwards recover'd, and Monsr. de Varenne was shott in the thigh at their attack as he was talking with me.

In three nights wee carryd on our approches to the edge of the ditch, and the next day, the Governour Don Pedro Savali sent out to capitulate, and march'd out of the Town the next day following which was the 25th.

While wee were busied at this Seige, the Enemy divided their Army; the Arch Duke and Count de Fuensaldagne with most of the Spanish foot and some horse, were at Notre-Dame-de-Halle,

The Pce of Condé with the greatest part of his at Tournay, the Lorrainers at Ath, and the Prince of Ligny[11] with about four or five thousand men at Mons.

And now the year was so far spent, that it was not thought expedient for us to undertake any other Seige, So that wee spent severall days in the same quarters where wee were when wee Satt down before St Guislain, from which place the Court departed, some few days after it was taken. During the time of our abode there, wee work hard both at that Town and Condé, adding new fortifications to them, but our cheifest care was to secure our Foragers, and to eat up the Country round about those garrisons; that by so doing wee might make it impracticable for the Enemy to beseige them in the winter. And to that intent wee continued in our Camp by St Guislain, till our men had quite made an end of the Forage thereabout, and wee took care allways to send out strong Convoys with our foragers, to prevent their being beaten or taken by the Spaniards. Sometimes Monsr. de Turenne himself went out with them; and when he did not, there was allways a Lieut Generall at the head of those partys, which had never less during our abode in that place then two thousand men to guard them.

Having taken these precautions, wee never received any affront or considerable loss in our Forage: yet notwithstanding all the care which could be taken, some small partys of the Enemys would be still abroad, and glean up here and there a man or two; it being impossible to restrain our Vedettes from running out beyond our Guards, where commonly they were surpriz'd; And of all the Enemies' horse, none did us so much mischeif as their Cravats,[12] who in litle partys would be perpetually upon our Foragers: but to prevent their designs as much as possibly wee could, Monsr. de Turenne order'd, That every Squadron of horse should send along with their Foragers, three or four Officers well mounted, so that when any of these Cravats fell upon their fellows, they might joyn twenty or thirty of them together, which were enough to beat off one of those straggling partys: By this means our Foragers were better protected then before, and many of the Cravats taken.

[11] The Prince de Ligne.
[12] See above, for the year 1654, p. 192.

The last Forage wee made while wee stayd in that quarter, was the greatest of any, and of the most danger, being to go as far as Chievres and the Abbey of Cambron; the first of which places is but the distance of a large league from Ath. This Convoy was commanded by men (*me*), and being to march so great a distance from their Camp into the midst of those places where the Enemies troopes were quarter'd, I had five Battalions and fourty Squadrons with two pieces of cañon along with me. And as I gave a particular account of one considerable Forage which was made in the foregoing year, I shall do the same of this.[13]

Having consider'd that I was to be ingaged so far in the Enemys Country, I thought it necessary to take what precautions I could, and to that purpose before day I sent a party of horse to a great wood, through which I was of necessity to pass, to stopp all the Foragers there, and to permitt none of them to go on beyond those limits, till I cam thither myself with the Troopes I commanded. This being perform'd according to my order, I march'd through the wood, and drew out upon the plaine before any one Forager was there. In the wood I left a Battalion, that from Mons, partys of foot might not intercept them when they return'd loaden. Then I gaue my orders, that the Foragers should not presume to disband, or march faster then the Convoy; but go along with me upon the same front on each hand of the Squadrons. In this manner I march'd till I came almost within a league of Chievres; and it was an extraordinary sight to see about ten thousand Foragers, most of them with scythes in their hands, with the Officers before them marching as they did, the front of them being almost half a mile in breadth: But when they came within sight of that part of the Country, which had not been already forag'd, it was altogether impossible either for me or their particular Officers to keep them in order any longer, or to hinder them from disbanding, and making what hast they could to forage. Which when I observ'd, I left the remainder of my foot, and some horse together with the cañon, upon the heigth where I was, near a Village; and myself with the greatest part of the remaining horse, march'd at a round trott after the Foragers, and when they were fallen to their work, I placed myself before them betwixt Chievres and Brugelet, by that means to cover them from

[13] Sentence omitted in the MS. *Campagnes* (p. 189).

those in Ath. At the same time sending the Count de Grandpré
with the rest of the horse the other way, ordering him to draw up
by a Village call'd Leuse, therby to Secure our Foragers from any
partys which might come out from Mons.

And upon this occasion I cannot forbear to mention the great
order and justice which was observ'd amongst Foragers; for he
who first enters into a Feild of Corne or Meadow, keepes possession, and none will offer to come within such a distance of him,
and not to leave him sufficient forage to load his horse: And who-
soever gets first into a Barne, or on a Hay-mowe, no man offers
to disturb him, or to size on any thing, till he has provided for
himself; so that First come first serv'd.

About noon I had an alarme, but it prov'd to be only Monsr. de
Rochepair,[14] who had been abroad with a party of about a thous-
and horse, and was returning to the Camp, without having done
any thing: I desir'd him to stay with me, not knowing what use
wee might haue of more men: And now hauing continued there
till all the Foragers had loaden, and were gone, I march'd back to
the Camp after them, loosing only half a score, who had past over
the brook by Cambron contrary to order, and were taken by a
small party of the Enemy. I have since been told by the Prince de
Ligne, and other Officers of the Spanish Army, That they had intended that day to haue fallen on our Foragers, and had appointed
a Rendezvous for most of their horse from Tournay, Mons, and
Ath, (and) haue met for that design; but that when I march'd out
with out Foragers, there was so great a noise in our Camp, that
some of the Prince de Ligne's small partys brought him intelligence to Mons, that our whole Army was on its march: wherupon
he sent immediate notice of it to the Rendezvous, and they all
march'd back into their severall quarters, apprehending to meet
with the Van (of) our Army: Thus in all appearance by this mistake, that Forage escap'd a great danger; for it would haue been
very difficult to haue gott off in safety, when so great a body of
horse should haue fallen on them.

Some days after this, all the Country about us being now quite
eaten up, wee past the River, and Camp at Outrage[15] on the 14th
of September, and on the 19th wee march'd to Leuse a Bourg in

[14] 'Rocheperre' (MS. *Campagnes*, p. 190).
[15] 'Hauterage' (MS. *Campagnes*, p. 291).

the midway betwixt Tournay and Ath, where wee rested for some days, till wee had also eaten up most of the Forage in those parts. During our stay there, wee took in the Castle of Briffeil, in which the Enemy had a garrison, who would not deliver it up till they saw our cañon in battery against them.

Having stayd as long as it was convenient in that quarter, wee began to think it necessary for us to go out of the Enemys Country; and on the 26th of September, wee march'd to Pommereuil near Pont de Haisne. The next day wee passed over that River, and camped at Angre upon the Hosneau (*Anirt sur l'Haisneau*)[16] about a league from Keuvrain up that brook. This quarter and all adjoining to it, had been so consum'd, that the very first night of our coming thether, our Foragers were forc'd to go out two leagues for nothing but for straw. So that had any one proposed to haue stayd there, about three or four days, it would haue been judged impracticable. Notwithstanding which Monsr. de Turenne maintain'd us there without want above a fortnight; which was impossible to haue done, had he not order'd us to provide ourselves with corn when wee went from Leuse: at which time our waggons were not only as full as they could hold, but every Trooper carryd a sack of corn behind him, the day wee came thether, which enabled us to subsist so long as wee did in that leane quarter; where there was so litle Forage in the neighbourhood, that I do not remember wee sent out above thrice while wee continued there.

At this place also I commanded the last Forage which wee made, and was forced to go almost as far as Bouchain before any thing could be found, most of our men coming loaden only with Straw. The occasion of our long stay in that place, was to furnish the two Towns which wee had newly taken with all manner of Stores and necessary provisions, and for finishing of some works which were absolutely needfull for their Safety.

When this was done, about the 11th of October wee march'd to Barlaimont, and on the 22d to the Abbey of Marolles; where wee thought wee should haue continued for some time: but having received intelligence that some troopes of the Enemy were drawing down that way, wee thought it expedient for us to remove from thence to a place called Vandegies-au-bois, where our Gener-

[16] Angri sur le Hainaut (MS. *Campagnes*, p. 291).

all received orders to march towards la Fere; the Court being then just advertis'd, that the Mareshall d'Hocquincourt was making a Treaty with the Prince of Condé, to deliver up to him Ham and Peronne, of both which places he was Governour. In pursuance of which order Monsr. de Turenne came with the Army on the 4th of Nouember to Mouy, a Village upon the River of Oyse, about two leagues above la Fere; where so soon as he arriued, he received a letter from the Cardinal to leave the Army there, and come himself to Compiegne where the Court then was, that they might consult together, what resolution was to be taken, in case the Mareshall d'Hocquincourt should not hearken to the offers which were made him from the King, and receive the Enemy into those two so considerable places, upon the River of Somme.[17]

Accordingly he went thether leaving the Army under my command, who was then the only Lieut Generall remaining with it, all the others having had leave given them before to go away, when they askt it, there being no probability of Action. By this accident I came to haue the command of the Army committed to me, at the very time when the Peace betwixt France and Cromwell was concluded and actually publish'd, and by which Treaty, I was by name to be banish'd France. The Army stayd at Mouy during some days, and there I received orders to march with it to Mondêcour on the 10th of Nouember. That Town is betwixt Noyon and Chauny, and there I stayd till Monsr. de Turenne return'd to the Army, which was about the 14th, when the affaire concerning Mr. d'Hocquincourt was wholy accommodated, and the Court was secur'd not to lose those two places. After which I obtain'd leave from Monsr. de Turenne to go to the Court, the Army being

[17] Condé's friend Madame de Châtillon had great influence with Marshal D'Hocquincourt. The latter installed himself in Péronne where he could conveniently receive overtures from both sides. Mazarin suggested that Turenne should move his army near to Péronne; but Turenne pointed out the risk of forcing D'Hocquincourt to 'some extreme resolution'. Should these invaluable fortresses fall into Spanish hands, the war might again turn into a civil war and the situation once more become desperate. D'Hocquincourt was asking for twenty thousand crowns. Give him fifty thousand rather than temporise, was Turenne's advice. Once Condé and the Spaniards are in Péronne, it will cost you more than twenty million, if not the loss of the kingdom. This was sound advice. Condé and the Spaniards were hovering within a few hours of Péronne. And when Mazarin offered D'Hocquincourt the sum he had asked for on condition that he should resign the governorship of Péronne and one or two other places to his son, whom the Court considered reliable, he came to terms, and the enemy withdrew into Flanders.

7. Vicomte de Schomberg

8. The Duke and Duchess of York and the Princesses Mary and Anne

at that time just ready to go into their winter-quarters, and no likelyhood of any more action that Year; for as long as there was any, I thought myself obliged in honour not to quitt the Army, thō I knew the Treaty betwixt the Crown of France and Cromwell, by Vertue of which I was presently to leave the Country, was already sign'd on both sides.

*1656**

UNTIL the conclusion of the treaty with Monsieur d'Hocquincourt, the Campaign of 1655 could not be considered finished; so the Duke of York did not think he could leave the French Army with honour while there might still arise some action, although he knew that the treaty between France and Cromwell was signed, whereby he was banished from the Kingdom. The Queen Mother of France as well as the Cardinal explained the reasons for this to the Prince on his arrival at Compiègne, and how they had been obliged to yield to a necessity so contrary to their inclination. And when the Court was returned to Paris, they not only expressed the desire they had to retain him in the service, but assured him that, if Cromwell would not consent to the propositions they had made to him in this matter, his pension would still be paid him in what ever place he might retire to, provided that he did not serve against France. He then accepted the offer that was made him to serve in Italy as Captain-General under the Duke of Modena, Generalissimo of the troops of France and Savoy in Piedmont. He had a strong inclination to get more and more experience in arms, and the tender love which his aunt the Duchess of Savoy had shown him on every occasion, caused him to embrace this decision with the more pleasure because he felt much gratitude for her kindness and because she ardently desired to have him near her.[1]

---

* The entry for 1656 has been translated *tel quel* from the French MS. It is slightly different from, and substantially shorter than, the corresponding entry in the *Life*. If we assume that both are based on the same original, it is clear that the person who made the French translation added one passage (as indicated below), but abbreviated or paraphrased the rest, passing over a few lines here and there, and omitting at the end nearly nine pages which figure in the *Life*.

[1] This first paragraph summarises very quickly the three paragraphs which conclude the entry in the *Life* (pp. 264–266) for 1655. Two points omitted in the French MS. are (i) that James affirms that Mazarin 'had been a very ill Minister, if he had not made that Treaty with Cromwell in such a juncture of affairs' (p. 265); and (ii) in reply to Mazarin's representations, Cromwell 'consented to my Stay in France, and to my serving in any of their Armys, excepting only that of Flanders' (p. 266).

At the beginning of February the Princess of Orange came to Paris to see the Queen her Mother. The Duke of York went to meet her between Péronne and Cambrai. It was there that the Prince for the first time saw Mistress Hyde, maid of honour to the Princess his sister, and whom he afterwards married.[2] The French Court came out of Paris with great civility to receive this Princess and carried her to the Palais Royal where they left her with the Queen her Mother.

A few days after this, on the arrival of the news that the King of England had gone from Cologne into Flanders,[3] all the Irish Colonels who had served in the French armies under Monsieur de Turenne and Monsieur de la Ferté, hearing of it, wrote to the Duke of York to assure him that they were ready to perform, as good subjects and men of honour, whatever he should appoint them.[4] He thanked them and recommended them by no means to suffer their soldiers to pass into Flanders piecemeal or in small parties, although the Spaniards might invite them, on the occasion of the King's having retired into their country; and that they should keep their Regiments together, as much for the service of his Majesty when there should be need of them, as for their own advantage; besides that their soldiers could not disperse themselves, as long as he was serving in France, without doing great prejudice to his private affairs, and that when it should be time to make use of their offers, he would advise them of it.[5]

One of the Colonels named Richard Gray[6] deserves that mention should be made of the handsome manner in which he quitted the service of the Spaniards after having been obliged so to do as much by their ill care as by his own duty. He had served King

[2] This circumstance has been hitherto unknown. The sentence does not occur in the printed *Life* (ed. Clarke) where the first mention of 'Mrs. Hyde' and the Duke's marriage occurs in the section immediately following the Restoration (I, 387).

[3] '... it being reported that the King of England was to go from Colen into Flanders' (*Life*, The Third Part, I, 267).

[4] The *Life* (p. 267) says the same in other words.

[5] The account in the *Life* (pp. 267–268) is substantially the same, but the order of phrases is different.

[6] 'And here his R.H. takes particular notice in his Memoires of the handsome carriage of one of those Colonells, when he quitted the Service of the Spaniards. This gentleman by name Col: Richard Grace, after having serv'd the late King Charles the 1st....' (*Life*, p. 268). The MS. shows that 'Grace' had originally been written, and then boldly corrected to 'Gray'—evidently by James's order.

219

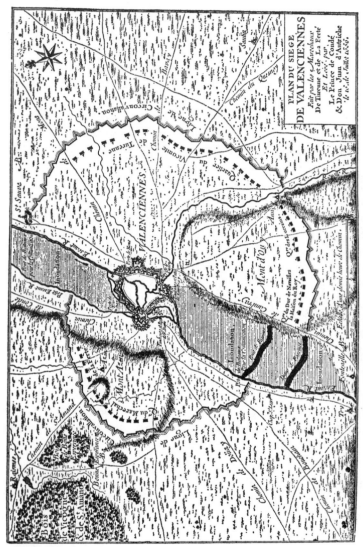

The Siege of Valenciennes, July 16, 1656

Charles the 1st in England until the capture of Oxford, and had sustained the cause of Charles the 2nd in Ireland as long as his party had been in arms in that Kingdom. When the war was over the Rebels had permitted him to take over a Regiment of his nation into Spain. He had concluded an honourable and advantageous capitulation with the Spaniards, but when his troops were disembarked to the number of twelve hundred men, it was so ill observed, and he himself so ill used, that he lost the half of his men before he could arrive in Catalonia. He nevertheless served in the Campaign with much valour;[7] but having been placed in garrison in an important fortress on the frontier, on learning that the King his Master had retired into France[8] and that the Duke of York was serving in the [French] Armies, he resolved to quit Spain, where he had no reason to hope for better treatment than in the past; but he did not think that, they having broken their word with him, he was for that reason freed from the obligation of behaving toward them as a gallant man and as became a gentleman.[9] He sent to propose to Monsieur d'Hocquincourt[10] that he should receive his Regiment on the same footing as the other Regiments of his nation that were serving in France, and on condition that he might afterwards go to serve his King wherever the King's affairs should require it. The offer was accepted, and he was earnestly desired at the same time to deliver up his castle. But he refused. He agreed only that the Marshal should send Cavalry on a certain day to a certain spot, to meet the Regiment. He then sent to the nearest Spanish garrison to give them notice that they should dispatch two hundred men to whom he would deliver up the Castle when he marched out of it; but that they should have care not to send a greater number which might cause him to suspect treachery; because then he would not deem it treachery to deliver the Castle to the French when he should be obliged to do so for his

---

[7] 'Notwithstanding which bad treatment, he serv'd in the Spanish Army with good reputation, till the end of the Campagne.' (*Life*, p. 268).

[8] Here the *Life* adds: 'where he was honourably treated.'

[9] The differences between the French MS. and the text printed in the *Life* are here very slight.

[10] 'To which purpose he sent to the Mareshall d'Hocquincourt, who at that time commanded the French Army in Catalonia, to let him know, that on such a day, which was mention'd by him, he would march off with his Regiment on these conditions, that . . .' (as in MS.). The *Life* is clearer and more circumstantial at this point.

own security and his regiment's. The evacuation was completed in good faith. He marched out of one gate, while the two hundred Spaniards entered by another; and he found the French horse at the rendezvous which had been fixed.

When it was known[11] that the King of England was not only in Flanders, but that he had signed a Treaty with Spain, all men believed that the Duke of York would also withdraw there. This Prince, who was used to speaking in confidence of his affairs with Monsieur de Turenne, was advised by him to write to the King his brother and offer to his consideration, that having served in France and received his education there, having moreover contracted friendship with the most considerable persons at the Court and in the Armies whose interest might one day be usefully employed for the advantage of his Majesty, he believed it would be to his interest to permit him to remain in France; whereas by quitting it, he ran great hazard of losing both his friends and the interest he had there. He believed he could render no great service in Flanders where it was enough for the Spaniards that his Majesty and the Duke of Gloucester were there. Besides this, there had been no mention made of him in the Treaty, and the Spaniards had not shown that they desired him to join them.[12] If they should happen later to ask for this, his Majesty could secretly consent to his remaining in France, while appearing vexed with him for his apparent disobedience; which would satisfy the Spaniards; and this connivance would be known only to the person who should carry the proposition and bring back the consent.[13]

The Duke of York was much pleased with this advice, he communicated it to the Queen his Mother who also approved it, and he resolved to send Charles Berkeley to make the proposition to the King. But at the moment when Berkeley was going to set out,

[11] The new paragraph in the *Life* begins: 'But to returne where wee left. After this address, which was made to the Duke from the Irish Collonels, there came certain news, That the King was in Flanders and that he had concluded a Treaty with the Spaniards. . . .' The narrative that follows differs somewhat from that in the MS. and is a little fuller.

[12] . . . 'et qu'ils n'avaient point témoigné souhaitter qu'il fut de la partie' (MS.). The narrative in the *Life* (p. 270) expresses a more marked vexation with the negligence and disdain displayed by the Spaniards on this occasion.

[13] This concludes the details of the scheme which Turenne proposed.

he unfortunately broke his leg, which obliged the Prince to make use of Doctor Frazer who was about to leave and join his Majesty. The latter acquitted himself very faithfully of this commission; but the King, far from consenting to the Duke's request, immediately sent him an absolute order to come and join him in Flanders with all possible diligence. He at once obeyed, and the French Court consented.[14]

When this Prince arrived at Compiègne at the beginning of September to take leave of the Court, there befell an accident which would have greatly embarrassed him in any other country. The Marquess of Ormond had been dispatched by the King of England, at the request of the Spaniards, to the blockade of Condé, which was to surrender in a few days. He sent in an order in the name of his Majesty to Muskerry who had an Irish Regiment in garrison in that place, and to the Chevalier Darcy, Lieutenant-Colonel of the Duke of York's Regiment, to quit the service of France by marching out of the town and to come and join him in Flanders. Muskerry answered that he had all the feelings of respect and obedience which a good subject must have for the King; but he did not think he could with honour quit the Service of France in which he had engaged, until he had previously obtained a passport, which he would ask for as soon as he should have joined the army. This behaviour[15] of the Marquess caused great displeasure at the French Court; but it did not hinder the Duke's being received there with much civility and being assured that his pension would still be paid, in case he did not actually serve against France.[16]

[14] The text here is markedly different from the longer passage in *Life* (p. 271). At this point, however, the text of the MS. as translated here, omits four pages which appear in the *Life* (bottom of p. 271 to lower part of p. 275) presumably because these relate to intrigues at the English court. The text of the MS. immediately following this point rejoins the text of the *Life* at p. 275.

[15] 'Ce procédé du Marquis deplut beaucoup a la Cour de France, mais il n'empescha point que le Duc n'y fut receu avec beaucoup de civilité. . . .' The reference is to Ormonde.

[16] Here follows in the *Life* (I, 276–277) a paragraph which describes the Duke's doings in Paris, and the letters awaiting him from Charles II requiring him to leave Sir John Berkeley in Paris. He saw that the design was to remove Berkeley from his service and impose on him Sir John Ratcliffe, 'an absolute creature of those who were most inward with his Majesty. But this their project did not take,' because the Duke obeyed the King by going to Flanders, although he took Berkeley with him.

This Prince, having sent his Equipage[17] and servants before him, set out from Paris on the 10th of September and lay the first night at Verneuil with Monsieur de Metz. The next day he proceeded in his carriage to Clermont in order to take the post there and go the same day to join his Equipage which had orders to await him at Abbeville.

On his arriving at the gates of Clermont, one of his servants whom he had sent before to hold the horses ready, came to tell him that Lockart, Cromwell's ambassador, was there and was lodging at the Post House,[18] which was the best in the town; whereupon he gave this man orders to have his horses brought to the door of the Post House. The Prince on arriving had his coach stop, took out his boots, got on horseback in the street and immediately continued on his way. There was equal surprise on both sides. Lockart feared the consequences. He knew that the Duke of York was as well liked by the people as he was held in consideration by all persons of quality in the Kingdom, and that the English of Lockart's party were equally hated by all men; these reflections alarmed him; he caused his horses to be saddled, assembled his men in the inn, and made them stand on guard with their swords and pistols. He himself stood at a window of the room which looked out on the street above the gate, having beside him the principal men of his retinue who like him were uncovered; 'tis probable that he stood thus to avoid taking off his hat and not be blamed for remaining covered. His footmen stood in the Court at the bottom of the stairs. Now the coach having stopped directly

---

[17] 'Ce Prince aiant fait prendre les devants à ses Equipages, partit de Paris. . . .' Furetière (Dictionnaire, 1690) defines this word as 'Provision de tout ce qui est nécessaire pour voyager ou s'entretenir honorablement, soit de valets, chevaux, carrosses, habits, armes, etc'. It therefore meant his carriage, attendants, baggage, and probably weapons.

[18] 'l'hotellerie de la poste.'

Sir William Lockhart was a Scottish gentleman who, as a boy, had sought his fortune on the Continent and distinguished himself in the French army. During the Civil War in England he had fought for the King, who knighted him. At the time of Charles II's adventure in Scotland he offered to accompany Charles as a volunteer in the expedition which was to end at Worcester; but Charles appears to have ignored his offer. He later came to terms with Cromwell and entered his service. His mission as ambassador to France and subsequently as commander of the English expeditionary force was highly successful. After the Restoration he retired to Scotland; but in 1674 Charles II sent him as envoy to Brandenburg and later appointed him as ambassador in Paris.

at the gate facing the window, the Prince saw him, and before he could get on horseback, all the people having eagerly run up to see him, the least word from him would have made them fall on the ambassador. Lockart was afraid but his fear lasted no long time and the Prince's departure reassured him.[19]

What the Court had done in civility to the Duke of York to avoid any accident was like to have caused a very painful one.[20] Lockart had been sent from Compiègne to Clermont to avoid his encountering the Prince, who had remained a few days in Paris but much fewer then the Court had supposed, after he had taken leave of them. His diligence in setting out was the reason for his finding Lockart still at Clermont. He was received with much civility in every town he passed through,[21] and arriving at Gravelines which was the first place belonging to the Spaniards, he was there met by the Marquess of Ormond on the orders of the King his brother; and his Majesty who was then at Bruges came to Furne to receive him.[22]

---

[19] The account of this episode in the *Life* is similar but longer and more detailed. The French text is a more concise paraphrase of it.

[20] . . . 'pensa en causer un [accident] fort fascheux,' that is, nearly caused a very awkward 'incident'.

[21] The *Life* (p. 278) specifies Montreuil, Boulogne, and Calais.

[22] This paragraph concludes the entry for 1656. It is written by the same scribe but in a smaller hand than the rest of the section in the MS., and was perhaps added somewhat later. The *Life* now gives a detailed account (nearly nine folio pages, pp. 279–287) of the pressure that was brought to bear on the Duke to get rid of his trusted followers, Sir John Berkeley, Harry Berkeley (his master of the Horse), and Henry Jermyn; to bring Sir James Darcey and his regiment from Paris into Flanders; and to compel him and the Duke to enter the Spanish service. This intrigue was the work of a faction then uppermost in Charles's councils; its leaders appear to have been Sir Henry Bennet (afterwards Lord Arlington), Sir John Ratcliffe, and the Earl of Bristol; Henry Killigrew was associated with it. Lord Jermyn, who with Henry Jermyn was strongly pro-French, wrote from Paris urging the Duke not to take service with Spain, as he had lived so long in France, had been treated with great kindness, and was in receipt of a pension. James felt nevertheless that he might with honour agree to the King's wishes and serve with the Spaniards. But when, on Christmas eve, he learned that the Spaniards proposed to administer an oath to everyone who came over to their side (which would mean that his own junior officers would be pledged to the King of Spain and not to the Duke); when Lord Bristol attempted further to damage Sir John Berkeley's credit; and when, finally, to add to his indignation, Charles compelled him to send Sir John away—in this juncture James determined to have no more to do with the Spanish proposal, but to withdraw into Holland—which he did.

1657 *

THE DUKE'S FIFTH CAMPAIGN, AND THE FIRST HE SERVED IN THE SPANISH ARMY

THE beginning of this Campaign was very glorious for the Prince de Condé. While he was reviewing his cavalry at La Bussière on the Sambre, whence they were to go to the general rendezvous of the army, he was advised that Monsieur de Turenne and Monsieur de la Ferté had besieged Cambrai, which he knew had only a weak garrison. He immediately, and without hesitating, marched in order to try to relieve it before the French could be informed of his march and had perfected their lines. He took his measures so as to arrive at night; and although the French

---

* This entry for 1657 has, like the entries for 1652 and 1656, been translated from the French MS. The *Life* here contains a section of 8 pages (pp. 288–296) which do not figure in the *Campagnes*. In this section of the *Life*, the Duke makes his way secretly into Holland and is about to embark in a French ship with the intention of returning to France when he is dissuaded by Charles Berkeley who points out that an English warship, exercising the right of search, may intercept him. He therefore proceeds to Utrecht, still hoping to rejoin the French. However, on receiving from Charles II promises of more satisfactory treatment, he returns to Bruges and it is now understood that he will serve with the Spaniards under Don Juan and the Marquess of Caracena. He dismisses Sir Henry Bennet and Harry Killigrew from his service, while Lord Bristol, another of his enemies, falls into temporary disgrace.

The next section, which is devoted to 'The Duke's Fifth Campagne, and the first he serv'd in the Spanish Army' (*Life*, pp. 297–329) opens with four paragraphs which likewise do not appear in the MS. *Campagnes*. These describe Charles II's and James's efforts to raise six regiments of foot, drawn from the English, Scots, and Irish then in France, to serve with the Spaniards. Over 2000 men are raised and the number would have been doubled but for Spanish jealousy and discouragement. The Duke nevertheless, being now in Brussels, wins the good will of Don Juan and the Spanish ministers, and takes the field at the head of the British regiments. The account in the MS. *Campagnes* is resumed at this point.

Here, and throughout this section of the *Life*, and also in the section for 1658, the narrative is in the first person; and this suggests that this part of the *Life* is a literal copy, as it purports to be, of James's autograph memoirs.

were on horseback and in good order, he forced a passage through the two lines of cavalry which stood in his way and which could not hinder so considerable a body of troops, whose only business was to reach the town; which was performed with very little loss. He arrived at the Counterscarp; and the Count de Salazar, governor of the place, so little expected this succour that the Prince de Condé was a long time at the palisade before they opened the gate for him. This surprise was the more agreeable to him [Salazar], because he was no great soldier, the garrison was weak, and if he had not been relieved at that time, he was going to abandon the town and defend the citadel. The place was ordinarily well provided with men, and the reason why it was not then well provided was that the Spaniards believed Cromwell was sending six thousand of his troops to join the French and that they were designing to attack some maritime town of the Spaniards. So they fortified all their garrisons on that side; and the Cardinal, having been informed that the garrison of Cambrai was weak, thought this a more favourable opportunity for taking it as he had for long greatly desired to become its Bishop and Prince;[1] and truly, had not the Prince de Condé been extremely prompt and suddenly and by chance decided to succour it, the town had been taken. For if he had been in Brussels when the Spaniards were warned of the siege, the French would have completed their lines before the Spaniards could have deliberated and resolved on the means of relieving the place.[2]

Monsieur de Turenne who had counted on the usual slowness and gravity of the Spaniards was exceedingly surprised at the Prince de Condé's promptitude, and having learned from some prisoners the number and quality of the troops that had entered the town, he judged it appropriate to raise the siege and give advice of this to the Court. The Prince de Condé, having left a sufficient garrison [in Cambrai], returned to Brussels and sent the rest of his troops to the general rendezvous which was near Mons.

This ill success [of Turenne's] disconcerted the measures that

---

[1] . . . 'crut l'occasion d'autant plus favorable pour la prendre qu'il avoit de longue main une forte passion d'en devenir l'Eveque et le Prince.' The passage in *Life* is milder and slightly more amusing: 'which he had more desire to take than any other, having, as I have been inform'd, a kind of longing to be made Prince and Bishop of it' (p. 300).
[2] The narrative in *Life* is more detailed and elaborate.

the French had taken for this campaign. They abandoned the design of undertaking any other considerable siege; they divided their army; Monsieur de la Ferté with one part went to attack Montmédy, and Monsieur de Turenne with the other marched towards the sea to join the English infantry that had disembarked, after which he returned the same way to watch the movements of the Spaniards. These, on the 19th of June, left the neighbourhood of Mons to go and camp on the Sambre a little above Thuin. On the 22nd the army passed the river, the next day it camped near Philippeville as if with the design of relieving Montmédy. Monsieur de Turenne made haste to get there before them; but the real design was to beguile and deceive him,[3] and fall upon Calais which it was hoped to carry in a few hours, at a point that was known to be weak. The Spaniards had been meditating this design even before the departure of the Archduke, who had sent engineers in disguise to reconnoitre the weaknesses of the place. They had not yet been able to find an opportunity of attacking it. They thought at last they would succeed and had taken measures so sound that it seemed the enterprise could not fail. It was conducted in such secrecy that the enemy had not the least suspicion of it. The Spaniards, on quitting Mons, had left a body of cavalry behind, which with the infantry that could be drawn from the neighbouring garrisons was enough to begin the undertaking.

After leading Monsieur de Turenne to advance towards Montmédy, the Spanish army suddenly turned back and began to march towards Calais on the 26th. Don Juan,[4] the Prince de Condé, and Caracena went in advance with the cavalry by the shortest way and left the Duke of York and Marsin with the infantry to follow with all diligence; the baggage and cannon were marching more in advance. The Prince de Ligne[5] had been chosen to execute this enterprise and, that he might have the principal conduct of it, he was sent a day's march in front of the army to put

---

[3] 'Mr de Turenne se hasta de gagner les devants; le dessein estoit de l'amuser et de luy donner le change, en tombant sur Calais, . . .'

[4] Don Juan was a son of Philip IV and the actress Maria Calderón. He had fought bravely in his early campaigns and his father, who had appointed him in 1656 as viceroy of the Netherlands, seems to have thought he might emulate the achievements of his sixteenth-century namesake. He was to distinguish himself mainly for his self-assurance and his siestas.

[5] The *Life* has 'The Prince de Ligny', which is an error.

himself at the head of the troops which had been left behind for this purpose. The Duke of York marched the first night to Tilly with the infantry; on the 27th he reached the suburbs of Mons; on the 28th Bruelles (?);[6] on the 29th, having passed the Scheldt at Tournai, he camped at Bouvines.[7] On the 31st he marched under the walls of Lille, passed the Lys at Armentières, and camped at Nieukerke.[8] The next day, 1st of July, he arrived at Hazebrouk and on the 2nd at Arques, a league distant from St. Omer, where, on arriving, he proposed to reach Calais before nightfall. But he received a letter from Don Juan who sent him word that the enterprise had failed and ordered him to remain at Arques until he received further instructions.

The Prince de Ligne had marched from Gravelines as soon as it was night to execute the design at low tide by seizing that part of the town which was outside the walls and adjoining the quay, after which one could make oneself master of the town in twelve hours. But he arrived half an hour too late; the water was so high that it was impossible to pass through, and he was obliged to draw off having done nothing but give a sudden alarm to the town and show the governor where the weakest point was, which the governor then took pains to fortify and so deprive the Spaniards of any hope of being able to surprise the place.

This long march having produced no other effect, the cavalry and infantry joined up at Quiernes, a league from Ayre, on the 4th of July and the cannon and baggage arrived a day or two later. The army marched on the 6th to Bourech near Lillers, remained there a few days and went and camped towards the 12th at Brouai; the next day at Lens, then at Roeux on the Scarpe, and on the 15th at Sauchy-Cauchy between Arras and Cambrai, and after camping there until the 21st it marched to Marcoing.

While time was being lost in making so many useless marches, Monsieur de la Ferté continued the Siege of Montmédy, which offered more resistance than he had expected, the place being

<hr/>

[6] The MS. has 'Briffeuille' crossed out and replaced in another hand (probably James's) by 'Bruelles'. Ramsay, *Histoire de Turenne*, II, cxviii, gives 'Bruxelles', and this is almost certainly correct.

[7] The MS. has: 'Il vint camper a pont a Tresin.' 'Tresin' has been crossed out and replaced by 'Bouvines'. I take 'Bouvines' (not of course Pont-à-Bouvines) as the correct reading.

[8] Neuve-Chapelle.

strong and defended by a good garrison. Monsieur de Turenne for his part was watching the Spaniards' movements without however going far from the beleaguered town, in order to prevent any relief from being thrown into it. The [Spanish] army having broken camp at Marcoing on the 27th marched to Ferracques, on the 29th to Origny where it only stayed one day and then went to camp at Eglancour until the 8th of August, when it marched to Feron; the next day to Macon near Chimai, and on the 10th to Amblain a league away from Mariembourg, where news came of the taking of Montmédy, which had defended itself so bravely and obstinately that it surrendered only after the enemy had lodged themselves in a bastion and set up a battery of six cannon there. It was learned at the same time that Monsieur de Turenne was marching into Flanders to undertake some siege. The [Spanish] army had to set off again on the 14th and did not stop until the 20th when it reached Calonne on the Lys, a league distant from St. Venant, which Monsieur de Turenne had laid siege to and where the lines were already so far advanced[9] that this consideration and the disposition of the forces did not allow the Spaniards to attempt to relieve the place. They simply thought how they might cut off the enemy's provisions and prevent the passage of a convoy of four or five hundred waggons which it was known was to march next day from Béthune to the French army. It was judged fitting for this purpose to break camp and take up a position at Montbernanson by which place it was absolutely necessary they should pass. The country across which the army was to march being covered [with enclosures] and intersected with hedges and ditches, workmen were commanded to march at the head of each regiment with spades and axes[10] to clear a way for them, so that the army could take up battle-order in the plain which was only a cannon's shot from the enemy. The army was

[9] The Spaniards were mistaken. Turenne had been able to do very little up to this time (Turenne, II, 80).

[10] 'Le pays par ou on devoit marcher estant fort couvert et entrecouppé de hayes et de fossés, on commanda des travailleurs pour marcher avec des beches et des haches a la teste de chaque Regiment. . . .' The narrative in the *Life* is more wordy and less circumstantial. 'And because the place where wee then lay, as well as the formost part of the ground, over which wee were to march the following day, was an inclos'd Country, wee had commanded men appointed to march with tooles at the head of each Regiment. . . .' (p. 305).

ready to break camp at dawn, and yet it only marched towards noon. The reason for this delay is all the more difficult to imagine because the success of the design depended on diligence. There was no neglect in warning Don Juan of this; the Duke of York advised him that the least delay would give the convoy an opportunity of entering the lines. But, despite everything that could be said, the army did not move until towards noon.[11] The Prince de Ligne, General of the Cavalry, was at the head of the right wing, the Prince de Condé at the left, and the Duke of York, whom Don Juan had desired to perform that day the office of Mestre de Camp General, was at the head of the infantry. Don Juan and the Marquess of Caracena marched before with their three companies of Guards, until, on arriving near the plain, they wished to take their siesta,[12] according to their custom.

The army could only move slowly in a country so enclosed. Nevertheless the Duke of York had but one enclosure to cross in order to arrive on the plain with the infantry, when he saw the enemy's convoy which, descending from Montbernanson, was marching with all diligence to reach the lines. The Duke, then, having passed the last hedge put his infantry in order of battle; and seeing that the Prince de Ligne was also on the plain with four or five squadrons, he sent to warn him of the convoy's approach, and that he had only to go forward and capture it all, the enemy having but three squadrons as escort. The Prince replied that he could see the thing as well as the Duke could, that nothing was easier than to seize the convoy, but that he durst not attack it without orders from Don Juan or the Marquess of Caracena. The Duke then went himself to find the Prince de Ligne and begged him not to lose so fair an opportunity by being too scrupulous; but he replied that he knew not how far Spanish severity would go; that by attacking without orders, it might cost him his head; especially if he did not succeed or if he should happen to receive the least reverse. The Duke replied that there was no ill success to be feared; that Monsieur de Turenne might indeed send out some

[11] The narrative in the *Life* is rather more amusing at this point: 'I am sure, some were not wanting to put Don Juan in mind of it, and myself for one; but wee began our march never the sooner for that advice' (p. 306).

[12] Cf. *Life*, p. 306: '. . . till they came within one Closs of the plaine, and there according to their usuall custom took their Siesta (or afternoon's Sleep).'

cavalry, but that he would not venture to send his infantry out of the lines. He added that if the Spaniards should happen to trouble him about this action, he consented to take all the blame of it on himself, and that the Prince might justly excuse himself on the ground of having done it only in obedience to the Duke since the latter was that day acting as Mestre de Camp General. But all these reasons availed nothing with the Prince de Ligne. The opportunity was lost. The convoy which recognised the danger redoubled its diligence; and when most of the waggons had entered within the lines, the three [Spanish] companies of Guards came to join the Prince de Ligne with orders to attack the convoy. He took with him only his own company of Guards. The Duke of York sent his. But the first four companies, which were led by the Count de Colmanar, Caracena's nephew, a young man without experience, marched forward so hastily and in such disorder that if the enemy's three squadrons had wished to dispute the ground, they would have beaten them. Berkeley, Captain of the Duke's Guards, seeing their bad manœuvre, followed them in good order and was of great help to them; for the three French squadrons having been forced to hasten on, the Spaniards pursued them as imprudently as they had previously advanced against them, and engaged them pell mell even inside the lines, for the enemy had not had time to shut the barrier; but they came out more quickly than they had gone in and fled without stopping until they had got behind Berkeley's company which had advanced to within a musket shot of the lines. There they rallied, but became so prudent and phlegmatic that, without taking pride in keeping the post of honour which belonged to them, they left Berkeley the honour of forming the rear guard, and in this order they returned to join the army; this they found drawn up in order of battle on the plain, within a cannon's shot of the enemy; where, after remaining some time, it drew back a little to the rear and camped on Montbernanson.

The enemy did not lose a single waggon of their convoy. They had some few men killed, wounded or made prisoner. The Marquis de Renty, a man of quality, and Tiernen or Quiernen who commanded the Régiment de Gesures, died of their wounds.

The next day[13] the Duke of York had a conversation on parole

[13] The *Life* says 'the same evening'.

with the Marquis d'Humières and some other French officers who came out of their lines on purpose to find an opportunity of talking with the Duke. He had with him an officer named Tourville, who commanded one of the Prince de Condé's cavalry regiments. This officer was to have the guard with a Spanish regiment on the following day, at the foot of the heights that were within a cannon's shot of the [French] lines. He knew that the French would not fail to fire on them at daybreak; and so he asked someone of his acquaintance, who were the Artillery officers in the French army. This man named them; whereupon Tourville asked him to present his compliments to one of them who was a personal friend, and to desire him to point his cannon at the Spaniards who were to be on his right and to be good enough to spare the left where he himself would be. The thing was carried out as requested. The Spaniards were regaled with quite peculiar distinction; they lost several men and horses before they were given orders to retire, and not a single shot was fired on Tourville's squadron.

The Duke of York has since learned that Reynolds who commanded the English troops Cromwell had sent to France, had been informed of the arrival of the Spanish army at Calonne, and so had asked Monsieur de Turenne if he would simply give him two thousand horse to support his six thousand English foot, to go and attack them there; hoping that the bravery of his infantry, who were accustomed to fighting in a country of hedges, would supply their want of numbers; but the General refused his consent, judging the thing impracticable and that it was unfitting to hasard these troops in an enterprise so rash.

After failing to capture the convoy, and considering that the enemy were too strong to allow of any hope of forcing their lines, the Spaniards deliberated[14] on what was to be done to oblige them to raise the siege, or what place could be attacked and taken before the enemy had achieved their design. The matter was decided at a Council of War which was held on the day following that of the arrival at Montbernanson. It was resolved to go and besiege Ardres; but the execution of this plan was delayed until the 25th

[14] 'On delibera . . .' *Campagnes* contains a superabundance of 'on', 'il' and 'ils', where a more precise indication is often desirable. The text of the *Life* is better in this respect. In the present instance, e.g., the *Life* has 'wee consider'd what course wee should take to oblige the Enemy, . . .' I have not scrupled on occasion to insert 'the Spaniards' or 'the French' as the case may be.

for fear lest the enemy, not having yet opened their trenches, might leave their present enterprise and come and engage Don Juan in battle against his will. This delay, the reason for which was poor, proved very prejudicial. Monsieur de Turenne lost no time; he opened his trenches the same night as the Spanish army arrived at Montbernanson. The Spaniards left on the 25th in the morning and arrived in front of Ardres before noon on the 27th. They first made haste to establish their quarters so as to prevent any help entering the place where it was known that there were no more than three hundred foot; but that day and night were lost in working at a circumvallation, which in everyone's judgment was very useless; whereas if they had attacked the place that night, they would probably have carried it.

The Spaniards are accustomed to flattering themselves easily on the success of their enterprises. The Marquess of Caracena's trumpeter coming from the French army before St. Venant, reported that the place was not as hard pressed as was supposed; whence the Marquess concluded that it was unnecessary to make as much haste as he was being urged, in besieging Ardres. But there arrived at the same time and with the same trumpeter a footman of the Duke of York's who had been several days in the enemy's camp and who assured the Spaniards that that very day or that night at latest, the place would be taken. Don Juan and the Marquess refused to believe it and judged the thing impossible.

This presumption and the negligence which had made them lose the opportunity of capturing the convoy that passed under their noses, exceedingly surprised the Duke of York who was not yet accustomed to Spanish formalities.[15] And this invites one to a digression which may come in here very appropriately, so as to cause less surprise at the faults they have been already seen committing and of those that will follow. Don Juan observed on Campaign the same forms of gravity and reserve[16] as if he had been in

---

[15] Here follows in the *Life* (I, 311) a passage which James omitted from the *Campagnes*:

'And I remember, that complaining to the Prince of Conde of the first of these errours, the night after the Convoy was gotten into the Enemys Line, I was answer'd by him, That he well saw I was Stranger to the proceedings of that Spanish Army, but that I was to prepare myself to see more and grosser faults committed by them, before the end of that Campagne; And so it prov'd, as the Reader will have occasion to observe.'

[16] The *Life* has 'gravity and retirdness', which perhaps conveys the nuance better.

Brussels. He was everywhere equally difficult of access. He and also the Marquess of Caracena, as has already been observed, were asleep very near the plain when the convoy was passing. Their servants who saw it coming down the hill, as did the rest of the army, never durst awaken them to warn them of it. But what is still more surprising is that Don Juan and the Marquess, who both had much good sense and wit and bravery, could be attached to formalities which they well knew to be prejudicial to their master's service and their own reputation.

The Marquess was a very good officer, had served for a long time, had passed through all the degrees[17] and owed his fortune to his merit; and had not Don Juan had, so to speak, the misfortune of being brought up as a Son of Spain, he was endued with qualities which could have made him a great man. But their scrupulous formalities ruined everything. When the army was on the march, they never rode at the head of it, except when in presence of the enemy. When half the troops were still out of camp, they would get on horseback and ride at the head of their three companies of Guards straight to the quarters which had been marked out for them, without troubling about the army, or taking pains to reconnoitre the situation of the ground or to know where the generals had their quarters; so, in case of an alarm or on the approach of the enemy, they knew nothing of the Camp, nor where the main guard was, nor the advance guards. Don Juan was most often accustomed, on arriving at his quarters, to go to bed. He supped there and did not rise until the morning. When the army was not marching he seldom went out or got on horseback.[18]

But to return to the siege of Ardres. On the 28th a Council of War was held in the Marquess of Caracena's quarters to resolve on what side the place should be attacked. When the generals were assembled they were all taken to the top of a tower that was there and were asked to reconnoitre the place with optic glasses;[19] and without any closer examination it was resolved that the Spaniards should attack a half moon between two bastions; that the

[17] 'avoit . . . passé par tous les degrez.' The *Life* has 'pass'd through all the degrees', i.e., risen from the lowest commissioned rank.

[18] In the MS. *Campagnes* the whole of this digression is marked with a line in the margin. In the *Life*, the following remark is added: 'so that the Major Generalls, in effect, did all the office of the Generalls.'

[19] 'lunettes d'approche,' i.e., telescopes. The *Life* (p. 312) has 'perspective glasses'.

Duke of York should attack the bastion on the right, and the Prince de Condé that on the left; and that, so as to lose no time, they should take measures to attach the miner to the body of the place that same night.

The Duke of York and the Prince de Condé, not being satisfied with having seen the place from the top of the tower, went to reconnoitre it more closely. Don Juan and the Marquess did not go in person to reconnoitre where they were to attack, they only sent a Major de battaille[20] to bring them an account of it; it not being the custom of the Spanish generals to expose themselves on such occasions. All things being now ready, the army opened the attack as soon as it was night, on a signal from Don Juan's quarters. The besieged had no men to defend the approaches, and so the troops advanced to the edge of the ditch, where they secured a lodgment before attempting to attach the miner. For the Duke of York's attack his own regiment was employed; Lord Muskerry who commanded it had a captain and a few soldiers from other battalions to strengthen him. The Duke took care to send him fascines and everything that he needed, and then went to visit the operations with the Duke of Gloucester. He found that Muskerry had ordered everything as it should be, that he had almost finished his lodgment at the edge of the ditch, facing the point of the bastion, and that he had already lodged the body of the battalion in the ditch of the ravelin which covered the point of the bastion. The Duke thought it was now time to attach the miner; but perceiving by moonlight that there was water in the bottom of the ditch, he sent a sergeant to sound it; who reported that the water was not deep enough to prevent the passage of the miners. He sent them down into the ditch with a sergeant and a few soldiers to carry the madriers[21] by means of which they were to lodge themselves. Day now beginning to dawn, the Duke of York and the Duke of Gloucester withdrew and returned to their quarters. No details will be given of the other attacks; one may simply say that as they had had the same success and attached their miners, it was not doubted but that the place would surrender in less than twenty-four hours. Word was taken to Don Juan and the Marquess of Caracena who were in their coach behind their attacking

---

[20] I retain this expression which is used also in the English text of the *Life*.
[21] Large planks. The French word 'Madriers' is used in the *Life* (I, 314).

positions and out of cannon shot of the enemy, that the Prince de Condé and the Duke of York had been to visit the operations of their own men. Don Juan replied: No hazen bien, which means, They act not wisely.

In the morning a little after sunrise, there came news that St. Venant was taken and that Monsieur de Turenne was advancing to relieve Ardres. A Junta was immediately assembled and it was at once resolved to raise the siege. The difficulty was to withdraw the troops from the attacking positions; there had been no time to make siege works and trenches for communication; so they could only draw back in the open. The operation began by bringing back the miners, which was done in the Duke's position[22] by the care of Lord Muskerry. Before communicating to the officers who were with him anything of the orders he had received, he [Muskerry] sent word to the miners to return as best they could and that, to cover their retreat, he would have his men open heavy fire on the besieged. He caused his soldiers to believe he was withdrawing them because he had been warned that that place was countermined; and the miners, under cover of heavy fire from the musketry, reached the lodgment without mishap. He then told his men about the order he had received, and commanded them to retire, when he should give the word, with all possible diligence to a place he showed them, out of musket shot, where they were to rally. The Duke of York on his side ordered a lieutenant with thirty horsemen[23] to approach the place as near as possible without exposing himself until he saw the soldiers returning from the attacking position, and then to gallop among them in order to bring away any officers or men who might fall wounded. The Duke followed them to see his orders executed and found that while his soldiers were drawing back from the attack, the lieutenant and his horsemen were stationed quietly behind a hedge within musket shot of the town. The Duke galloped up to the lieutenant to repeat the order he had given; the other obeyed and to make amends for his neglect rode to the edge of the ditch; and although the besieged opened heavy fire, no officers except Captain Knight[24]

22 'à l'attaque du Duc,' i.e., in the position which his attacking troops had occupied.
23 'trente Maistres.' Certainly mounted men, probably not N.C.O.s.
24 The *Life* reads: 'Captain Kinf', for which the editor suggests 'Keith'. The MS. has 'Knight', the *gt* having been inserted in dark ink as a correction. The rest of this paragraph differs markedly from the corresponding passage in the *Life*.

and but a few soldiers were wounded, and none died, which was as fortunate as it was extraordinary. A few miners were lost from the other attacks. After the troops had everywhere drawn back with very little loss, the baggage train was sent towards Gravelines and the whole army followed. This march was extremely painful. On arriving at the edge of the lowlands, they were obliged to halt until the cannon and baggage were on the dike or causeway which leads from Polincour to Gravelines and which the heavy rains had made almost impassable. The rain that continued without ceasing, the tempest, the darkness of the night, the road heavy with mud and the frequent halts they had to make, distressed the troops and threw them into so great a disorder that it was impossible for the officers to prevent their breaking ranks and seeking cover where they could. In the morning there were not ten men together in any one regiment; all that could be done was to reassemble them next day. On the 30th the army camped at Broukerke. The French army had its share of bad weather on the night it marched across the plain from St. Omer to Ardres, when the Spanish army raised the siege.

On the 31st the Spanish army passed the Colme, and the troops were quartered at Drinkam and in the surrounding villages, to recover a little from their great fatigue. The country was so enclosed that it would have been very difficult to camp in battle order; but the enemy was so far off that there was no risk. On the 2nd of September the army marched towards Mont Cassel and, the troops having been quartered in the neighbouring villages, they remained until the 7th. Then, having learned that Monsieur de Turenne was near La Motte-aux-Bois, the army marched to[25] Wormhout, where they had news on the 12th that the French had taken La Motte-aux-Bois and were approaching now for the second time. The Spaniards therefore repassed the Colme next day with the resolution of defending the passage of that river and camped along its banks. They were posted from the Fort of Linck nearly as far as Likere; the Duke of York's line extended from the place where the Spanish quarters ended to as far as Bergue sur Vinox,[26] and the Prince de Condé's as far as Bergue itself. All the bridges were broken and earthworks were raised behind the fords

[25] Not 'from', as the *Life* says.
[26] And not 'bergue, St. Vinox' as in the *Life*.

until the 17th, when it was learned that Monsieur de Turenne was advancing to take them on the flank, he having passed the Colme above Linck. Most of the native Spanish regiments with some cavalry were at once detached to occupy Gravelines. The three Italian regiments commanded by Don Tito del Prato were sent to the fort of Mardyck; and the rest of the army drew back behind the canal that runs from Bergue to Dunkirk; the Prince de Condé having his quarters at Bergue, Don Juan at Dunkirk, and the Duke of York at Coukerk;[27] and cannon were planted all along the canal where they found batteries all ready.

A day or two after the Spaniards had left the Colme, the French arrived before Mardyck and laid siege to it. This was partly in fulfilment of the treaty with Cromwell by which they pledged themselves to put into his hands some maritime town in Flanders, and Mardyck was the only one they could attack so late in the season; because great care had been taken to provide Gravelines and Dunkirk with everything necessary for a long and vigorous defence.[28]

The Duke of York, who was intending to observe the enemy when they arrived before Mardyck, took with him the Horse Guards who were outside the gates of Dunkirk and advancing to within cannon shot of the city,[29] he left the Guards behind to secure his retreat in case he should be pursued. He then, with fifteen officers and other men well mounted, rode up so near to the French army that some officers of the Regiment of Picardy, which was on the march, advanced some way and fired on him with the fusils[30] they were carrying when on horseback. When they reached the quarter which had been assigned them[31] and the soldiers began to build their huts, these officers and several from other regiments rode out again to drive back the Duke; but some of them who came nearer this Prince recognised a big greyhound they had seen with him in France and asked if the Duke of York was there. When they were told that he was, they cried out *Sur parole*, desiring to speak with him. He then stopped, and found among them several persons of the first quality who were all of old acquaint-

[27] Probably Oudekerke.
[28] This part in the *Life* is verbose and repetitive.
[29] Obviously Mardyck, and not, as in the *Life* (p. 318), Dunkirk.
[30] The word used in the *Life*.
[31] The position which this French regiment was to occupy in the siege of Mardyck.

ance. They alighted from their horses; the Prince did the same; and they conversed together for nearly an hour until Monsieur de Turenne ordered them to come back. There were quite two or three hundred officers: the Marquis d'Humières, the Comte de Guiche, Castelnau, indeed most of the persons of quality and notable officers in the French army. The Duke of York had no more than twenty persons with him, among whom was a Spanish officer of horse who, seeing him turn back when he heard himself named, was surprised and asked what he intended to do. The Duke ordered him to remain beside him, and said that no one had anything to fear. This episode is related particularly that it may be observed what civility is used in that country even between enemies or persons of opposed parties, and that the Duke, although in the service of Spain, had no fewer friends in the French army. Some English who were present at this conversation wished to follow the same example, and they fared ill for it as will be seen hereafter. The Duke of York does not positively know whether the Spaniards took umbrage at these courtesies; but at the end of the campaign Monsieur de Marsin advised him, personally, to abstain from them henceforth. He told him that the Spanish character is suspicious and circumspect; and that, although they gave no sign of it, they might not be at all satisfied. The Duke of York replied that if his behaviour aroused their disquiet, they were much in the wrong; that they had been unable to observe in his conduct during the whole campaign anything but great fidelity and application in their service; that he would always continue in the same way, and that in the event of a fight he would attack anyone of his acquaintance in the same way as even the most zealous Spaniard might do. But, he added, as for conversing when opportunity offered with persons who had served so long with him, he thought he could give himself this satisfaction without being of prejudice to the Spaniards; and that, to show them that he had no other intention than of following the customs of ordinary civility, he had not suffered any of the Prince de Condé's officers to be with him on such occasions, because he did not think it reasonable that they should be there and that the Spaniards might justly think ill of it. The Duke always after that observed the same circumspection when he wished the officers of the French army to enter into conversation with him.

On arriving before Mardyck the French set to work immediately on their lines on the Dunkirk side and on the approaches to the fort. The forage in the neighbourhood having been eaten up, they were obliged next morning to go and look for some on three great farms which were at only a half cannon shot from the Spanish trenches: these had been preserved through the influence their owners[32] had with some officers of the Spanish army. There was even a regular guard[33] to prevent anyone's touching them. The commander of this guard, when he saw the French approaching with horse and foot, could not but judge for what purpose they were coming. But, following the laudable custom of the Spaniards, he drew back without daring to set fire to the farms, because he had received no order to do so.

The cannon in the Spanish lines opened fire when the vanguard of the enemy approached. The Duke of York, whose quarters were only half a mile from there, galloped up and found that the French were already working to get cover and entrench themselves[34] so as to defend themselves in case of attack. Meeting the Prince de Ligne who was that day filling the office of Mestre de Camp General, the Duke asked him what he intended to do and whether he wished to let the enemy forage quietly in front of his eyes. The Prince replied in his usual way, that without the orders of the Marquess of Caracena or of Don Juan, he durst undertake nothing. Thereupon the Duke answered that before they could arrive, the French would be entrenched and it would no longer be possible to dislodge them or to burn the forage. The other responded that that was true, but he would undertake nothing without positive orders. The Duke told him that he was himself going to attack the enemy with his own troops and asked the Prince only to draw up his infantry along the line. But the other replied that, the bridge being in the Spanish quarter, he could not permit him to pass that way, because if there was anything to be done it was for the Spaniards to do it. Thus all these proposals served no purpose, and while orders were awaited from Dunkirk, the French foraged without being disturbed by anything but the cannon

---

[32] They were relatives of the Spanish officers (*Life*, p. 320).

[33] A horse guard of about 100 men (*Life*, p. 320).

[34] The *Life* says they 'were beginning to lodge themselves at the farme houses, and preparing for their own security . . .' (p. 321).

which kept firing on them. The noise brought the Prince de Condé from Bergues. The Duke of York at once informed him of what had passed between himself and the Prince de Ligne. The Prince de Condé was not at all surprised, and assured the Duke that when he had served with the Spaniards as long as he, the Prince, had, he would get accustomed to seeing them commit many great faults without being astonished. The enemy having foraged as long as they pleased drew back, leaving behind them about one hundred horses that the cannon had killed. It is not known how many men they lost, but no dead bodies were found, whether because they had taken them away or because they had buried them on the spot in some place which could not be discovered.

Two or three days later the fort of Mardyck surrendered, and, in accordance with the treaty with Cromwell, it was put next day into the hands of Reynolds; and shortly afterwards the French, having repaired the breaches and filled in the trenches, marched back to quarters in their own country for rest and forage. The Spanish army continued in camp where they were, and it was announced that they would retake Mardyck. The sickness caused by the unhealthful air was so general that, except for the native-born Spaniards, few officers and soldiers escaped fevers[35] and more than half were at one and the same time incapable of doing duty. The troops commanded by the Duke of York suffered the worst; he himself was almost the only person among the officers or volunteers of quality, or the members of his household, who was not attacked. The Duke of Gloucester left the army, sick; and the Prince de Condé was holden with such a fever that the doctors feared for his life. Soon after this the King of England came to Dunkirk to solicit Don Juan concerning some private business and to remind him of some promises which he had made his Majesty in relation to England.

The English in Mardyck started repairing the old fortifications round that fortress, work which was all the more easy as the ditches had not been filled in and only a small part of the parapet had been levelled. Don Juan being warned of this resolved to march there one night with the whole army in order to destroy in a single day[36] the defence works which they had been building for a

---

[35] '... few ..., excepting only the naturall Spaniards escap'd agues' (*Life*).

[36] 'en un jour.' Apparently an oversight. The *Life* has 'in the space of a night'.

month. This was more out of ostentation and to make his men believe that he designed to retake the fort, than from any hope of success.

The day having been appointed for this expedition, he marched out of Dunkirk at the head of the army and accompanied by the King of England. The darkness was so great that they had to proceed by torchlight; which when the enemy perceived, they thought the Spaniards were going to storm the place or at the least lay siege to it, and they prepared to defend themselves by lighting torches round the fort. When the army arrived within rather less than cannon shot, they extinguished their torches. His Majesty, Don Juan, and the Marquess of Caracena then halted with the cavalry, while the infantry was advancing. The Spaniards, commanded by * * *[37] Maréchal de Bataille, marched to that part of the outworks that looked towards Dunkirk; the Comte de Marsin with the Prince de Condé's foot, to the part that looks towards Gravelines; and the Duke of York, at the head of his troops, posted himself between the two. When they approached the fort, the enemy kept up a continual fire of cannon and musketry, and the little frigates that were in the canal[38] did not cease firing either. The infantry suffered very little because they got straight into the shelter of the old outworks; but the balls which passed over their heads fell among the cavalry and killed men and horses. His Majesty having gone forward to see what the infantry were doing, the Duke of Ormond who was with him had his horse killed under him by a cannon shot. Each corps, on arriving at its position, sent its workmen forward with soldiers to support them; but the ditch was too deep in the Duke of York's position and he was obliged to send them round to where the Spaniards were to attack. In the meantime he had the ditch filled with fascines[39] and caused a passage over to be made so that he could support them if the enemy made a sortie. While the workmen were beginning to raze the fortifications,[40] the soldiers who had been detached in support kept up a continual fire on the enemy, and continued to do this until early dawn when,

[37] There is also a blank in the *Life* (p. 323).
[38] This 'fosse', presumably a canal running inland from the sea, was called 'the Splinter' (*Life*, p. 323).
[39] The military term: they were bundles of faggots.
[40] 'applanir les ouvrages.'

the outworks being razed, the army drew off in good order and arrived at Dunkirk when it was beginning to be broad daylight. The enemy were surely more surprised by the retreat than the attack, and they so little expected the Spaniards to retire so soon that they were still firing when the troops had been gone a good half-hour. There were not more than twenty horsemen, a captain of Gloucester's regiment and three or four soldiers killed; there were eight or ten wounded. The English in the fort, as was learned since, had only one man killed. And they believed so firmly that they would be besieged that they dispatched a messenger to Monsieur de Turenne to warn him of it. He assembled his troops who were in forage quarters and began to march to their help; but, on being advised that the Spaniards had drawn off, he returned to his quarters.

A few days after this an attempt was made to seize the English frigates which were lying in the canal. The first design had been to burn them,[41] but this being judged too difficult, it was resolved to try and surprise the two larger ones, the 'Rose' and the 'True Love', which mounted six or eight cannon each. For this action twelve shallops were armed and sent out in very calm weather. Don Juan warned the King and the Duke of York and they went along the shore accompanied by all the persons of quality and the principal officers to see what success the enterprise would meet with. There was a kind of mist. When they came over against the frigates, an English seaman was heard calling out: 'What ship's boat is that?'; and on no one's replying, this man, seeing another shallop that was going to board the frigate, raised the alarm and fired a cannon shot which broke the leg of one of the rowers. This accident and a few musket balls that were fired at the same time terrified the shallops which drew off shamefully without attempting anything further.

Since Reynolds had seen the civilities which the French took pleasure in showing the Duke of York when they found an opportunity of speaking with him, he also desired to have one; and having, for this purpose, roamed several times in the direction where he knew the English were accustomed to ride when they came out of the town[42] on horseback, he one day sent for Lord Newbourgh

[41] By means of fire-ships. The *Life* explains why this plan was impracticable (p. 325).
[42] Presumably Dunkirk.

244

and Colonel Richard Talbot. The former had by chance received great civilities from Reynolds on several occasions in England, and Talbot was under obligation to him for having saved his life in Ireland. This caused them willingly to enter into parley with him. After some discourse he asked them if the Duke of York did not come sometimes to take the air that way; and on their replying that he came fairly often, he said that if the Duke was willing that Reynolds should have the honour of speaking with him, as he did with them, that would give him great pleasure. They promised to propose this to the Duke and said they thought he would make no difficulty. On their return they informed the King and the Duke, who riding out that way more often than they had been accustomed to, Lord Newbourgh asked his Majesty's permission to go and speak to Reynolds. This being granted, he asked George Hamilton to accompany him, and riding up to the mounted sentry of the Mardyck garrison, told him to have his General advised that he desired to speak with him. Reynolds came at once, having with him only a gentleman named Mr. Crew, and first asked Lord Newbourgh who were the men he could see some way off against a dune. The other only named the Duke of York, whereupon Reynolds asked, 'Can I not then go and speak to him?' Newbourgh sent Mr. Hamilton to the King and the Duke to inform them of what Reynolds desired. His Majesty ordered the Duke to go. He took with him only Hamilton and Berkeley the Captain of his Guards. As soon as Reynolds saw him advancing he came to meet him, and was going to alight to salute him [on foot]; but Crew dissuaded him. Except for that, he conducted himself with much civility and respect. He began to discourse with great compliments, addressed the Duke as Highness and prayed him not to regard him as sent by Cromwell but as being in the service of France; adding that he was as much disposed as any Frenchman to render him the respect that was his due. The Duke replied as civilly as he could, considering him a man who might one day be very useful. It even appeared to him that Reynolds had something to say that he did not wish Crew to hear; but as Crew was too close, he used obscure expressions which showed that he hoped to be able one day to render service to the Duke. The conversation lasted nearly a half hour and they separated well satisfied on both sides. It is not known what intentions Reynolds may have had; but

245

this interview and other civilities which he showed the King and the Duke cost him dear. He forbade the frigates to fire when either of them was riding by the sea; he sent presents of wine to Lord Newbourgh asking him to dispose of it to those of whom Newbourgh knew he felt much respect. Some officers who were serving under him took umbrage at this; Cromwell was advertised of it; and a Colonel named White chartered a vessel expressly to go and accuse him. Reynolds being informed of it embarked on the same vessel to justify himself. But a shipwreck settled their difference.[43] The negligence of the ship's master was cause of it. A frigate warned him by several cannon shots that if he did not change course he would be stranded on the sand-banks called the Goodwins; but whether because he scorned the signal or did not hear it, he ran on to the bank and not a man was saved.

It has been known since then that Cromwell had been so much offended by what Reynolds had done that he was resolved to order him to England and to deprive him of his command,[44] if he did not clear himself of suspicion by offering good reasons; but the accident that befell him finished everything. A certain Colonel Lockhart, a Scotsman who had married a relation of Cromwell's, succeeded to Reynolds' command.

The King, having finished what he had to do with Don Juan and the Marquess of Caracena, went to Bruges and then to Ghent and Brussels. The Duke of York remained at Dunkirk in command of the army. The Spaniards had been still keeping the population in the hope that they would retake Mardyck, with a view more easily to obtaining a large subsidy from the Province of Flanders; and to make this appear more likely, great magazines

[43] 'mais un Nauffrage les mit d'accord'—a cynical remark (not in the *Life*) which reminds one of La Fontaine's cat who when acting as judge of two small animals, '... mit les plaideurs d'accord en croquant l'un et l'autre.'

[44] James's interpretation of this episode must be regarded as extremely doubtful. John Reynolds was a Cambridgeshire man, who had made his reputation as an excellent officer in Ireland and had been knighted by Cromwell, prior to being sent to France as commander of the forces that were assisting Turenne. He had married Elisabeth Russell, a sister-in-law of Henry Cromwell; and thus, like others of Cromwell's generals, including Sir William Lockhart, he had become closely associated with the Protector's family. These circumstances make it very unlikely that he was disloyal. It seems certain that he exchanged 'civilities' with James, which the latter probably misunderstood. It is true, of course, that he died at sea soon after the interviews described. Apart from this, James's account of the affair is to be treated with scepticism.

were established of fascines and gabions[45] and all things necessary for a siege. Nevertheless the order was given to send the troops into winter quarters on New Year's Day; and the Duke who had remained all that time at Dunkirk, returned to Brussels a few days after Don Juan and the Marquess of Caracena had arrived there.

---

[45] From the Italian 'gabbione'. They were wicker baskets full of earth.

*1658**

BEING now come to Bruxelles in the beginning of January, 1658, I made no long stay in that City; for so soon as I had dispatched my small affaires, I went to my sister who was at Breda, where my Brother the Duke of Glocester had been already for some time to recover of his ague, which at my arriuall had just left him. After I had remain'd there till the midle of February, wee went all three together to Antwerp there to meet his Majesty.

While wee resided in that place, there were strong reports of something to be undertaken in England; and that all things were in such a readiness, that at the breaking of the frost, when the Six flutes[1] which were brought in Holland could come to Ostend, Soldiers should be put immediately on boord them, who together with some men of war, which lay ready there and at Dunkirk, were to be landed in some part of England, where it was also said wee had intelligence of forces which would joyn ours at their arrivall: But at the same time there were others who were so far from giving credit to those rumours, that they were of opinion nothing could be done: for looking more deeply into the matter they saw that both the King and the Spaniards, by these reports, aim'd on either side to excuse themselves for non performance of the Treaty made betwixt them; thō 'tis true the Spaniards by not performing their part, render'd it impossible for the King to comply with his engagements, at least to do what otherwise he might haue done.

And now while this discourse was at the hottest, the Earle of Bristoll having almost quite lost himself with the Spanish Ministers, was endeavouring his uttmost to ingratiate himself with the Prince of Condé; who at that time also, had neither any great esteem nor kindness for him. Being full of his design, he came one day to me in the Princesse's chamber, and began a discourse with

* Reprinted from the *Life*, I, 330–368. The MS. *Campagnes* is an almost word-for-word translation of this section.

[1] Flute. From French 'flûte'; cf. Dutch 'fluit'. It was a warship used as a troop carrier. The *O.E.D.* cites the *London Gazette*, No. 77/2 (1666): 'Two Men of War ... with three Flutes of 18 or 20 Guns.'

me concerning the busines of England: After a long conversation with me upon that subject, he sayd, That thō he doubted not but our designs there would meet with the desired success, yet he (it) would not be amiss to think before hand, what wee should do in case of a miscarriage; and that one of the things which he thought most necessary to be look'd after (which also more immediatly concern'd me) was to consider of some meanes to preserve the troopes which wee had already, and to increase their numbers by all the meanes wee could imagine; which if done, would render me more considerable with the Spaniard, besides the common advantage which would redound to the Royall party; That for the present he had nothing to propose towards the compassing of this design, but desir'd me to take it seriously into my thoughts, and he would also do the like; and that in case I would permitt him, he will speak with me again, when he had any thing in a readiness to offer: Thus wee parted, and he spoke no more to me upon that Subject during two or three days.

In the mean time this discourse had given me a very hott allarm, not doubting that I should haue some extraordinary proposition made to me, which would not be to my advantage: and that consideration put me upon ghessing of what nature it might be: It happen'd as I was rowling over these things in my imagination, one of my Servants told me of a discourse, which an Officer belonging to the Prince of Condé had held with him some days before; by the relation of which, I immediatly ghess'd what would be propos'd to me, and accordingly gave my Sister the knowledge of it; advising with her, what answer I should make when it should be offer'd to me.

A day or two after this, the Earle of Bristoll came again to me, and after another eloquent preambule, and a protestation that what he was going to propose to me was not only for his Maties Service, but for my particular advantage; in short his proposition was, That his Maty should joyn his troopes to those of the Princé of Condé, by which means they would be So considerable, that the Spaniards must be forced by necessity to comply with the promises, which they had made to the King for the recruiting of his forces, which it was apparent they had no inclination to do, having no great care or consideration of those which he already had; That as to what concern'd the command which I should haue, there might be care taken to accommodate it, the Prince of Condé being very easy to live withall, and having a great esteem of me.

He us'd these and many other arguments to perswade me to be of his opinion: To which I answer'd, That it was a busines of great importance, and ought to be Seriously weigh'd, before any resolution could be taken in it; that accordingly I would consider of it, and speak with him again. I say no more to him at that time, that he might not perceive the dislike I had of it. When he was gone, I not a litle troubled how to govern myself in this affaire; for I saw very well it was a snare layd for me: If I should haue approv'd the proposition, I had certainly lost my self with the Spaniards, who would haue taken it very ill, that I should haue put them upon the hardship of refusing any thing to the Prince of Condé, who was then So Strong, and So necessary to them; and I my self could not but be unwilling to consent to a thing, which would haue been prejudiciable to my reputation: for thō I had serv'd in Severall capacities under Monsr. de Turenne, I did not think that after having served so long, and commanded the King my Brother's forces the year before, it became me to come under any other person. On the other side, if I had openly discover'd any aversion to it, I should haue expos'd my self to the ill offices, which might haue been done me with his Maty upon that account; by their representing to him, that for a punctilio of my own, I was willing to obstruct what was intended for his Seruice, and also I should haue had the Prince of Condé my Enemy: all which considerations, together with the confidence I had that the Spaniards would never consent to such a proposition, whensoever it should be made to them, strengthen'd me in the resolution of appearing wholly passive in the matter, so as neither to put it forward nor obstruct it.[2]

Some time after this his Maty went to Bruxelles, and I with my Sister return'd to Breda, where having stayd with her three or four [days], I went back to Bruxelles to waite on the King: So Soon as I was return'd, they began again to talk with me concerning that affaire; And one day particularly, the King call'd me and My Lord Bristoll into the Chancellor's closett, where the matter was

---

[2] These four paragraphs, describing Lord Bristol's machinations and James's embarrassment, are translated very closely and even literally in the MS. *Campagnes* (pp. 232–235).

debated; And I who since my return thither, was more then ever confirm'd in my opinion, that the Spaniards wou'd never be induced to suffer it: Accordingly I spoke but litle, and at length it was concluded amongst them, that the Earle of Bristoll should conferr with the Lord Barklay (*Berkley*), how to propose it to the Spaniards, and after what manner the whole affaire was to be conducted. In order to this, they two had a meeting once about it, and no more; for by this time My Lord Bristoll began to see, that it was a matter not to be effected: because the Prince of Condé, having consider'd that it would give great umbrage to the Spaniards, and withall finding that it could not possibly be compass'd, went himself to Don John, and acquainted him with the proposition which the Earle of Bristoll had made to him, at the same time shewing his own dislike to it. That Conversation made an end of the whole affaire, and of the Small remaining credit of My Lord Bristoll with Don John and the Spanish Ministers: But on the other side, gave them a very good impression of me; for inquiring into the bottom of it, they easily found the great aversion I had to it: But as it prov'd of advantage to me in relation to the Spaniards, so he (*it*) did me harm with the Prince of Condé, who ever afterwards quite alter'd his way of living with me; and on the contrary liv'd much better then he had done the year before with all those, whom he knew to be no freinds to me and to my concernments.

In the begining of the spring, as soon as the frost was broken, the Six flutes above mention'd were taken by the English, betwixt Holland and Ostend; and so a conclusion was put to all the discourse of attempting any thing in England for that year.

All our thoughts at Bruxelles were now taken up with our preparations for the ensuing Campagne; and, as the time of action was approching, the Spaniards applyd their greatest care in providing for those places, which they judg'd were in greatest danger of being beseiged by the French Army: for all our Intelligence agreed, that this year the Enemy would undertake some considerable Seige. The thought of this gave great perplexity to the Spaniards; for not having a body of foot sufficient to man their important fronteer towns, as they ought to haue been furnish'd, they were forced to leave some of them very slightly guarded.

His Maty press'd them very much to recruit Dunkirk with a

strong garrison, letting them know, that he was assur'd by his letters from England, and by others which he had found means to intercept from thence; That the first thing the French would undertake would be to beseige that Town, they being press'd to it by Cromwell; and that accordingly both in France and England all things were preparing for it: And this was not only once said to them, but repeated every week, as the letters which were sent from England still confirm'd it: But all these advertisements wrought no effect upon the Spanish Councells; they giving litle credit to them, as being perswaded that the intelligence was false, and that such reports were contrived artificially by the Enemy, to oblige them to leave Cambray, or some other of their inland Towns, unprovided of defence; what had happen'd the year before, at the place last mention'd, had rais'd such apprehensions in them as outweigh'd all the reasons which had been given them by the King: And besides, they beleev'd, the Cardinal had still a longing to that Town, so that neither his Treaty with Cromwell, or any other consideration, would hinder him from undertaking that Seige, unless it were so well provided for, and secur'd against him, as to render it too difficult a peice of work: With these and other reasons, rather plausible then strong, they flatter'd themselves into a beleef, that Dunkirk was not in any danger of being attacked that year. Wherupon they did not only leave it very slenderly guarded, but also without furnishing it with such a proportion of ammunition as was requisit; at the same time disposing most of their foot into the Towns of Artois, as Ayre and St Omer, and into the fronteer places of Haynault, and reinforcing the garrison of Cambray with a considerable body of horse and foot; but as for Dunkirk, they added nothing to the ordinary garrison. Neither was this all, for they neglected the finishing of two Forts of four bastions each, which they had begun upon the Canal betwixt that and Bergue, which if they had once perfected and man'd, would haue render'd the Seige of Dunkirk a much more difficult peice of work; for the Enemy must of necessity haue master'd one of these two Forts, before they could haue begun a formall Seige.

I cannot forbear upon this occasion, to make this remarque, araising from what I have observ'd when I was either in the French or Spanish Army; That of all the Fortifications of this nature, or Intrenchments for the defence of Rivers, I never Saw any which the Spaniards made, that were of great advantage to them; for either they were not finish'd time enough to defend them, or were render'd useless by the French marching about, and falling into their flanque, as I have already mention'd in the year 1655, when Monsr. de Turenne endeavour'd not to force the great retrenchment which they had made all along the River betwixt Condé and St Guislain, but fetching a compass about, went to Condé and tooke it, therby making frustrate all the great labour they had taken. And indeed 'tis very difficult in such Countrys to make any works which will prove of use; for an Army which is once Master of the feild, will with a litle time and patience find the means, either of forceing their passage over such a work or river, or, by marching about, get into the Enemies Country some other way: So that in my opinion, thō it may be necessary on some occasions to make them, yet a Generall never ought to rely upon them.

The French, according to their custom, drew first into the feild this year; and in their way to Dunkirk, at Cassel, took prisoners of warr the Duke of Glocester's Regiment of foot, which consisted of four hundred men; they having been very unadvisably sent thither by Monsr. de Bascourt a Mareshall de battaille, under whose command were all the Troopes which acted on that side of the Country, it being a place not possibly to be defended: And at the same time he sent my Regiment of about five hundred men, with some other small foot Regiments which were quarter'd at Hondescote, with some few horse, into St Omer, thinking the French would haue sate down before it. But when, by their passing by him, he saw their design was upon Dunkirk, he endeavour'd, thō too late, to haue cast some men into it; and only made a shift to get in himself with some few horse. Much about the same time the Marquis de Leyde (*Léede*) Governour of that Town, gott in also with great difficulty, he being at Bruxelles soliciting for supplys of men and ammunition, when the first intelligence arrived, that the French were marching thither: At which time, and no sooner, they order'd all the troopes, which were in Nieuport, Dixmuyde, and Furnes, (of which they were jealous thō without reason, because they were all English, Scots, and Irish) to march for Dunkirk, (*reserving*) only the King's Regiment of foot, which was upwards of four hundred, and then lay at Dixmuyde; but these also came too late, the Town being block'd up already. So that the Marquis de Leyde found himself beseiged in a place, the main strength of which consisted in the outworks, which were very large, all of earth, and very easy to be approched. To all this great extent of ground which was to defend, his garrison was no ways answerable, for it consisted but of a thousand foot, and eight hundred horse, and his provisions of pouder and other necessarys were very scanty, even with reference to the Small number of his men.

The certain intelligence of this Seige being come to Bruxelles about the end of May, gave no small trouble to the Spaniards, especially when they saw all hopes of putting succours into the place by Sea were wholly vanish'd, by reason that the English Navy under the command of Generall Montague was now come before it; So that the only prospect which they had of releeving it, was by the Army; And therfore it was immediatly resolved in a Councell of Warr, (where were present all the Generall Officers) that the Army should draw together at Ypres with all imaginable hast; pursuant to which, the orders were immediatly dispatch'd for all their troopes to meet at the Rendezvous appointed.

Accordingly on the 7th of June all the Army and the Generall Officers were there. At their first meeting they resolv'd to march to Furnes, and on the 9th they camp by Nieuport; On the next day betwixt Odekerk and Furnes, whither came to us the Mareshall d'Hocquincourt, who was lately come out from France by way of Hêdin a Town in Artois, of great importance, upon the River of Canche; which upon the death of the Governour, by means of the Lieutenant du Roy and his Brother in law, revolted from the obedience of the King their Master, and call'd the Spaniards to their assistance, with whom they finally agreed to deliver the Town up to them, in consideration of a Summ of mony; and accordingly having receiv'd it, the Spaniards were put into possession of the place.

As for the said Mareshall, he had all along maintain'd a secret correspondence with the Lieut du Roy, as having designs at the same time of flying out into Rebellion, and of alluring most of the Noblesse, and Commonalty of the Vexin, and lower parts of Normandy, to haue joyn'd with him: But his contrivance being discover'd before he was fully in a readiness to put it in execution (a fate which for the most part attends such undertakings) he was forced to consult his own safety, by flying as speedily as he could. Notwithstanding which it was beleeved by many, that had not this instant Campagne prov'd So very unsuccessfull to the Spaniards, some disturbance would haue follow'd in those parts.[3]

To return again to our main business.[4] On the 11th it was resolved in a Councell of Warr, at which were present Don John, the Prince of Condé, the Marquis de Caracena, the Mareshall d'Hocquincourt and the Pce de Ligny (Don Estevan Gamarra and myself being accidently not there) That on the 13th, wee should march with the whole Army as near as wee could conveniently to the lines of the Enemy, amongst the Sand-hills, and there incamp; that by placing our selves so closs to them, wee might be in a readiness to attack them, when wee saw our proper time; and that on the 12th, the day before our appointed march, all the Generall Officers should go with two thousand commanded foot and four thousand horse, to view the place where they would camp, and themselves pitch upon it.

But before I proceed any further, I shall give a more particular account of what pass'd at this Councell; because that most of those who were present at it, haue since endeavor'd to clear themselves, either from giving that advice which I have mention'd, or even of consenting to the resolution which was then taken. And this Relation which I am now giving, I had from one of those who was assisting in it, and was desirous amongst the rest to clear himself from the imputation of giving that advice, or consenting to it.

So Soon as the persons whom I have already named were sett in Councell, Don John informed them of the cause of their meeting, That it was to consult on the most proper method of releeving Dunkirk: He let them know the present condition of the place, which was such as requir'd a speedy succour; and after having inlarg'd upon these heads, he propos'd to them that the Army should march to Zudcote, and camping there amongst the Sand-hills, as near as they could to the Enemies Lines, should watch their opportunity of attacking them. After this proposition there was a long silence, and no one arising to oppose it, he said, Since I see you all approve of what I haue proposed, let us now consider after

---

[3] The MS. *Campagnes* continues to follow the above text very closely.

[4] 'Pour revenir aux mouvemens de l'armée d'Espagne' (*Campagnes*, p. 242), because the narrative in the French MS. is in the third person.

what mañer, and what time, wee shall march thither: Vpon which it was resolv'd, that they should all go the day following to view the ground for incampment, and observe the Line of the beseigers.

I shall not take upon me to accuse or excuse any who were then present at this hasty resolution; thõ I have read a Relation which was printed and published by a freind of the Marquis de Caracena, wherin the Author endeavour'd to lay the whole weight of that resolution on Don John; and I have also read the answer to it, where-in Don John was justified, and it was made to appear, that in case the Marquis had so been pleas'd, he might easily haue inder'd that march, by only declaring himself against it, he having practis'd that very way in things of far less consequence then this; for his power was such, that he had but to Say he thought it not for the King's seruice to put in execution such a resolution, and Don John must acquiesce in it: in Spanish it is more strongly exprest, No sera de servicio del Rey; and this power he made use of the year before at la Cappelle.

But resolv'd it was; and in pursuance of it, wee[5] went on the 12th, with our four thousand horse, and the commanded foot, with intent to view the Enemies Line, and chuse the place for our incampment. Being advanced as far as Zudcote, wee halted there, and first made choice of our ground to lodge the Army, before wee went nearer to discover the Enemy: This was done by the Marquis of Caracena, Don Estevan de Gamarra, and my self, who taking some horse along with us, went a cross the Sand-hills, till wee came to the Strand. In the mean time Monsr. de Boutteville was gone with our Cravatts along the hight way betwixt the Sand-hills, and the meadow ground, advancing towards the Enemies horse guard so far, that he began to Skirmish with them, and forced them to give back a litle; by which means he had the opportunity of coming within a convenient distance of their Lines, and viewing them.

As he was returning to give the Generalls an account of what he had observ'd, he met the Mareshall d'Hocquincourt, who earnestly desir'd him to turn once more, Saying he would charge the Enemies horse guards; and notwithstanding that Monsr. de Boutteville us'd many arguments to disswade him (as having

[5] 'Les Generaux furent envoyez le 12 . . . avec 4000 chevaux . . .' (MS. *Campagnes*, p. 244).

already done what he intended, and brought back a prisoner or two with him, which he had taken amongst the Sand-hills) yet the Mareshall continued obstinate, and over-perswaded him to go back, by which he did not only ingage himself, but almost all the reste of the Generall Officers at a great distance from their troopes: for the Prince of Condé Seeing him go that way, walk'd after him, and Don John, hearing the Prince was gone on towards the Line, did the like: and last of all, I, having observ'd all that could be Seen where the Marquis and I had been together, and coming that way, where I heard that those whom I haue already mention'd were gone before, put on at a large gallop after them, and came up to them just as Monsr. d'Hocquincourt had forced the Enemies horse guards to retire. In performing which, Henry Jermyn on our side, and the Marquis de Blanquefort, at present Earle of Feversham nephew to Monsr. de Turenne, on the other, were both of them shott through the thigh.

The Mareshall d'Hocquincourt was now come within muskett shott of a redoubt, which the Enemy had advanced upon a heigth, somewhat before their Lines; when at the very moment that I came up to him, he received a shott in the belly from the Sd Reboudt, of which presently after he dyd: Vpon this wee drew off, the Enemy at the same time beginning to advance upon us; and the Prince of Condé with his people, being very busy in taking the papers out of the Mareshall's pockets, not knowing whither they shoull be able to bring off his body, a Gentleman who belong'd to the sd Mareshall came to me, and desir'd me to face about, to give them the leysure of bearing off his Master's corps; which at his request I did, and so with some difficulty the body was brought away. But had the Enemy press'd hard upon us, wee had not only been forced to haue left it behind, but all the Generall Officers there present had run the hazard of being made prisoners, they having no other horse with them besides Cravatts, who were not capable of sustaining a vigourous charge, and being distant from their own troopes above a mile. But at length when all was over, up came the Marquis de Caracena with three troopes of Guards to our assistance, who chid us all for having expos'd ourselves as wee had done.

After this wee return'd to the body of our Army, but so disorder'd by the fatall accident which had happen'd to the Mareshall d'Hocquincourt, that wee march'd back to our Camp by Furnes, without viewing any part of the Enemies Line or taking any other consultation about our going thither. The day following wee remov'd to the place which wee had chosen for our encampment; having our right to the Sea, and our left to the Canal of Furnes. Wee lay with our foot upon one Line before our horse, which reach'd from the Sand-hills next the Sea, as far as the ditches, which are nearest to the foremention'd Canal: our horse were on two Lines behind our foot, and as for our baggage, wee left it behind at Furnes; for our traine of artillery, by good fortune, it was not yet come to the Army: so that wee had neither cannon nor tooles, nor hardly powder enough for our foot; without all which necessarys wee came and camp'd within less then twice cannon shott of the Enemies Line.

Wee came thither with the Van of our Army about eleven of the clock in the forenoon. And, as I haue been since inform'd, it was evening before Monsr. de Turenne could be drawn to beleeve, that wee were there with our whole Army, or that wee came with a design of camping in that place: But about that time a prisoner was brought, who assured him of both. Wherupon, without consulting one moment with any person, he immediatly took the resolution of marching to us the next morning, and fighting us.

Accordingly he gave out orders for all his troopes to be in a readiness at that time: And sent for the English, that were *quarter'd at Mardyke*,[6] to march up to him; which they immediatly obeyd, and march'd all night, having a great compass to take, and were by day-break at his quarter: But while the French were preparing to come out upon us, the next morning, wee took no measures in our Army as if any Enemy were to be expected; for when the orders were given in our Camp at night, there was no prohibition made to our horse of going out to forage, till the pleasure of the Generall should be further known, as is usuall in the like cases: But they were permitted to go abroad, as if no Enemy had been near us. And that it may be seen, how litle some of our Generall Officers beleev'd the French had any such intention (or at least would haue it thought that they so beleev'd) happening myself to be at supper that night with the Marquis de Caracena, and the Company falling into discourse on the Subject of our

[6] 'qui estoient vers Mardick' (MS. *Campagnes*, p. 247).

coming thither, and what the French might probably attempt against us, I said, That for my own particular I lik'd not our being there upon such termes as wee were then, having no Lines nor any thing to cover us from the Enemy; and that it was my opinion, if they fell not upon us that very night, I was very confident they would give us battaill the next morning: To which both the Marquis and Don Estevan de Gamarra answered, that it was what they desir'd: To which I reply'd, That I knew Monsr. de Turenne So well, as to assure them they should haue that Satisfaction.

The next morning about five of the clock, our horse guard brought us intelligence, that they saw some horse drawing out of the Enemies Lines, which they suppos'd came with design to beat them in; upon which our whole Army tooke the alarme, and stood to their armes, and the Generalls went out to discover what the Enemy was doing. I was the first who came to our horse guard, and going as far as the outmost Sentrys, I plainly saw that their whole Army was coming out of their Lines; Their horse, with four small feild peices, advancing along the high way betwixt the Sand-hills, and the meadow grounds, and the French foot drawing out on their left hand, having thrown down some peices of their Line that they might march out at least a Battailion a front; and farther on their left hand, which was nearer to the Sea, the English were drawing out, whom I easily knew by their redcoats: Of all which having taken a distant view, I went back to give an account of it, and before I reach'd our Camp, I mett with Don John, who asking me, what were the intentions of the French? I answer'd him, That they were drawing out to give us battell; which he seeming not to beleeve, said, their design was only to drive in our horse guards. I replyd, That it was not the custom of the French to march out with such a body of foot, as I had seen, compos'd of the French and Suisse Guards, the Regiments of Picardy and Turenne, all which I knew by their colours, as well as the English by their redcoats, and with so great a body of horse as those I had observ'd with their cañon before them, with a bare intention of forcing in our horse guards.

Before I could add any other arguments for the confirmation of my opinion, or Don John had the leysure of replying, the Prince of Condé came up to us, who had also been at one of our horse guards, and gave the same account which I had done; and seeing

the Duke of Glocester there, he ask'd him, If he had ever seen a
Battell? who telling him, he had not; the Prince assured him, that
within half an houre he should behold one:[7] And now, there being
no farther room to doubt of the Enemies intention, all the Generall Officers parted from each other, and went to their respective
posts; with resolution to attend the coming of the French, and to
fight them where wee were, having the advantage of the ground,
which wee must haue lost had wee advanced towards them.

Our Army was drawn up after this following manner: Our
Foot, which were about six thousand, were divided into fifteen
Battalions, and were all upon one Line, excepting two of them;
They reach'd from a high Sand hill into the meedows adjoyning
the Canal of Furnes: The naturall Spaniards had the right hand
of all, who consisted of four Regiments; Don Gaspar Boniface his
Regiment was plac'd upon the high Sand hill, nearest to the
Strand; Behind which was that of Francisco de Meneses, facing
towards the Sea, to be in a posture of opposing any which should
offer to fall into their flanck: On the left hand of the first which I
have mentiond, was that of Don Diego de Goni, commanded by
Don Antonio de Cordoua, on whose left hand was placed the Marquis de Seralvo at the head of his Regiment; next to whom were
the King's and the Lord Bristoll's Regiments, both which made
up one Battalion alone, and was commanded by the Lord Muskerry; And for a reserve behind those two Battalions, Coll:
Richard Grace with the Lord Newbourgh's Regiment,[8] making
likewise one Battalion. On the left hand of the Regiment of York,
were three Walloon Battalions, after them one of Germans, composed of four Regiments; Next to which upon the last Sand hill,
towards the Canal of Furnes, was plac'd Guitaud's Regiment of
Germans, being the first of the Prince of Condé's foot: The rest
of them, which were three Battalions, were drawn up betwixt the
Sand-hills and the Canal, by the high-way side and in the meedows.

On the Sand hills, where our Foot was drawn up in this order,
wee had a great advantage of the Enemy, there running a ridge
from one side to the other, upon which they were posted; so that

[7] This is the passage which Ramsay 'improved' so wittily (see Translator's Introduction, p. 35).

[8] 'Il y avoit derriere ces deux Battaillons Les Regimens de Richard Grace et du
Lord Willoughby qui ne faisoient qu'un bataillon qui servoit de reserve' (MS.
Campagnes, p. 251). 'Willoughby' may be the correct reading here.

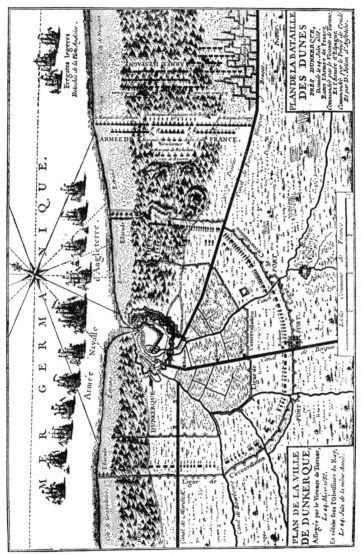

The Battle of the Dunes, June 14, 1658

the Enemy must be constrain'd to charge us up the hill, which every one knows is a greater disadvantage on the Sand, where the footing is loose, then on firm ordinary ground. As for our Horse (which should haue been eight thousand thō at that time they were scarcely half so strong, the greatest part of them being gone out to forrage and not returning till after wee were beaten) the Spanish Horse were drawn up in two Lines behind our Foot, amongst the Sand hills; The Prince of Condé's in more Lines behind his Foot, betwixt the Sand hills and the meadow-grounds; in many places there being not room for above three or four Squadrons a front: so that I am not absolutely certain, in what number of Lines they were drawn up.

In this order wee stood expecting the Enemy, whose Army, according to my best remembrance, were marshall'd in the manner following. Their Foot were drawn up in two Lines of seven Battalions each: The first Line was commanded by a Lieut Generall Monsr. de Guadagne, and compos'd of one Battalion of the French Guards which had the right hand, and march'd along under the Sand hills by the high way side; Next to which was one Battalion of the Suisse Guards, which went along by the top of the Sand hills, next the high way; On whose left hand was the Regiment of Picardy makin one Battalion; and then on the same front that of Turenne, which was the last of the French Battalions on the first Line; on whose left hand were three of the English Regiments, each of which made a Battalion, the last of them reaching as far as the Sand hills next the Sea: And before each Battalion of this first Line, they had commanded Musketeers[9] (which was the only time that ever I knew forlorne hopes us'd beyond the Seas in any battell) But as Monsieur de Turenne advanced, seeing wee had some foot in the meadows, he took the right hand Battalion of the second Line, and made it march on the right hand of his Horse in the meadows; this Battalion was commanded by Monsr. de Montgomery one of his Nephews. As for their second Line of Foot, it consisted of the same number of Battalions, three of which were English, and the rest French.[10]

[9] 'les Enfans perdus' (MS. *Campagnes*, p. 252), the 'technical' name given to this kind of musketeers in France.

[10] The last two sentences (after 'commanded Musketeers', i.e., 'enfants perdus' or 'forlorne hopes') do not appear in the MS. *Campagnes* (p. 252).

THE BATTLE OF THE DUNES

For their Horse, they had about five or six Squadrons betwixt their two Lines of foot; and their right wing came along the high way, just beneath the Sand hills, commanded by the Marquis de Crequi, a Lieut Generall, having as many Squadrons a front as the ground would bear, which in divers places was not above three or four; before whom march'd four feild peices. Their left wing commanded by Monsr. de Castelnau a Lieut Generall, came along the Strand, with feild peices attending them; and severall of the English small Fregatts having the advantage of the tyde of flood, stood in as near the shore as possibly they could see amongst the Sand hills. This was the order of the French Army: And in this manner they advanced upon us, while wee only stood our ground, and expected them.

The first who engaged us were the English led up by Major Generall Morgan; their Generall Lockart (for what reason I know not) being with Monsr. de Castelneau at the head of their left wing. But immediatly before their falling on, Don John sent me, and desired me to go to our right hand, and take a particular care of that part, where he saw the Englis were advancing; Which I did, taking no troopes along with me from the middle of the Line, where I then was, excepting only my own Troope of Guards, and a hundred commanded men, with two Captains, and Officers proportionable out of my next Battalion, to reinforce the naturall Spaniards. Which Foot I joyn'd to Boniface, where I judged they would make their greatest effort, and which was (of) the greatest importance to be maintain'd, it being the highest of the Sand hills on that side, and advanced somewhat farther then any of the rest which were thereabout, commanding also those which were nearest to it.

This was all I had leisure to do, before the English attack'd us; who came on with great eagerness and courage: But their heat was such, that they outmarch'd the French, so that had the opportunity been taken, they might haue paid deer for their rash bravery, But they, whose busines it was to haue taken that advantage, either tooke no notice of it, or had some other reason, unknown to me, why they sent not some Horse to fall into their flanques; Whatsoever the occasion was, the opportunity was let slipp, and the English came up without the least disturbance to make their charge.

Boniface, as I haue already said, was posted on the highest Sand hill, which was somewhat advanced before any of the others, so that the battell began there. It was Lockart's own Regiment which charged those Spaniards, and was commanded by Lieut. Coll. Fenwick; who so soon as he came to the bottom of the hill, seeing that it was exceeding steep, and difficult to ascend, commanded his men to halt and take breath for two or three minutes, that they might be more able to climb and do their duty.

While they were thus preparing themselves, their commanded men[11] opening to the right and left, to give way to their main body which was to mount the higth, were continually firing at Boniface; and as soon as the body were in a condition to climb, they began their ascent with a great shout, which was generall from all their foot. But while they were scrambling up in the best manner they were able, the Lieut. Coll: fell in the middle way, being shott through the body; which yet hinder'd not the Major, who was called Hinton (since a Captain in the Duke of Albemarle's Regiment)[12] from leading on his men together with the rest of their Officers, who Stopt not till they came to push of pyke; where notwithstanding the great resistance which was made by the Spaniards, and the advantage they had of the higher ground, as well as, that of being well in breath, when their Enemies were almost spent with climbing, the English gain'd the hill and drove them from off it: The Spaniards leaving dead upon the spott, seven of eleven Captains which commanded in the Regiment, together with Slaughter and Farrell, two Captains whom I had joyn'd to that Regiment just before: besides many of their reform'd Officers (their stands of Pykes being for the most part made of such)[13] Yet this ground had been so well disputed, that the English, besides their Lieut. Coll: lost Severall Officers and Soldiers.

And now, having thus far carryd on their busines successfully, so soon as they had put themselves again in order, and recover'd breath, they came down the Sand hill, which I observing, went to charge them with my own Guards and those of Don John; but being come up almost within reach of their pykes, I found the

---

[11] 'Leurs enfants perdus' (p. 254).

[12] The fact that this Cromwellian officer was retained after the Restoration does not appear in the MS. *Campagnes* (p. 254).

[13] 'et plusieurs officiers reformez dont la plupart estoient piquiers' (MS. *Campagnes*, pp. 254–255).

ground to be such, as render'd it almost impossible for me to break into them: notwithstanding which I was resolv'd to endeavour it, and accordingly charg'd them thō to no purpose: for what with the advantage of the ground, and with the stout resistance they made in that first charge, I was beaten off, and all who were at the head of my own Troope, were either killed or wounded; of which number I had been one, had not the goodness of my armes preserv'd me. The cheife Officers of my Troope escap'd better then those belonging to Don John; for of mine, only Charles Berkley the Capitaine of my Guards was hurt, and of the other, only the Count de Colmenar who was Captain of it, came off unwounded, amongst all the Officers: neither did their common men fare better, the loss falling so heavily amongst them, that thō I endeavour'd all I could to rally them, it was not possible for me to perform it. But I had better fortune with those of my own Guards, for I gott all of them together who were yet in a condition of doing duty, which were not above forty.

When I had rallyd this small party, I went to Boniface, where first Don John, and after him the Marquis de Caracena had been endeavouring to rally them, but not being able to do it, were gone off. When I came up to that Regiment, I was not able at first to make them stand; but while I was trying my authority amongst them, I saw there one Elvige a Lieutenant of the King's Regiment, who had been commanded along with the hundred men whom I had sent to strengthen that Battalion; and asking him, what was become of his Captains? he answer'd me, they were both slaine with most of their Soldiers; and that he was the only Officer of that party that had escap'd unhurt. Upon which I commanded him to stay with me, and call his men together, which he did, and crying out aloud to them, That the Duke was there, those who heard him faced about immediatly, and came up to us. At the same time seeing the Major of that Spanish Regiment, I call'd to him, That he should make his men follow the example of those few English, it not being the custome of Spaniards to run when any others stood; and upon the Major's reproching them with that, they stopt, and drew up in good order. And now the Marquis of Caracena coming back once more, demanded of me, Why I charg'd not the Enemy with my Horse? I answer'd him, I had already done it, and (*been*) worsted for my paines; farther telling him, That considering the present posture of the Enemy, it was impossible to be done, and at the Same time shewing him, what I had affirmed, from behind the next Sand hill.

Presently after this (the Marquis being gone again) Lockart's Regiment, which, as I have already said, had beaten off our Horse, advanced not directly forward, but bent a litle towards their left hand; and wee lost sight of each other, by reason of the unevenesse of the ground (a Sand hill being interpos'd betwixt us) so that by the time I had got the Regiment of Boniface in order, and those few Horse which I had with him, this English Battalion was come even upon a line with us, just upon my right hand, a Sand hill only being betwixt us: Wherupon I faced touards the Sea, and marching at the head of my Foot, as I came up to the top of the Sand hill, I perceiv'd the English coming up on the other side to me: upon which I gott from betwixt them, commanding the Major who was with me at the head of Boniface, to charge them in the front, whilst I with my Horse would fall into their flanque.

When I had given this order, I put myself immediatly at the head of my forty Guards, and charg'd that Battalion So home, that I broke into them, doing great execution upon them, and driving them to the edge of the Sand hill next the Strand. As for the Battalion of Boniface they did not charge, seeing I had already broken the English; but discovering from the top of the Sand hill, where they were, that our whole Army was in route, they scatter'd, and every man endeavour'd to gett off, which few of them were so lucky as to perform.

Tis very observable that when wee had broken into this Battalion, and were gott amongst them, not so much as one single man of them ask'd quarter, or threw down his armes; but every one defended himself to the last: so that wee ran as great danger by the butt end of their musketts, as by the volley which they had given us. And one of them had infallibly knock'd me off from my horse, if I had not prevented him when he was just ready to haue discharg'd his blow, by a stroke I gave him with my sword over the face, which layd him along upon the ground.

The Duke of Glocester, who during the action of all that day had seconded me, and behav'd himself as bravely as any of his Ancestors had ever done, had his sword either struck out of his hand by one of the Enemy, or it flew out of his hand by a blow

266

which he had given; but which of the two I remember not: It happen'd that a gentleman, one Villeneuue, Ecuier to the Prince de Ligny, who was next him, saw this accident; wherupon he leap'd down immediatly from his horse, took up the sword and delivered it to my Brother, who with his pistoll in his hand, stood ready to secure him till he was remounted. But immediatly after, the same gentleman was shott through the body; notwithstanding which it was his fortune to gett off, and to recover of his wound.

I had no sooner made this charge, but I was obliged to make what hast I could to get away; for a Squadron of the French Army from the Strand, had gott up amongst the Sand hills, just as I was charging, and had [broken] into my flanque;[14] So that they had undoubtedly cutt me off with my small party, had they not been charg'd themselves, at the same time, by the Prince de Ligny, who thō he did not defeat them, yet he gaue them a litle stop; which opportunity I took to get off, and the Prince, after he had made his charge, escap'd another way.

By this time not only all the Regiment of Boniface was cutt in peices, but the rest of the naturall Spanish Regiments were all taken in their Severall posts by the Horse; for they were not charg'd by the English as they ought to haue been, had our Countrymen march'd directly onwards: but so it happen'd, that when the other two Regiments of them, saw the resistance which was made by Boniface, they all bent that way, marching by the flanque, only firing at the other naturall Spaniards as they pass'd along, and marching up the Sand-hill after Lockart's Regiment.

While these things were passing on our right hand next the Sea, our left wing received as hard measure from the Enemy as wee had done; for the four feild peices, which as I sayd, advanced along the high way, under the Sand-hills, terribly gaul'd both our Horse and Foot which were before them: So that the Foot Guards and the Regiment de la Couronne (the last of which was commanded by Monsr. de Montgomery, and having been taken out of the Second Line by Monsr. de Turenne, as I haue said, was placed on the right hand of the Guards in the meadow grounds) seeing that wee had three small Battalions betwixt the Sand-hills and the Canal, they advanced against them, but our Battalions making a very fainte resistance ran away. Upon which the French

[14] 'Ilz alloient le prendre en flanc' (MS. *Campagnes*, p. 258).

horse advanced before their foot, as many Squadrons a front as they could march, commanded by the Marquis de Crequi, a Lieut Generall, and were charg'd so vigorously by the Prince of Condé's horse, that they were beaten back behind their foot: yet at length, notwithstanding all he could do, they having horse and foot against horse alone, they[15] forced him from his ground, and oblig'd him to run for it, as fast as his neighbours had done before him; thō he did what was possible to be done, in both capacities, both as a Generall, and as a Soldier; in so much that at the last of the three charges, which he made with his horse, he was in great hazard of being taken.

As to what pass'd on the right wing of the Prince of Condé, upon the Sand-hills betwixt him and the place where the naturall Spaniards were drawn up; The Regiment de Guitault[16] (which was posted upon the Sand hill next to the high way along which came the right wing of the French Cavalery) did not Stay for a charge from the Suisses, but fir'd at too great a distance and presently ran away: The four next Battalions did the like, none of them Staying to be throughly charg'd; which cowardise of theirs, and the defeat of Boniface his Regiment, who were beaten from their ground, strook such a terrour into our horse, which were drawn up behind our foot on the Sand-hills, that the greatest part of them, especially those of the Second line, ran away without being charg'd, or even without seeing an Enemy, thō most of their Officers were not wanting to their duty, in endeavouring to stop them: Those few who had courage enough to Stay, perform'd their parts like men of honour, as shall be mention'd in its proper place.

The next of these three Regiments, of which I have spoken, was my own, which stood a litle longer then their neighbours on the left hand; But a voice coming behind them, that the foot should save themselves, that Battalion broke also, the Soldiers leaving their Officers, and running away; which Coll: Grace seen (*seeing*) who was drawn up behind them, thought it was high time for him to endeavour to save his Regiment, and march off in good order at a round rate in three divisions; by observing of which dis-

---

[15] 'They' were mainly Bussy-Rabutin who commanded the cavalry and Gadagne who brought up infantry to support him.

[16] Not 'de Guiscard', as Clarke supposed.

cipline, and keeping them together, he had the good fortune to gett off a cross the high way, to the Canal of Furnes, along which he made his retreat without losing a man. But my Regiment was attended with worse luck: for thō Monsr. de Roc[17] with his Regiment of horse went up and charg'd the Cardinal's Gensdarmes, killing with his own hand Monsr. du Bourg who commanded them, and beating that Squadron; yet they who should haue seconded him being gone, and more horse coming on to charge him, he was forced also to make the best of his way, and shift for one. Those horse which he had beaten soon overtook my Regiment, so that excepting My Lord Muskerry, who was fortunate enough to get a horse accidentally, not a Soldier or Officer escap'd.

Much about the Same time, one Michel an old German Collonel, with his Regiment of horse, charg'd the Battalion of Turenne after they were march'd down from the hill, on which the Spanish foot had been drawn up; but he was not able to break them, they receiving his charge in so good order, that they kill'd him with the greatest part of his Officers, and beat off his Regiment of horse without any loss but of the Lieut Collonel Betbesé, who was slain at the head of the pikes with a pistoll shott. Besides these two Collonels, I know not of any Spanish horse that behav'd themselves well in this battell, or if they did, it never arriv'd to my knowledge.

I must go now a litle back to give a further account of my own fortune: As soon as I came off from charging and breaking that Regiment of English, I thought it but reasonable to endeavour my own escape, the French horse having already incompass'd me on every side, and none of our men standing: But not knowing what success wee might haue had in our left wing where the Prince of Condé was, I resolved in the first place to go thither, and see in what posture our affaires were there. I had not now above twenty horse remaining with me; the rest of my Guards which were with my Lieutenant, being parted from me as I came from amongst the English: The Smalness of my number prov'd my best security; for with those who still continued about me, I was strong enough to deal with any loose men, and yet was not so considerable as to provoke any bodys to disband after me: And by Some of the Enemys wee were taken for one of their own partys; for as I

17 Mr. de St. Roch' (MS. *Campagnes*, p. 261).

was coming off, I saw four or five of their Troopers falling upon an Officer of mine, on Lieut Victor, since a Captain at Tangier: I went up to them, taking them indeed for some of our own horse, and called out to them in french, That they should let him alone, for he was one of our own Englishmen: Accordingly they dismiss'd him, giving him his sword which they had taken from him, and went off themselves, mistaking me for one of their own Officers: Thus both I and they were in an errour, and I knew not my own mistake till Victor told me of it afterwards.

I continu'd my way forward, and made a shift to pass through the French, trotting in good order, 'till I overtook Coll: Grace and his Regiment before they gott out from amongst the Sand hills; going by the Regiments of Picardy and Turenne, which were then as far advanced as where our men had been incamped the night before; and coming down into the high way, under the Sand hills, I found all the Prince of Condé's Troopes already beaten, he having then made his last charge; So that he was constrain'd to run with them, and as I sayd, with great difficulty escap'd. The throng being very great in the Village of Zudcote, through which the high way went, and the Enemy pursuing us with great eagerness, I had no other means to avoid being taken, then to disingage myself from the crowd, and to take another way, which was round about the Village leaving it on my right hand. And to shew how near I was to be made prisoner, a Collonel under the Prince, one (de) Morieul, meeting me just as I came down the Sand-hills, and not following my example of taking round the Village, but mingling with the crowd, immediatly after he was parted from me fell'd into the hands of the pursuers, and was made a prisoner. As for me, I gott safe into the way again on the other side of the Village, where Don John, the Prince of Condé, the Marquis de Caracena, and others, were already gott before me. Soon after which, wee were obliged to make a litle stand, and face about, to give Don John de leisure to change his horse, his own by some accident being fallen lame; which being done, wee sett spurrs again to our horses, and did not stop, 'till the Enemy had left pursuing us.

I shall not take upon me to give a particular account of what was done in this engagement by our Generall Officers, because I have received no particular information of it: Only this I know in

grosse, that all of them behav'd themselves very bravely, excepting Don Estevan de Gamarra; the rest of them so far exposing
their persons, that they escap'd not without great hazard. For the
Prince of Condé, and myself, I have already given a Relation of
our fortunes: And concerning Don John, I have been inform'd,
that he stayd so long, that he was in danger of being taken: And
the Marquis de Caracena was so near it, that before he gott out
from amongst the Sand hills, a horseman of the Enemys had layd
hold on his bridle; but the Marquis at the same time striking him
over the face with his cane, (having nothing els in his hand) so
stun'd him, that he let go his hold, and so the Marquis had leisure
to escape. To what concerns the Prince de Ligny,[18] I have already
mention'd how handsomly he behavd himself when he charg'd;
but how he gott off, I am not certain: But for Don Estevan de
Gamarra who commanded as Mestre de Camp Generall, and was
at the head of the foot, he went away at first, and never stopt till he
came to Nieuport.

I have not yet given an account of the Battalion, which was
compos'd of the King's Regiment and the Earle of Bristoll's, and
I should be very injurious to the first of these two, if I should pass
them by in silence. They were posted, as I haue said, next the
naturall Spaniards; and notwithstanding that they saw all on the
right and left hand of them already routed and gone off, yet they
continued firm (I mean that part of the Battalion which was compos'd of the King's Regiment) for they were all English; As for
the other part of it, which was form'd of My lord Bristoll's men
who were Irish, they indeed went away, when they saw all their
freinds about them beaten; neither was it in the power of their
Officers to hinder them, thō they endeavour'd it; but seeing their
paines were to no effect, they ran for company, excepting Captain
Stroad (*Stroud*) an English Gentleman, who was Captain Lieut.
of that Regiment; for he came and put himself at the head of the
remaining part of the Battalion, with his own Countrymen: But
this was not the only discouragement which these English had,
for both the Lieut. Collonell and Major had forsaken them before
the Irish, the first upon pretence of going for orders, and the other
upon an account which was not a jot more honorable. The Lieut.
Coll: was rewarded for his paines as he deserved; for being mett

[18] de Ligne.

by some of the lose French horse, who were then gott behind them, he was shott into the face, somewhat below the eye, and the bullet came out behind his neck; of which wound he narrowly escap'd with life: He was also unhors'd, and being in this condition, one of my Guards, the only man amongst them who behav'd himself ill and who was not an Englishman, accidentally found him, and help'd him off.

But none of these misadventures did at all daunt the King's Regiment: They continued to stand firm, and maintain'd their ground, thō they beheld the first Line of the French passing by them on their left hand, and the Cromwellian English on their right, till the second Line came up to them. It was the Regiment of Rambures which advanced to charge them (their Collonel commanding that Line, and being at their head). This Officer seeing not a man standing of all our Troopes, excepting this small body which was before him, went up to them himself, a litle before his men, to offer them quarter; To whom they return'd this answer, That they had been posted there by the Duke, and therfore were resolved to maintain that ground as long as they were able: He replyd, That it would be to no purpose for them to stand out, their whole Army being already routed, and having left the feild. They answer'd again, That it was not their part to beleeve an Enemy: Upon which he offer'd them, that if they would send out an Officer or two, he would himself carry them up to a Sand-hill which was behind them, and then they should perceive, that what he affirm'd was true: Accordingly they sent out two Officers, Captain Thom: Cooke and Aston,[19] whom he conducted as he had promis'd to the Sand-hill which he had nam'd; from whence they could easily discover, that none of our Army was left standing excepting only themselves, after which, he brought them down again to their own men. Wherupon they told him, That in case he would promise they should not be deliver'd up to the English, nor be stripp'd, nor haue their pockets search'd, they would lay down their armes and yeeld themselves his prisoners; to which he immediatly agreeing, and giving his word for the performance of those Articles, they accordingly yeelded, and his promise was exactly kept to them: by which their honorable carriage, they far'd much better then the other Regiment which deserted them; some

[19] 'Ashton' (MS. *Campagnes*, p. 266).

of whom were slaine, and the rest taken and stripp'd afterwards.

I haue now give the best account I am able of the whole Action, and it remains, that I should say something of the number of the Slaine on both sides and of the Prisoners. As for the Slaine, they amounted not in all to above four hundred;[20] amongst which on our side there fell the Count de la Motterie and of the Spanish troopes, Collonel Michel, with most of the Captains of Boniface, one of Seralvo, and another of Goni (*Gomez*), as also Don Francisco Romero Governour of the two Troopes of Guards, with two or three more of his Officers: Of those whom I commanded, there were kill'd three Captains, Slaughter of the King's Regiment, * * *[21] of my own, and Farrell of the Lord Bristoll's, besides some Lieutenants and Ensignes, and two Brigadeers of my Troope of Guards. Of the Pce of Condé's Troopes, I remember none of quality but the Count de Meille a Lieut. Generall, with some few Captains. Of the Spanish Officers, were taken the Marquis de Seralvo, Risbourg, Conflans, Belleveder, the Prince de Robec, Don Antonio de Cordoua, Don J. de Toledo y Portugal, Don Joseph Manriques, Don Luis de Zuniga, Le Baron de Limbeck, Darchem, Baynes, all Collonels of horse or foot, and Mr. de Montmorency, Captain of the Guards to the Prince de Ligny. Most of these were abandon'd by their men, and were taken, because they would not make such hast away as their Soldiers had done: I cannot say what Captains and other inferiour Officers were made Prisoners, only, that of the naturall Spanish Regiments of foot, few or none escap'd, because they behav'd themselves very honorably; But of the horse, the number of Captains and Officers under them, was no way proportionable to the number of Officers in my Troopes. Of my own Regiment, not an Officer escap'd taking, excepting My Lord Muskerry who commanded it; and of the private Soldiers, not twenty. As for the King's Regiment, it was intirely broken. The Earle of Bristoll's Regiment had the same fate with mine, few or none getting away; but of his Guards not above five or six were taken. As for the cheif Officers under the Prince of Condé, Monsr. de Coligny et[22] Boutteville, both Lieut

---

[20] The French version makes it plain that these casualties were on the Spanish side (MS. *Campagnes*, p. 267).
[21] The French MS. does not supply this blank.
[22] i.e., and Monsr. de Boutteville.

Generalls, were made Prisoners with Meille (who dyd of his wounds) and Monsr. des Roches Captain of his Guards: He lost no many of his foot, for they not doing their duty as became Soldiers, and being near the Canal, had an easy opportunity of escaping; his horse, thō they fought bravely, yet lost fewer then the Spaniards, and amongst them all not one Collonel.

How many of the Enemy were slain, the Duke knew not certainly, only in generall, that their loss was very inconsiderable both as to the number and the quality; for I haue not heard of any other Officers who were kill'd on their side, then Monsr. de la Berge (who had been Captain of Mr. de Turenne's Guards, and was then Major Generall of the Foot, which is less then either a Lieut Generall or a Mareshall de Camp) Monsr. de Bebsey[23] Lieut Collonel of Monsr. de Turenne's Regiment of Foot, and Du Bourg Lieut of the Cardinal's Gensdarmes: Of the English sent by Cromwell, Fenwick Lockart's Lieut Collonel,[24] with two Captains, four Lieutenants, and four Ensignes; Of the English common men about a hundred; and the Major of the Same Regiment, with two Captains, and some Lieutenants and Enseigne's hurt.

As for the baggage and cannon, wee had none to lose, our traine by good fortune not being come up to us; and our baggage being left behind at Furnes, at which place wee rally'd our beaten Army.

And here I must not forgett to mention, what Monsr. de Gadagne a Lieut Generall in the French Army, and who commanded the French Foot that day, did on my behalf, when our Army was intirely routed, and none left standing on the feild, hearing that I was taken prisoner by the English, he took two or three Squadrons of the French horse along with him, whose Commanders were his particular freinds, and went with them across the feild to the place where the English then were; fully resolv'd, in case my fortune had been such, to haue rescued me by force out of their hands: But coming amongst them, and after a diligent inquiry finding there was no truth in that report, he return'd back with that satisfaction to his own command.

At our first coming to Furnes, and for some days after the Battell, wee thought our loss had been more considerable, then after-

---

[23] 'de Brebsey' (MS. *Campagnes*, p. 268).

[24] 'Des Anglois de Cromwel Fenwick et Lockart Lieutenans Colonels . . . furent tuez' (p. 268). This is an error. Lockhart was a General, and he was not killed.

wards it prov'd; for most of our foot Officers, as well as our common Soldiers, gott off, some by making their escape from the Enemy, others, and especially the Officers, by giving small summs of mony to those who (*had*) taken them; of which number was Don Antonio de Cordoua, with many other Collonels and persons of note: So that by that time wee came to Nieuport, which was about the 26th of the same month, all our Regiments of foot, excepting the King's and the naturall Spaniards, were almost as strong as when they came into the feild.

As for Monsr. de Turenne, so Soon as he had beaten us, he march'd back into his Lines, and continued his Seige, So that within * * *25 days afterwards, Dunkirk was surrender'd to him; which had not been so soon given up, if the Marquis de Leyde the Governour, had not been wounded, of which hurt he dyd with in few days.

Wee remain'd at Furnes till the 26th, about which time the news was brought us, that the Town was to be deliver'd up, and then wee drew back to Nieuport. So soon as wee came thither, wee had another Junto, to consult what wee should do when the Enemy were masters of Dunkirk. Vpon which it was proposed by Don John, that wee should put our Selves all along the Canal betwixt Nieuport and Dixmude, and endeavour to defend it. Some who spoke after him, agreed to this, and others did not directly oppose it. But when it came to my turn to speak, I declar'd my opinion against it, and gave my reasons, because wee had not a sufficient strength of foot to maintain that post against a Victorious Army, ours being also dishearten'd by their late defeat: I also desir'd them to consider into what miserable condition wee should be reduced, in case that passe should be forced upon us; for then it would be too late, and perhaps impossible to think of securing our great Towns, since the Enemy would haue their choice of attacking, and also of mastering which of them they pleas'd; besides what other unknown mischeifs might arise from so hazardous an undertaking.

Having us'd these and other arguments against it, I propos'd that wee should divide our Army, and disperse it, as wee should judge most convenient, amongst our great places on that side of the Country where wee were, a particular regard being had to those

25 The French MS. does not specify the time, except that it was 'not long'.

Towns, which in probability wee might expect to be next be-seiged; That this provision being made for their Security, what place soever should be attack'd, might be in a condition of making a vigorous resistance, or at least defend itself so long, that when it should be taken it would be too late for the Enemy to sitt down before another; That during this seige, wee might haue leasure to draw the rest of our Troopes together, and withall might watch our opportunity of attempting somewhat against the Enemy.

Vpon this motion of mine the whole affaire was again brought under a debate, and it was resolved at last, to divide our Army. Myself and the Marquis de Caracena were left in Nieuport, which place wee beleev'd would be next attempted: Wee had with us about two thousand foot, and as many horse. The Prince of Condé went to Ostend, with a sufficient body of men for the defense of that strong place; Don John with some foot and a con-siderable body of horse put himself into Bruges; and the Prince de Ligny with the remainder went to Ypres. At our coming out from this Junto, the Prince of Condé ask'd me, Why I would venture to contradict Don John, as I had done? To which I answer'd him, Because I had no desire to be forced to run again, as wee had done so lately at Dunkirk.

This resolution being thus taken, the troopes began their march the same day to the severall posts which were assign'd them: And within * * *[26] days after, Monsr. de Turenne with the body of the French Army came to Dixmude, and the Marquis de Crequi with the Van came and camp'd within litle more then canon-shott of Nieuport, betwixt that place and Dixmude, intending the next morning to haue pass'd the Canal which runs from Nieuport to Ostend, and to cutt off all our communication with that place; at the same time also the whole Army was to haue come up to him, with intention to beseige us. But the next morning as they were ready to haue march'd, Monsr. de Turenne receiv'd orders from the Cardinal, not to attack till further directions from him, nor to undertake any other action, the King his master being fallen desperatly ill of a fever at Calais: By which accident wee escap'd a Seige, and a most evident danger of being taken; for so careless had the Spaniards been, that when the Marquis de Crequi was come, and camp'd within our neighbourhood, wee had not ammu-

[26] 'peu de jours aprez' (MS. *Campagnes*, p. 271).

nition sufficient for fifteen days; So that notwithstanding the great strength of our garrison, wee could not haue defended the Town long.

But within a day or two after, wee were plentifully furnish'd with powder and shott from Ostend: So that if wee had been attacked, wee should haue been able to haue made a good defence. And to inable ourselves the better to sustain a Seige, wee began a new Conterscarpe, and five half moons, with a *langue de Serpent* without the Canal, which incompass'd the old outworkes, which wee finish'd in the space of eight days, and then open'd our sluces to drown the Country round about us; but it had not the effect which wee expected, the ground about the Town being higher then it was suppos'd to haue been, however it did us some Seruice.

As for the French Army, the body of it continued about Dixmude, and Monsr. de Crequi lay within cannon shott of us, during all the time that the King of France was in danger by his fever. In this intervall our Generalls had a meeting at Planquendal, a Village which lys upon the Canal betwixt Bruges and Nieuport; where it was resolv'd that so soon as the French Army should march from Dixmude, Don John, the Prince of Condé, and the Marquis de Caracena, should draw together to Bruges as many men as could be spar'd out of the other Towns, into which they had put their Army, with which body they should observe the motions of Monsr. de Turenne; and that I should still remain at Nieuport, with another body of horse and foot, thō of a less proportion then the former, to secure and take care, as well as I was able, of that place, Ostend, and Bruges.

This was the summ of their resolutions at that meeting; and as myself and the Marquis were going back to Nieuport, wee had a hott alarm, and were obliged to trott for two or three miles riding, for fear of being intercepted, before wee could reach that Town; Monsr. de Varennes a Lieut. Generall of the French, being come down to the Side of the Canal to view it, and having pass'd some of his Horse over it, which gave us that allarm. Soon after this, the body of the French Army remov'd from Dixmude, but Monsr. de Crequi was left with the Troopes under his command, at the place where he then was incamp'd: Vpon notice of which, the Marquis de Caracena, in pursuance of what had been concluded at the last meeting, went from Nieuport, taking with him some Squadrons of Horse, and such Foot of the naturall Spaniards, as having been taken in the late Battell, and had made their escape out of the French Army, or bought themselves off, and with them march'd to the Rendezvous appointed, to joyn with Don John, and the Prince of Condé.

I think it not materiall enough, in this place, to make a relation of all the petty skirmishes, and driving in of each others Guards, which pass'd betwixt us and Monsr. de Crequi; nor of the litle stratagems and deuices which were used, to take or beat the advanc'd Guards on either side, both of Horse and Foot, which wee were obliged to keep within muskett-shott of one another; So that there hardly pass'd a day without action, thō not considerable enough to be related.[27]

Not many days after the Marquis de Caracena had left Nieuport, Monsr. de Crequi drew off from his post in our neighbourhood, to go and joine Monsr. de Turenne who lay neer * * *.[28] And had not an accident interveen'd, in all probability he had not march'd away so quietly: for about noon, I had intelligence from my out guards, that the Enemy was preparing to remove, and that already their baggage was going out of their Camp: Wherupon I went immediately to see whither that report was true, and at the same time gave order, for six hundred commanded Foot to be drawn out of all the Regiments, and to come to me with what expedition they could make: As also, that all my horse should get ready with the same diligence, and draw into the Conterscarpe, on that side of the Town which was next to the Enemy; my intentions being to try what could be done upon their reere, in their going off.

Being come to my outworkes, I found the intelligence to be true, and that not only their baggage was gone out, but that the troopes already were beginning to march: I therfore sent again for the Cōmanded Foot, as also for my own Troop of Guards, and two or three Squadrons more, to come immediatly to me: The Horse came accordingly, but not the Foot; for they linger'd so long, that before they were with me, the Enemy was drawn off at so great a distance from the Town, that I thought it not safe to

[27] This paragraph is omitted in the MS. *Campagnes* (p. 273).
[28] Not specified in the MS. *Campagnes* (p. 273).

attempt any thing upon them. So that there pass'd nothing betwixt us, but only a slight Skirmish of Some loose Foot on either
side, and one charge of Horse which was given by Some of our
Volunteers, without order, to a small party of the Enemies Horse
who brought up their Reer upon the dyke, in which a mettled
page of mine, one Litleton, charg'd so home, that he was taken.

The slowness of the Foot, which ruin'd this design, was occasion'd by the loss of a small Vessell, which happend to be cast
away that morning closs by the Town, having run on ground
before day at high water, so that when the tyde went off, she was
left dry upon the Sands; which being seen by our men, they went
to plunder her, and the Ship being laden with wine and brandy,
most of our foot Soldiers had made themselves so drunk, that
when they were commanded to their armes, it was not in the power
of their Officers to take them from their liquour, et[29] gett them
together time enough to come to the place where I expected them.

As for the remainder of this Campagne, I shall not give a particular account of it, because I was not present in the feild; Only
this in short: The Prince de Ligny, with the body which he commanded about Ypres, was defeated by Monsr. de Turenne, who
accidentally lighted upon him with the Van of his Army near
* * *,[30] where he expected not to find him; And having cutt off all
his Foot, followed him to Ypres, and beseig'd that place which he
took within few days, and then march'd to Oudenarde, which he
also master'd, it being a place of great importance, thō at that time
of litle strength, Scituated upon the Scalde.[31] In this Town he
left a strong garrison, as also in Dinse, and most of the places on
the Lys: So that this blow given to the Prince de Ligny, prov'd
to be of worse consequence to the Spaniards, then the defeat which
wee receiv'd near Dunkirk; for had it not been for this last misfortune, in all probability the French had done litle during the rest of
the Campagne, besides the taking of Gravelines, after the time
which they were obliged to loose, while their King lay so disper-
atly sick at Calais: But the defeat thus given to the Prince de
Ligny, put into their hands the opportunity of taking in so many
Towns, as otherwise they durst not haue attempted.

[29] and.
[30] Not specified in the MS. *Campagnes* (p. 274).
[31] Scheldt.

This I speak knowingly, having been inform'd of the whole matter since that time, by one who could give me the best relation of it. But to return to my own affaires at Nieuport: Not long after the Marquis de Crequi had left his quarters near that Town, Monsr. de Turenne being marchd toward * * *,[32] I drew out the troopes which remain'd with me, and march'd with them to the Suburbs of Bruges, governing my motions by the intelligence I had of those which were made by the Enemy, and still keeping behind one of the Canals, that I might avoid the hazard of engaging upon unequall termes, or of receiving the least affront: by this means also taking care, that the Enemy might not get betwixt me and any of the Towns which were intrusted to my particular inspection.

About the 16th of September, I march'd back to Nieuport, where I received the wellcome news of Cromwell's death; which I sent immediatly to Don John, at the same time desiring him to send Some other who might take upon him my command; it being of absolute necessity for me to go to Bruxelles, and attend the King my Brother upon this new alteration of affaires in England.

Monsieur de Marsin was he that was order'd to releeve me; who arriving at Nieuport on the 21st of September, I immediatly made what hast I could to Bruxelles, and return'd no more to the Army, the Season of the year being too far spent before I could leave the King; so that there was not any need of my presence at the place of my Command: And when the French Army was march'd back into their own Country, and our Troopes dispos'd into their winter-quarters, I went to Breda to the Princesse my Sister, where I continued for some time.

[32] Not specified in the MS. *Campagnes* (p. 275).

1659 *

THE Death of Cromwell, and the disturbances which most men foresaw would ensue upon it (his Son Richard having neither the parts nor vigour of his Father to govern and keep in order the Army) had rais'd the spirits of the Royall Party, which before were very low, by having so often attempted and so often miscarryed in their endeavours to restore the King: So that now forgetting all the hazards which they had already run, and dispising those to which they were again to expose their lives and fortunes, they fell to work afresh; and by the Severall changes which happen'd afterwards in a litle space of time amongst their Enemies, had the opportunity of carrying on their design with a greater liklyhood of success then ever:[1] for they had not only provided themselves with armes and mony for a rising, but had engaged in severall parts of the Kingdom many considerable men of the Presbyterian Party; and besides them, divers other persons whom either their interest, or their misled judgment, had hurryd into actuall Rebellion either against the then present King, or his Father: In the West of England, Collonel Popham, In Wales, * * *[2] Mansfield, In Chesshyre, Sir George Booth, In Lincolnshyre, Collonel Rossiter, In Norfolk, Sir Horatio Townshend; besides Sir William Waller, and many other men of great interest in the Countries where they liv'd: Of the Army, Coll: Charles Houard, Coll: Ingolsby, and others who by the death of Cromwell, and the laying aside of his Son, had either lost their commands or were in fear of losing them; such especially as had been of that Party which advised Cromwell to take the Crown upon him: In the City, Major Generall Brown, and in the Navy, Generall Montague. As for Genll Monk, who commanded in Scotland, it is doubtfull whither at that time he had it in his thought to perform, what afterwards he brought So well to pass.

---

* Reprinted from the *Life* (I, 367–379). The narrative here is in the third person as in the MS. *Campagnes* (pp. 277–287).

[1] All the above is slightly abbreviated in the French MS. (p. 277).

[2] There is no gap in the French MS.

Most of these who have been nam'd, were so far ingaged by those whom his Majesty intrusted with the managment of his affaires in England (who were these following Lord Bellasise, Col: John Russell, Sir William Compton, Coll: Edward Villars, Lord Loughbourow, and Sir Richard Willis) that the first of August was appointed for a generall rising through all England: And his Maty had resolv'd to be there in person to head them, together with the Duke, at their first appearing in the feild. Everything was accordingly prepar'd, and the King had already taken his measures, how and at what place he should land, and from thence to go where the risings were to be: But being in this readiness, and the time almost come for the embarquement to put this great affaire in execution, it was all dash'd and brought to nothing by the treachery of one man.

This person was Sir Richard Willis, as it was afterwards discover'd to his Majesty by the means of Mr. Moreland, he being one of those who was intirely trusted by the King in the managment of this design, and of THE SELECT KNOTT (as they call'd them) and having been so all along, was corrupted by Cromwell for some * * *[3] before he dyd; and constantly betrayed to him during his life, and after his death to those who succeeded him, our whole affaire, thō not the persons of any of his freinds (for such was the agreement he had made with that Party) undertaking either to frustrate any of the King's designs, or at least to advertise them so early, that they might secure themselves from any such attempt: And he never fail'd them in any thing he promis'd; nor was ever press'd by Cromwell or others after him, to discover any particular persons who were carrying on his Majesty's Seruice;[4] neither did he betray any of them in this present juncture, thō he had it in his power to haue put the Duke of Ormonde into their hands, when he was privatly in England.

And now, according to his former practises, he set upon it to break this whole design: which he compass'd, by perswading THE SELECT KNOTT,[5] when all things were in a readiness and the day appointed just at hand, to deferr the rising for ten

[3] This should read 'some little time before he died' 'peu de temps avant sa mort' (MS. *Campagnes*, p. 279).

[4] The above passage is abbreviated in the MS. *Campagnes*.

[5] This expression is not translated in the MS., where we simply hear of the 'Chefs de la Conjuration'.

days longer; using such arguments to work them into his opinion, as indeed were plausible enough, thō not convincing, if they had been throwly consider'd. But there was no room left for suspicion of such a man, whom they look'd upon as one firm to his Master's seruice, and to be as forward as the best of them for such an undertaking; So that his advice prevailing, orders were accordingly dispatch'd to all who were ingag'd, that they should not take up armes till farther directions were sent them: Only Sir George Booth had no notice given him of this countermand, of whose intentions to rise, Willis accidentaly knew nothing; But at the same time he sent over to Bruxelles, and advertis'd the King that the busines was put off, when both the King and Duke were just ready to haue come for England.[6]

This journy being thus deferr'd, his R. H. thought he had time enough before him to make a visit to his Sister, who was then at Honslarcdyke near the Hague, and to be back again with his Maty before he should sett out from Bruxelles: But it prov'd otherwise; for the day after his R. H. departure from that place, the news was brought thither, that Sir George Booth was up in Chesshyre, with a considerable body of men. Vpon which intelligence, his Maty beleeving his freinds might also rise in other parts, as encouraged by this example, thō the last day appointed was not yet come, thought it proper for him to go over into England by the way of Calais; at the same time sending the Duke notice of it, that he might follow him: And the next day he sett out privatly from Bruxelles, taking along with him of his Servants only the Duke of Ormonde, Lord Bristoll, Daniel O'Neale, and Titus.

As for the Duke, so soon as he had received the King's letter, he came away for Bruxelles without stopping any where: He enter'd privatly into the Town and went immediatly to Mr. Secretary Nicholas' lodgings, from whence he sent word to the Chancellour, that he should come thither to him, that he might know from him what farther directions his Maty had left for him; which were only these, that he should make hast after him to Calais, where he should know more, and that the Duke of Glocester should still remain at Bruxelles till farther orders. Having received this short account, he made no longer stay then just to put on his disguise, in which he was resolved to go to England; and taking

[6] This paragraph is rapidly paraphrased in the MS. *Campagnes.*

283

with him only Charles Berkley and a Trumpetter, he travell'd day and night till he had overtaken his Majesty at Hazburck, short of St. Omers, where it was concluded that the King should go to Calais, and the Duke to Boulogne; where he was to provide a Vessell which might be in a readyness to transport him into England, but not to stirr till the King sent his commands from Calais. Thus they parted, and his Maty arrived that night at his journys end, as he had design'd; but his R. H. got not to Boulogne till the next morning.

The Duke has been since inform'd, that from the very time his Maty left Bruxelles, the resolution was taken of his going to Fontarabie, he not having any opinion that Sir George Booth's business would succeed, But that however he thought it not amiss to go by Calais, that in case some others of his freinds should rise, and new hopes be given him, he should be in a readiness to go over: if not, then to continue on his journey to Fontarabie. Whither this was true or not, is uncertain; but if it was true, the Duke was not made acquainted with it: for he did so firmly beleeve that he should pass over into England, that the same day he arriv'd at Boulogne, he sent Charles Berkley to the Lieut. Governour, to desire his assistance in procuring a boat for his passage into England, pretending that he had obtain'd leave from the Duke to go over privatly about some concerns of his own; and that the Lieut. Governour might haue no suspicion of the Duke's being there, his R. H. writt a letter to him, dating it from Bruxelles, which letter Mr. Berkley deliver'd to him, and according to his desire he was immediatly furnish'd with a small Vessell; and now the Duke stayd only for his Maties further orders for Calais, beleeving he should receive commands for his passage.

Within a day or two, the King came himself to Boulogne, in his way to Abbeville, and told the Duke, That by the last letter which he had received at Calais, he had heard of no other rising, then only that of Sir George Booth; for which reason he thought it not convenient for either of them, as yet to adventure over the Seas; That, for himself, his intentions were to go along the Coast towards Dieppe and Rouen, and if he heard any better news, then to pass over into the West to Popham, or into Wales to Mansfield: But for the Duke, he was order'd to hover about those quarters where he then was, and had permission given him to receive and open all letters which should be directed to the King; and, for the rest, it was left wholly to him to govern himself as he thought fitt, according to the intelligence which he should receive: Notwithstanding which, some few days after, Doctor Allestree refus'd to give him a letter, which he brought out of England with him, for the King.

After these directions, the King left his R. H. and went on to Rouen, from thence to St. Malo, and so by Rochelle to Thoulouse; from thence to Sarragossa, and then back again to Fontarabie, hearing the conference at that place was not yet ended betwixt the French, and the Spaniard. His Maty at his departure from Boulogne had left Mr. Titus with the Duke, and within few days after they went together to Calais, there to informe themselves more particularly of the news from England; where Titus mett with Mr. Dawson newly arriv'd out of Kent, who told them, that the very day wheron he expected the King and the Duke at Linecourt, a Troop of Horse came thither, thinking to haue found them there, and that it was not without great difficulty he escap'd from them, and gott over into France: This accident being related to the Duke, surpris'd him very much, knowing how few were intrusted with the secret of their designing to go to that house; But afterwards when the practises of Sir Richard Willis came to light, he was known to be the person who had discovered that design to the Rebells.

There happen'd likewise another accident, while the Duke was then at Calais, which had like to haue given him some trouble, and might also haue been of bad consequence to others. It happen'd that an over-officious Captain, a Huguenot, who was in the Garrison of that Town, advertis'd the Lieut. Governour, Monsr. de Courtebonne, that the Duke was there in a disguise, and that he himself had seen him, knowing him very well, as having been in the French Army while the Duke serv'd there, and withall he gave notice where his R. H. was lodg'd: Upon which the Lieut. Governour commanded the gates to be shutt, and taking a Guard along with him went to the place, conducted by the Huguenot Captain. It was a blind ale-house[7] in a by-part of the Town, where he was led with an opinion of finding the Duke: But coming thither, he found the Informer was mistaken, for the person prov'd to be Mr.

[7] 'un cabaret borgne' (MS. *Campagnes*, p. 283).

Edward Stanley, Brother to the Earle of Darby, who was newly come to Calais, as were also many English gentlemen; who hearing of the rising in England, came from all parts with intention to go over and serve their King.

But the Lieut. Governour not content with this, and being told by the same person, or some other, that the Duke was in Town, went on with his inquiry, and search'd the house of one Mrs. Booth an English-woman, where commonly her Countrymen us'd to lodge, leaving no part or corner of the house unsearch'd; but thō the Duke lay not there, yet by accident he had like to haue been found there: for he was going to that very place, when Titus met him in the street, and told him that the gates were commanded to be shutt, and that a search was actually making for him; for which reason he refrain'd from going thither, and gott into a house where the Lord Berkley and the Lord Langdale were, and there he continued till night, and then return'd to the Inne where he had taken up his lodging.

The Lieut. Governour after this, made no further inquiry, but caus'd the gates to be open'd again an hour before night. Of all this the Duke was soon advertis'd; and some advis'd him to go out of Town the same night before the gates were shutt, that he might be so much taker (*farther*)[8] on, in his way to Boulogne; but he refus'd that Counsell, because perhaps there might be a trap layd for him, and the gates on purpose left open to apprehend him as he returned out. He therfore judg'd it not secure for him to give them such a mark of knowing him, as they would haue, if he went out so hastily at so undue an hour. But betwixt twelve and one he had a hott alarm at his lodging, and verily beleev'd they were come to take him; for he was waken'd with great knocking and bouncing at the door of the Inne, and going to the window, he heard, as he thought, the noise of Soldiers; neither was he mistaken in that opinion, for so they were: But their busines was not to search for the Duke, it was only to bring home the master of the house, who was dead drunk and brought home betwixt four of them.

The next morning his R. H. in pursuance of what he had resolv'd, went away for Boulogne, and return'd no more to Calais

---

[8] The text of the MS. *Campagnes* reads simply: 'pour aller a Boulogne', and the next few lines are summarised in a short sentence (p. 284).

during all the time of his residence in those parts. Some time after, Captain Thomas Cook came thither from Paris, with letters to the Duke from the Queen his Mother, and commands to find out his Maty. These letters likewise inform'd him, that Monsr. de Turenne who was then about Amiens desir'd to speak with the King in reference to his affaires in England. Upon which the Duke went[9] immediatly to Abbeville, hoping there to haue found the King; But his Maty was departed from thence, and all his R. H. could hear of him was that he was gone towards Dieppe, and thither he sent Captain Cook after him; who missing of him there also, went in quest of him as farr as Rouen, but his Maty was gone from thence also on his way to St Malo: Wherupon Cook return'd to the Duke, and gave him account of his fruitless diligence.

The busines was of too great importance to be neglected, and therfore his R. H. resolv'd on going himself privatly to Monsr. de Turenne: when he was come to him at Amiens, Monsr. de Turenne told him, He had desired to speak to the King his Brother, but since his Maty was not to be found, he would do him the same seruice in the Duke's person: Therupon he offer'd him his own Regiment of foot, which he would make up twelve hundred men, and the Scots-Gendarmes, to carry over into England with him; That besides this, he would furnish him with three or four thousand spare armes, six feild peices with ammunition proportionable, and tooles, and as much meale as would serve for the Sustenance of five thousand men for the space of six weeks, or two months; and farther, would furnish him with Vessels for the conveyance of all this into England, and permitt the Troopes that his Maty had in Flanders, to march to Boulogne and there imbarke, with orders to follow the Duke as fast as Vessells could be provided for them; advising his R. H. to send directions to them, that they should march immediatly to St Omers where a pass should meet them.

And that all these preparations might be compass'd with more ease and certainty, he offer'd the Duke to pawne his plate and make use besides of all his interest and credit, to make up such a sum of mony as should be thought necessary for the carrying on of the business: Concluding all with this expression, That his

[9] 'prit ... la poste pour Abbeville' (MS. *Campagnes*, p. 284).

R. H. might easily beleeve he had no orders from the Cardinal, who was then at the Conference, to perform all this; but what he did was freely of himself, out of no other motive then kindness to the Duke, and to his family.

Tis not hard to imagine, that his R. H. accepted of this noble Offer with great joy, and that he lost no time in designing where to land with these forces. The place resolv'd on was Rye, and that in case the Country should come in to him, he should march on to Maydstone and Rochester; if not, then to fortify that Town, which by reason of its situation might be made so strong within few days, that Lambert should not easily haue forced him out of it; and he would haue found him work enough in that Seige, to haue divided the forces of the Rebells, and disorder'd all their methods.

These things being thus resolv'd, and order'd, the affaire was put into a forwardness; and Monsr. de Turenne gave the Duke a letter to (*the*) Lieut Governour of Boulogne, wherein he was commanded to furnish his R. H. with all the Vessells, and Fisherboats which he could get together in all his Government of the Boulonois. The Duke gave this letter himself to the Lieutenant du Roy, with another from the Mareshal d'Aumont his Governour which the Queen has procur'd and sent to the Duke from Paris, by which the Lieut was likewise order'd to assist his R. H. with Vessels, and all things he could desire.

The busines was now so far advanced, and in such a readiness, that the Duke of Bouillon, and others[10] of M. de Turenne's Nephews, were to haue gone Volonteers with the Duke; and the next day was appointed for his R. H. and his Soldiers to imbarke at Estape,[11] to which place the Troopes were already upon their march, when letters from England brought the unwelcome news of Sir George Booth's defeat by Lambert. Upon which the Duke, being then at Boulogne, went to Mr. de Turenne who was at Montreuil to informe him of it; who in that juncture thought it not advisable for his R. H. to adventure into England, but counsell'd him to haue patience and expect a better opportunity, which could not be long wanting to him, by reason of the disorders and distractions which must of necessity happen amongst them in England: Notwithstanding which reasons, the Duke press'd him

[10] 'Le Duc de Bouillon et le Comte D'Auvergne' (MS. *Campagnes*, p. 286).
[11] Etaples.

to consent that he might go, telling him that he beleev'd the King might be landed in the West, or somewhere in Wales, and be there ingag'd in difficulties and dangers; and that if his conjecture should prove true, there was no other way of saving his Maty and gaining time for him to attempt any thing considerable, but the Duke's going over, and making a diversion: But these arguments could not prevaile on Monsr. de Turenne to give his R. H. the leave which he So earnestly desir'd; for he replyd, That he was very confident his Maty was not gone for England, and that thō he were, it was not reasonable for the Duke to hazard himself, when there was no probability of Success: He therfore counsell'd his R. H. to return to Flanders, and there to expect some news from the King his Brother, and fresh intelligence from England. And when he had concluded with this advice, knowing the Duke wanted mony, he lent him three hundred pistoles, and gave him a Pass. And thus an end was put to this design; and the Duke returned to Bruxelles.[12]

[12] The five preceding paragraphs, which describe Turenne's offers to James and his subsequent advice are translated fairly literally and in detail in the French MS. (pp. 284–287). The remainder of this section in the French MS. (from the bottom of p. 287 to the end) corresponds to the entry for 1660 which is reprinted below.

The entry for 1659 in the French MS. stops at the point where the Duke is described as 's'en retournant a Brusselles' (p. 287). But the three paragraphs that follow in the *Life* (I, 379–380) appear, translated, in the French MS. under the heading '1660'.

1660[*]

IN this way he pass'd through Peronne; where he privatly
visited the Governour of that place, the Marquis d'Hocquincourt,[1] an old acquaintance of his, whom he had known in the
French Army, who us'd him with all imaginable civility and kindness. The 11th of September he reached Cambray, and from thence
went straight to Bruxelles: where he found, that notwithstanding
the Duke of Glocester had deliver'd to the Marquis de Caracena
the letters which his R. H. had written from Boulogne for the
marching of his Troopes to St Omer, yet the Marquis would not
permitt them to stirr out of their quarters; thō he was sufficiently
press'd to it by the Duke of Glocester: But he still answer'd, he
did not beleeve Mr. de Turenne durst let them pass through any
part of his King's Dominions, without order, which he knew he
could not haue. Nor would he suffer them to draw down to the
Sea-side, to which he was also urged by the Duke of Glocester,
when he found he could not obtain his first point. What his reasons were for refusing these two requests, the Duke could not
learn; but as it happen'd, the denyall prov'd to be of no prejudice
to his Majesties affaires; Only it gaue opportunity to See what was
to be expected from the Marquis, if things were left to his management.

This design being thus blasted, and no hopes left of attempting
any thing in England at that time, the Duke past the remaining
part of this year at Bruxelles, expecting the King his Brother, who
arrived thither from the Conference at Fontarabie a litle before
Christmas.

And to shew here, what litle expectation even the most intelli-
gent Strangers had at that time, of those Changes which happen'd
so soon afterwards in England; his Maty, as he came back from
Fontarabie through France, press'd the Cardinal very earnestly

* Reprinted from the *Life* (I, 379–380 and 381–382). This corresponds with the
last three pages of the French MS. *Campagnes*.

[1] The son of the Marshal who had deserted to the Spaniards and been killed in
1658.

290

for leave to Stay, thõ never so privatly, with the Queen his Mother, which small favour he was not able to obtain; and therupon was forced to return to Bruxelles much against his inclination, having only Stay'd some few days with the Queen at Colombe (which he tooke in his way) a civility which could not well be refus'd him.[2]

The hopes concerning England being now reduced to the lowest ebb, in the beginning of the year, 1660, an offer was made to the Duke, of commanding in Spain against Portugal, and also to be their High Admiral with the Title of Principe de la Mare; which office, the Duke has been told, was never given to any but the King's Sons or near Relations, and whoever enjoys it commands the Galleys as well as Ships, and wherever he lands he commands as Vice Roy of the Country whilst he stays in it; he has also the fifts of all Prises, and a great Salary, besides other considerable perquisits: So that this was not only a very honorable post, but also a very advantageous one even as to profit, which was what the Duke then wanted. He therefore readily consented to the offer which was made to him, the King his Brother ratifying it with his free permission.

And now his R. H. was preparing to go for Spain in the ensuing spring, when that Voyage was happily prevented by the wonderfull Changes, which were almost daily produced in England: And when the motion was once begun, it went on so fast, that his Majesty was almost in his own Country, before those abroad, especially the Spaniards, would beleeve there was any Revolution towards it; for even after Sir John Greenfeild[3] was come over to the King from Genll. Monk, they yet beleev'd him as far as ever from his Restoration, and were so possest of that opinion, that they let him go into Holland. And at last when his Maty was at Breda not many days before he embarked for England, the Marquis de Caracena endeavour'd to perswad him to return to Flanders.

He pretended he had busines of importance to acquaint his Maty with from England, some persons being come over from thence to Bruxelles, who had great offers to make to him: And he

---

[2] This paragraph appears in the French translation on p. 289, immediately *after* the paragraph relating the Spanish offer.

[3] 'Le Chevalier Grenville' (MS. *Campagnes*, p. 289).

sent the Count de Grammont with letters to him on that occasion, desiring his Maty would be pleas'd to give himself the trouble of coming but as far as Antwerp, or at least to West-Wesel, he not being able to wait on him (as he knew he ought) any where out of his Master's Dominions. But his Majesty had no inclinations to venture his person in the hands of the Spaniards, not knowing what the consequences might be; And besides he could easily judge, that it must either be a pretence to draw him thither, or indeed a thing not worth his journy, his return to England being then ascertain'd.

But because he would give the Marquis no reason of complaint, he sent the Duke to Bruxelles, and desir'd the Marquis to impart the business to him; When his R. H. came thither, he found it was only Coll: Bampfeild who was come over with some ayry proposition from Scott, and some of that Party: From whence the Duke concluded, that his Maty had done wisely not to stirr from Breda.

When his R. H. stayd a day or two with the Marquis, he returned to the King his Brother, who some few days after went to the Hague, where he was very well received; and embarking himself at Schevelin about the latter end of May, (23d) on board the English Navy, commanded then by Generall Montague, he landed with his two Brothers, The Duke of York and the Duke of Glocester, at Dover, the * * *[4] (25th) of the same month, and made his entry into London on the 29th, which happen'd to be his Birth-day.

---

[4] 'le 28 du mesme mois' (p. 290). '28' is entered in the MS. in a different hand, perhaps that of James himself.

INDEX

A

Abbey of Mont St Eloy, 166–8
Ablon, 102–4
Agecourt, Capt. d', 77, 81
Allestree, Dr., 285
Angeau, Marquis d', 119
Anne of Austria, 100, 111, 218
Anne, Queen of England, 8, 10
Anne-Marie-Louise d'Orléans. *See*
  Montpensier
'Archduke'. *See* Léopold
Arcy, M. d', 174, 223
Ardres, 233–8
Arras, 156–90
Aston, Capt., 272
Aubrey, John, 3
Aumont, Marshal d', 119–20, 124, 288
Auvergne, Philippe d', 44
Auvergne family. *See* Bouillon; Turenne

B

Bampfield, Col., 292
Bar (or Barr), M. de, 169, 178, 189
Barkley (cornet), 117
Bar-le-Duc, 113–15, 117–22
Barr. *See* Bar
Bascourt, M. de, 253
Bassecourt, M. de, 126, 127
Bastille, 93
Battles: Arras, 178–90; The Dunes,
  255–75; Porte St. Antoine, 85–94.
  See also Sieges
Baume, Francois de la. *See* Valon
Baynes, Col., 273
Beaufort, Duc de, 82, 90, 94–7
Beaujeu, M., 77, 78, 139, 140, 161
Beauregard, M., 174
Beauveau, 161–2
Bebsey, M. de, 274
Bellasise, Lord, 282
Belle Cense Regiment, 88
Bellechassaigne, Lt., 138
Bellefonds, M. de, 186
Belleveder (officer), 273

Bergue, 238–9
Berkley (or Berkeley), Charles, 173, 174,
  222–3, 232, 245, 251, 265, 284, 286
Berkley, Sir John, 57, 58, 71
Berlo, Baron de, 66, 69
Betbesé, Col., 269
Biscara, 189
Blanquefort, Marquis de, 257
Bléneau, 60–3
Bodervitz, Col., 181
Bohemia, Queen of, 2
Boniface, Gaspar, 260, 263–5, 267, 273
Booth, Mrs., 286
Booth, Sir George, 281, 283, 284, 288
Bossuet, J. B., 40
Bouillon, Emmanuel-Théodose de la
  Tour d'Auvergne, Cardinal: role in
  preservation of *Memoirs*, 14–15; life
  of, 37–42; Preface to *Memoirs*, 52–3
Bouillon, Frédéric-Maurice, Duc de:
  life of, 38–39; and Mazarin, 86, 100;
  advises court, 97
Bouillon, Godefroid-Charles-Henri, 39,
  43
Bouillon, Godefroid-Maurice, Duc de,
  39
Bouillon, Henri de. *See* Turenne
Bouillon family, 38–9, 44–5
Bourgueville, Bernardin, *See* Clinchamp
Bout-de-bois, Col., 181
Boutteville, M. de, 165, 256, 273
Breuauté, Marquis de, 189
Brie-Comte-Robert, 101–2, 104
Briol, Comte de, 143
Briole (or Briolle), Baron de, 69, 189
Briscara (volunteer), 173
Bristol, Earl of, 30, 34, 115, 117,
  248–51, 260, 271, 273, 283
Broglio, Comte Carlo de, 70, 169, 178, 189
Broussel, Pierre, 96
Brown, Gen., 281
Brussels, 248, 251, 290–2
Buckingham, Duke of, 182
Bussy, Comte de, 45
Bussy-Rabutin, M. de, 208

293

C

INDEX

J

James II, King of England: achievements, 1; life summarized, 1–11; youth, 1–5; poverty, 5, 289; in French Army, 5–8, 57–218; in Spanish Army, 7, 226–80; as Lord High Admiral, 8–9; Catholicism of, 9–11; reign, 10; Memoirs, 13–23, 25–36, 52–3; documents on, 25–36; literary style, 36–7; affection for Turenne, 53; caught on ambling mount at battle, 75; negotiates with Lorraine, 77–8; aids Charles in mediating treaty, 78–81; observes enemy for Turenne, 104; and Turenne join skirmishers, 104; soldiers too drunk to march, 112; Irish regiment offers to serve with, 122; engagement near Arras, 162–3; in battle of Arras, 178–85; on forage duty, 213–14; compelled to leave France, 216–18; takes leave of French court, 223; meets Cromwell deputy, 224–5; arrives in Flanders, 225; prepares to attack Calais, 228–9; opposes Spaniards' delay before attack, 231–2; French fire on his Spanish allies, but spare him, 232–3; Spanish disapproval of personal reconnoitering by, 236–7; conversations with French annoy Spanish, 239–40; recognized by greyhound, 239; Spanish ignore advice they attack enemy, 241–2; troops ill, 242; Reynolds seeks interview with, 244–6; English commander's civility to, 244–6; Bristoll tries to persuade join troops with Condé's, 248–51; at Battle of the Dunes, 255–75; enemy troops mistake for own officer, 270; French friend believes prisoner, tries to rescue, 274; advises Spanish army after Dunes, 275–6; at Nieuport, 276–80; prepares to invade England, 283–4; in disguise at Calais, 285–7; Turenne offers aid with invasion, 287–9; Spain offers high command to, 291; mission to Caracena, 291–2; lands in England, 292
James, Duke of Monmouth. *See* Monmouth

James Stuart. *See* Stuart
Jermyn, Henry, Lord, 78, 80, 81, 167, 173, 257
John, Don. *See* Juan
Joyeuse, M. de, 173–4
Juan, Don: life of, 228n; takes siesta, loses enemy, 231; stickler for formalities, 234–5; character of, 235; disapproval of personal reconnoitering, 236–7; marches on Mardyck, 242–3; attempts to seize English frigates, 244; at Dunkirk, 239, 255–9, 263–5, 270, 271; at Bruges, 276, 278; James asks to be relieved of command, 280

K

Knight, Capt., 237
KNOTT, THE SELECT, 282–3

L

La Baume. *See* Valon
La Berge, M. de, 274
La Ferté, Duc de: life of, 72n; at battle of St. Antoine, 82–5; to St. Ménéhou, 112; fury at Turenne's entering St. Michel, 116–17; besieges Ligny, 118; delays deprive Turenne of victory, 120–1; takes Ligny, 122–3; and siege of Mousson, 143, 147, 150; at Arras, 159, 163, 168, 169, 177–89; threatens to rip open messenger, 163; unwillingness to do battle, 168–9; at King's council, 202; mistake at siege of Condé, 207; besieges St. Guislain, 210; besieges Montmédy, 228–30
La Feuillade, M. de, 201
La Fèvre, Antoine, 96
La Fuitte, Major, 83
La Guillottiere, M. de, 178
La Loge, Capt., 89
Lambert, John, 288
La Motte, 66, 69
La Marck, Charlotte de, 38
La Motterie, Comte de, 273
Landor, Walter Savage, 13
Landrecies, 200–1
Langdale, Lord, 286
Laon, Vidame de, 151
La Rochefoucauld, Duc de, 46, 91